Walk

LightFoot Companion

to the

via Francigena

Canterbury
to
St Peter's Square, Rome

ISBN 978-2-917183-09-0

Also by Babette Gallard and Paul Chinn
Riding the Milky Way - Long Riders' Press 2006
Riding the Roman Way - Pilgrimage Publications 2007
Reflections - A Pictorial Journey Along the via Francigena 2008
LightFoot Guide to the via Francigena - Canterbury to Besançon 2008/9/10
LightFoot Guide to the via Francigena - Besançon to Vercelli 2008/9/10
LightFoot Guide to the via Francigena - Vercelli to Rome 2008/9/10
LightFoot Guide to the Three Saints Way - Winchester to Mont St Michel 2008
LightFoot Guide to the Three Saints Way - Mont St Michel to St Jean d'Angely 2008

Our special thanks go to:
Barbara Edgar, for her tireless and ever vigilant proof-reading
Jannina Veit Teuten, for allowing us to use a selection from her beautiful water-colours painted whilst on the via Francigena.

Author's note

The Companion is a cultural and historical information guide to the via Francigena, with subheadings. While following the route I discovered so many interesting facts about people, places and events, each with its fascinating tangent, that there was a very real risk the book would never be completed. So, for the sake of everyone involved, not least my unfortunate partner, I have endeavoured to make a sensible selection that you will hopefully find as compelling as I do. If, while reading it, you find any gaps, inaccuracies or indeed anything that could be improved, please let me know. I am happy to accept suggestions and will be even more happy to say that the next edition of the Companion to the via Francigena has been produced in collaboration with its readers.

Babette Gallard

CONTENTS

Pilgrims and Pilgrimages

Pilgrim - person who journeys to a sacred place; a traveller or wanderer.
Peregrini - those who go through fields (per agros), transients.

 The meaning and dilemna of the pilgrimage journey is dramatically expressed by Yourcenar's autobiographical novel 'Le Labyrinth du Monde'. Her protagonist, Zeno, is troubled by the paradox of the journey's end: "Once you have arrived, you go back in the opposite direction". Yourcenar uses Zeno's confusion to define the journey as the discovery of those intermediate zones where soul and flesh are intermingled, where dream adapts to reality and where life and death become interchangeable. Pilgrims who journey to a specific destination, irrespective of the danger and hardship, often view the experience as the search for the true meaning of life, even though they are aware that there is in fact no single or final answer - a dilemma expressed by the image of the 'Labyrinth', an ancient symbol which can arouse anxiety and fear, but also the desire for adventure and challenge. The image of the spiritual Labyrinth is both sculpted and inlaid on the floors of many churches along the via Francigena. In Pontremoli, one can see the labyrinth of 'St Peter's de conflentu'. On its upper ledge the labyrinth depicts a knight challenging death, overlooked by a winged beast representing the devil. On the sides there are a dragon biting its tail and an hourglass, symbols that together indicate the rapid and eternal circle of time. Within the maze one can also see the abundance of cathedrals with the Garden of Eden at their centre. From here the arms of the cross branch off as four rivers that flow towards the four divisions of the world. Similar examples of this version of the labyrinth can also be seen in Piacenza and Lucca.

To set out on a pilgrimage is to throw down a challenge to everyday life.
               Phil Cousineau - the Art of Pilgrimage

Religion points to that area of human experience where in one way or another man comes upon mystery as a summons to pilgrimage.
                  Frederick Buechner

Pilgrimage is an evocative word. Most religions have places of pilgrimage, some simple and austere, others magnificently embellished. A pilgrimage is a journey - the notion of sacred motion or travel running deep in human religion and dating back to when early humans would climb hilltops to be closer to God or go to a specific site designated for the act of worship. Spiritual talk is full of the language of travel : walking the walk, leaving behind, stepping forward and following God's paths on our spiritual journey of life. There are all manner of reasons for making such a journey. Pilgrims may hope to obtain spiritual succour, peace of mind, a sense of unity with other like-minded people or more material benefits such as cure from disease or disability, but irrespective of the notion, every pilgrimage needs a focal point. At the beginning of the second millennium, a huge number of pilgrims began crossing through

Europe in search of the lost Celestial Land, the Patria Celeste. They travelled to three major destinations: Rome, the city of the martyrdom of Saints Peter and Paul (founders of the Christian church), the Holy Land (site of Calvary) and Santiago de Compostela in Spain, the Apostle James'' final resting place. Thus Europe hosted a vast network of roads, paths and routes leading towards these pilgrimage sites and though the journey was often arduous and dangerous, the pilgrims kept coming in their thousands, right up until the 17th century when the pilgrimage experience finally fell out of fashion.

St. Helena ... Empress, Saint and first recorded Christian pilgrim to Rome

Helena was a humble innkeeper's daughter from Bithyna. It was said that as a girl she had been one of the supplementary amenities of her father's establishment, regularly available to clients, at an extra charge. Helena married Constantius and was the mother of Emperor Constantine I (born 274), but she was abandoned by her husband so that he could marry, Theodora, Emperor Maximus' adopted stepdaughter. Without any ties, Helena was able to embark upon a pilgrimage to Jerusalem in 324 and arrived in Rome with her son Constantine in 326. Later, aged 70, she made another pilgrimage to tour principal shrines in the Holy Land and is said to have unearthed the True Cross, which she sent back to Rome. Her discovery was endorsed by the Emperor who built the Church of the Holy Sepulchre to house it. The length of her stay in the Holy Land is unknown but she probably died there.

The Pilgrimage Renaissance

In 1986, just 2,491 pilgrims collected the Compostela certificate at the end of the St. James way, but by 2009 this figure had risen to above 150,000 - a renaissance that can be primarily attributed to the European Cultural Route designation that was first given to the St James Way and later (1994) to the via Francigena. For some of these contemporary pilgrims, religion may still be the motivating force, but for a large percentage it is more likely to be an opportunity to achieve personal goals or take time out before making a major life decision.

The via Francigena Yesterday and Today

The via Francigena was first mentioned in the Actum Clusio (876), a parchment held in the Abbey of San Salvatore al Monte Amiata (Tuscany). In medieval times, north-south roads through Italy, particularly those from the western Alps, were often referred to as 'the 'via Francesca' or 'via Francigena'. Other accounts also name the northern sections as the 'Chemin des Anglois' and the southern section as via Romea, but in fact the via Francigena is an amalgamation of several possible routes with only two unifying factors: their ultimate

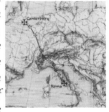

destination (Rome) and the provision of links between religious communities offering pilgrims a place to rest and recuperate. At its height, when the Holy Years were proclaimed in 1300, tens of thousands used the route, with the obvious consequence that nearby communities thrived and grew. The northern via Francigena, as we know it today, was first documented in 990 by Sigeric the Serious, Archbishop of Canterbury. After receiving his cope and pallium (a circular band of white wool with pendants, worn by archbishops) from the Pope, he recorded his return journey, listing the places he passed  through and identifying them as "submansiones". Nothing in the documentation suggests that the route was either new or uncharted, but Sigeric's manuscript (now held in the British Library) has become the focus for academic research and the re-creation of this modern-day pilgrimage route. In November 2005, Italian politician Romano Prodi announced that he would revitalize the via Francigena and in spite of resigning from politics himself, his work has gone on. In 2007, the 0km foundation stone was laid in the forecourt of Canterbury Cathedral, identifying both physically and symbolically, the starting point for the via Francigena. Today, the Italian Ministry of Culture is dedicating time and resources to the

signing of an official route and development of local support for pilgrim travellers, in the hope that the via Francigena will one day equal the popularity of the St James Way. In addition associations of pilgrims are uniting to breathe life back into these walks and once or twice a year they set off from North, South, East and West to reach at their journey's end in Rome. In the southern sections of Italy, Pilgrim numbers on the via Francigena have increased significantly, though in northern Italy the numbers are still relatively low (around 300 to 400 travellers each year), but as one draws nearer to Rome the total rises to over 2,500. Over three quarters of those following the route do so on foot, but there is a growing number of horseriders and particularly cyclists. The youngest pilgrim registered in 2009 was just nine years old,

whilst the oldest was a Swiss woman aged 85. There has also been a significant rise in the number of establishments of all types offering accommodation to users of the via Francigena. In Italy the newly improved official route is a great improvement over all previous routes and benefits significantly from being recommended and owned by the local communities or local branches of hiking groups such as the CAI (Club Alpino Italiano). The route succeeds in continuing to reduce the amount of the journey needed on the busy SS and SP roads and where this is unavoidable recommendations have been made to the ministry and the communities for additional safety measures. Some route improvements come at the cost of additional distance and sometimes more strenuous hiking. The signing activity is being undertaken at a community level, though at the time of writing, a number of them still have to start the work, with the result that signs can stop abruptly at a community frontier. Pilgrims should not plan to depend on the signs alone as there is already evidence of erosion/vandalism of installed signs.

The Southern via Francigena (not described in the book) snakes down through lower Lazio into Campania and Puglia, where it continues after a sea voyage from Brindisi to the Holy Land and the final stretch on foot to Jerusalem. The route goes through numerous little known, but fascinating places and several National Parks including parco degli Aurunci, parco dei Lepini, parco dei Castelli Romani, parco dell'Appia Antica and nature reserves like those in Ninfa and on Lake Giulianello. The walk also follows Roman and medieval roads and passes by important basilica from the twelfth-century, ancient churches like those at Segni and Carpineto Romano and the remains of Roman temples.

Pilgrim Credential/Passport

With the increasing development and recognition of the via Francigena, the ancient systems associated with the more well known St James Way to Santiago de Compostela are also being adopted on this less well known route to Rome. To gain admittance to religious hostels along the road, pilgrims must now present a credential to prove that they are hiking, cycling or riding the route. Each day, as pilgrims pass through towns, they will receive stamps in the credential and at the end of their journey in Rome, they can present it to one of two places to confirm that they have completed the last 100 kilometers (from Acquapendente to Rome) - the minimum requirement for receipt of the 'Testimonium'.

Serious - Archbishop of Canterbury, 990–994

Nothing in his history identifies Sigeric as being more 'serious' than anyone else at the time. The

epithet may have originated from his learning, or could have been derived from transliteration of his name into Latin as Serio. Sigeric took holy orders at Glastonbury Abbey, where he was educated and subsequently elected Abbot of St Augustine's. In approximately 986 he was consecrated to the See (the official seat of a Bishop) of Ramsbury and Sonning and finally transferred to the See of Canterbury in 990. Today, Sigeric's only real claim to fame is his journey from Rome to Canterbury, but he was also notable for a number of decisive acts for which future generations should be grateful. While Sigeric was an abbot, Ælfric dedicated a book of translated homilies to him and advised King Æthelred to found Cholsey Abbey in Berkshire in honor of King Edward the Martyr, as well as having Edward memorialized at Shaftesbury Abbey. Later, it was Sigeric who advised King Æthelred to pay a tribute to the invading Danish king, Sweyn Forkbeard, in 991. Æthelred presented Sweyn with 10,000 pounds of silver and in response Sweyn temporarily ceased his destructive advance into England, though he did return later for a further tribute. Sweyn's ever-increasing demands in the following years resulted in a debilitating tax known as the Danegeld, payable by the inhabitants of Æthelred's territories. In 994, Sigeric paid tribute to the Danes and secured the protection of Canterbury Cathedral. Sigeric died on 28 October 994 and was buried in Christ Church, Canterbury. His will left wall hangings to Glastonbury as well as a valuable collection of books to his church in Sonning.

After receiving his cope and pallium (a circular band of white wool with pendants, worn by archbishops) from the Pope, Sigeric recorded his return journey, listing the places he passed through and identifying them as "submansiones".

Iste sunt submansiones de Roma usque ad mare.]
Roma. Il Johannis VIIII. III Bacane.IlIl Suteri
Sce Valentine. VII Sce Flaviane. VIII Sca Crist
Aquapendente. X Sce Petir in Pail. XI Abricula.
Quiric. XIII Turreiner. XIV Arbia. XV Seocine.
Burgenove. XVII Aelse. XVIII Sce Martin in Foss
Gemiane. XX Sce Maria Glan. XXI Sce Peter Curra
XXII Sce Dionisii. XXIII Arne Blanca. XXIII Aqu
XXV Forcri. XXVI Luca. XXVII Campmaior. XXV!II
XXIX Sce Stephane. XXX Aguilla. XXXI Puntremel.
Sce Benedicte. XXXIII Sce Moderanne. XXXIV
Phi<lemangenur. XXXV Metane. XXXVI Sce Domnine.
XXXVII Floricum. XXXVIII Placentia. XXXIX Sce A
XL Sce Cristine. XLI Pamphica. XLII Tremel. XLl
XLIV Sca Agath. XLV Everi. XLVI Publei. XLVII A
XLVIII Sce Remei. XLIX Petrecastel. L Ursiores.
Maurici. LII Burbulei. LIII Vivaec. LIV Losanna
LVI Antifern. LVII Punterlin. LVIII Nos. LIX By
Cuscei. LXI Sefui. LXII Grenant. LXIII Oisma. I
Blaecuile. LXV Bar. LXVI Breone. LXVII Domaniar
Funtaine. LXIX Chateluns. LXX Rems. LXXI Corbur
LXXII Mundlothuin. LXXIII Martinwaeth. LXXIV Du
LXXV Atherats. LXXVI Bruwaei. LXXVII Teranburh.
LXXVIII Gisne. LXXX Sumeran. (il manoscritto nc
la mansione con il numero d ordine LXXIX

Giovanni Caselli has been a Fellow of the Royal Anthropological Institute of Great Britain (1972) and a Member of the Institute of Archaeology of Great Britain (1985). He is the author and illustrator of many history books for young adults and as an expert in the history of land communications and settlement has lectured on the subject at the Institute of Archaeology of London, at the University of Malta and in Italy.

via Francigena - RIVER OF HISTORY

"Roads are the rivers of history", I remember reading this in a book when I was very young and beginning to become interested in history. Equally one may say that roads are the bloodstream of nations. People, goods and most of all ideas, have travelled along roads and all these have left their mark.

"All roads lead to Rome", is an old saying, but not only in the Italian tradition. Even nations which were never part of the Roman Empire have it. After St. Augustine of Canterbury converted the Saxons, several of their kings made the journey to Rome. Some of them died there and a special section of the Vatican became a Saxon enclave for visitors from Britain. From then on and until the Reformation, the Pope's guards were all Saxons. Saxon Archbishops had to go to Rome for their official investiture when they received the "pallium", an ecclesiastical vestment, from the Pope himself.

There are many early medieval records of kings (among them King Alfred and King Cnut), abbots (like Ceolfrid of Wearmouth and Jarrow), Irish saints (like Saint Columbanus of Bobbio) and Canterbury archbishops going on a journey to Rome, but only one such record enables us to reconstruct the route and, of course, put it on today's map and travel it. Archbishop Sigeric of Canterbury, an otherwise obscure figure, barely making a minor appearance in British history, recorded his return journey from Rome and this document, dating to the 10th Century, still survives. William Stubbs, a 19th century English historian, discovered Sigeric's account of his journey from Rome which took place in 990-992 and transcribed it, interpreting the 80 place-names, or submansiones of the route, where the prelate and his entourage spent their nights,

In 1985, as the millennium anniversary of this journey approached, I thought of trying Sigeric's route to see what the expert eye could detect on the banks of that "river of history". And, as always happens, the experience on the ground was full of unexpected surprises. I will never forget the excitement of this true journey through space and time, from Canterbury to Rome. It was not so much the great cities, like Laon or Rheims, but the smallest villages or farms, which reserved the greatest surprises for the time traveller. In France I discovered barns that had been Templar's chapels and old houses called "hospital" (meaning hostel). The road through the Marne, between Rheims

11

and Chalons-en-Champagne, known as the *Voie Romaine*, looked as if the Romans had just left it and then, as if that were not exciting enough, I discovered the *Chaussée Brunehaut* - a term

which in Northern France identifies a Roman Road and in popular tradition also signifies that it is a road built by "Queen Bruhehilde, wife of Julius Caesar"! In Switzerland, I came across ruins of Roman villas with splendid mosaics, while the Saint Bernard Pass itself is practically a museum. The original Roman road, cut deep in the rock and bearing deep ruts, can be walked for some hundreds of yards. During the Dark Ages English pilgrims were attacked by the Saracens who, for a time, controlled the pass. From there and across the Italian border, Roman bridges and Roman milestones can be seen in every village all the way down to Aosta - a splendid little town with massive ruins towering above the modern buildings and ancient monasteries of Sigeric's time, founded by Irish saints. Vercelli and Santhià, are Roman and medieval treasure troves. The "Vercelli Book" in the Cathedral Library -one of the oldest of the four Old English Poetic Codices - is an anthology of Old English Prose and verse dating back to the late 10th

century. From here the River Po was crossed at a place where a ferry has now been put back into service for the benefit of modern pilgrims, thanks to the advice I gave to the local people. In Fidenza, the great Romanesque and Gothic cathedral of the small town depicts friezes with rows of via Francigena pilgrims that give us a very good idea of what the travellers of the

12th-13th century looked like on the road. Over the Apennines I also found fantastic Romanesque artworks and roads frequently called via Romea – the medieval name of any road leading to Rome.

The via Francigena in Tuscany is, in my view, the most evocative. Lucca was rebuilt by an Irish saint, St. Finnian, in the 7th century on the ruins of the Roman city and the town was subsequently administered by an Irish nun for a good part of the 8th century. After Lucca, having crossed the Arno, the road takes travellers to the excavations of San Genesio, just below San Miniato, a lost city whose cathedral is now only a trace in a sunflower field. Then onto San Gimignano and Siena, two locations that do not require any further description from me, except perhaps to add that they both owe their existence to medieval traffic along the Francigena, where it was crossed by the droves of shepherds going to the coast from the Apennines. Siena grew rich by renting the grassland of the Maremma in Winter. The oldest bank in Italy, Siena's bank, Monte dei Paschi di Siena, literally means "Savings from the renting of pastures". The greatest painter of Siena, Simone Martini was a Frenchman from Tours. After Siena the road winds among the rolling hills of Val d'Orcia and you feel as if you are walking in a dream or a timeless world painted by a surrealist artist. Then come the ragged vast landscapes between Monte Amiata and Radicofani, where in Sigeric's times there was just one inn called "Mala Mulier" (Dishonest wife). Here, in about 715, two monks from Wearmouth and Jarrow vanished. They were carrying the largest illustrated book ever produced as a gift for the Pope - a Bible made of the skins of 1500 calves and needing a pack mule to

carry it. In the 16th century, a large book was bought by the Medici library from the monks of San Salvatore of Mount Amiata for their library in Florence and in the 19th century, scholars discovered that that book was the English book described by the Venerable Bede. Further south, the via Francigena enters the flat tuff plateau of Lazio and retraces the Roman via Cassia. After walking through the town and on the rim of Lake Bolsena, the traveller will taste the fine wine of Montefiascone , which induced even a pope to say "it is, it is, it is of the best".

After all this the pilgrim will finally tread shiny Roman paving stones, skirting vast Roman ruins and, after visiting but then leaving aside the town of Viterbo, he will cross streams on Roman bridges, feel the proximity of Rome and ultimately reach Mons Gaudii" (a vantage point thus named by pilgrims from before Sigeric's times) from which he will see the Holy Dome of St. Peter's and the Vatican .

At the journey's end the traveller will be a richer person, elevated by the experience and the acquisition of knowledge obtainable only by sailing along this "river of history" .

For more information about Giovanni Caselli go to:
http://www.giovannicaselli.com
http://www.giovannicaselli.it
http://www.giovannicaselli.it/LA%20VIA%20ROMEA%20PAGE%201.htm
http://www.donsmaps.com/caselli.html

The CPR was formed in late 2006 and its founding meeting was held on the 18th November. It is the British Association representing those making a pilgrimage to Rome by foot, bicycle or horse. The objective of the confraternity is to aid those making a pilgrimage to Rome by foot, bicycle or horse with practical help and information.

What routes do the CPR cover? *The via Francigena and all traditional pilgrimage routes to Rome. Our primary efforts are to re-establish the via Francigena as a popular pilgrimage route.*

Is the CPR a secular organisation? *The group is non-denominational in that it is not tied to any one church, however the title 'pilgrim' is in our objectives to distinguish ourselves from a hiking group.*

Is the CPR a British organisation? *The members present at meetings and any physical facilities are likely to be from Britain, but the purpose of the organisation is to help all English speaking people.*

Way-marking - *We limit our way-marking to England and work with Canterbury City Council and Kent County Council to mark routes for walkers and cyclists from Canterbury to Dover.*

Accommodation - *The pilgrimage to Rome is a long and expensive journey. We have established a database of accommodation of all costs that can be updated quickly and conveniently.*

Newsletter - *Our newsletter publishes articles about the pilgrimage and aspects of the route such as journals, new routes, historical information, new publications, book reviews, information about meetings and conferences etc. and is a method of communication between members of the confraternity. It is published primarily by e-mail though hard copies are available.*

Pilgrim Passport - *A pilgrim passport is published by the confraternity.*

Website - *The website www.pilgrimstorome.org.uk is central to providing members and those interested in the pilgrimage to Rome with information.*

Meetings - *There is a Practical Pilgrim Day and AGM held every year in the Spring and an Autumn meeting which is based on a topic relevant to Rome or the pilgrimage routes.*

Membership *is open to all interested in pilgrimage to Rome by foot, cycle and horse. The cost is £10 per year or £20 for 3 years for those based in the UK and £20 for 5 years for those outside the UK who are unable to attend our meetings.*

Via Francigena Yahoo Group (VFYG) *http://groups.yahoo.com/group/via-francigena/ was established in October 2004. It is an open group which all those interested in pilgrimage to Rome by foot, cycle and horse are welcome to join. The benefit of such a group is the question and answer process as well as the reports and feedback provided by pilgrims on the route or by those who have completed the pilgrimage. There is also much information in the Files and Links sections of the website. The site is moderated on a reactive basis but as the members are pilgrims this is hardly ever necessary.*

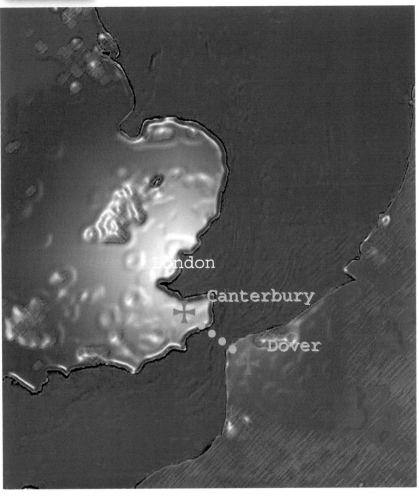

Where the sea meets the moon-blanched land,
Listen! you hear the grating roar
Of pebbles which the waves draw back, and fling,
At their return, up the high strand,
Begin, and cease, and then again begin,
With tremulous cadence slow, and bring
The eternal note of sadness in.

Matthew Arnold

15

Kent

Our journey starts in the county of Kent, often referred to as "The Garden of England", because of its abundance of orchards and hop gardens. The major geographical features of the county are determined by a series of ridges and valleys running east-west across the county. Kent's location between London and the continent has led to its being in the front line of several conflicts, including the Battle of Britain during World War II. East Kent was named Hell Fire Corner during the conflict and England has relied on the county's ports to provide warships through much of the past 800 years; the Cinque Ports in the 12th–14th centuries and Chatham Dockyard in the 16th–20th centuries were of particular importance to the country's security. Kent has a nominal border with France halfway through the Channel Tunnel and France can be seen clearly from Folkestone in fine weather.

The area has been occupied since the Palaeolithic era. The Medway megaliths were built during the Neolithic era and there is a rich sequence of Bronze Age, Iron Age and Roman era occupation, as indicated by finds and features such as the Ringlemere gold cup and the Roman villas of the Darent valley.

The extreme west of the modern county, as it is defined today, was occupied by Iron Age tribes, known as the Regnenses. It is possible that another ethnic group occupied what is now called The Weald and East Kent. East Kent became a kingdom of the Jutes during the 5th century and was known as Cantia from about 730 and as Cent in 835. The modern name of Kent is derived from the Brythonic word Cantus meaning "rim" or "border". This describes the eastern part of the current county area as a border land or coastal district. Julius Caesar named the area Cantium, or home of the Cantiaci in 51 BC. The early medieval inhabitants of the county were known as the Cantwara, or Kent people.

In the 11th century, the people of Kent adopted the motto Invicta (meaning undefeated), following the invasion of Britain by William of Normandy. Their continued resistance against the Normans led to Kent's designation as a semi-autonomous County Palatine in 1067. Under the nominal rule of William's half-brother Odo of Bayeux, the county was granted similar powers to those granted in the areas bordering Wales and Scotland. During the medieval and early modern period, Kent played a major role in several of England's most notable rebellions, including the Peasants' Revolt of 1381, led by Wat Tyler and Wyatt's Rebellion of 1554 against Queen Mary I. Later, in the early 1800s, Kent became associated with smugglers working along its coastline. Groups like The Aldington Gang brought spirits, tobacco and salt to the county and transported goods such as wool across the sea to France, while also creating an adventorous mystic that inspired Rudyard Kipling, among others. During World War II, much of the Battle of Britain was fought in the skies over the county. Between June 1944 and March 1945, over 10,000 V1 flying bombs, known as "Doodlebugs", were fired on London from bases in Northern France. Many were destroyed by aircraft, anti-aircraft guns or barrage balloons, nevertheless, both London and Kent were hit by around 2,500 of these bombs.

Canterbury

The Canterbury area has been inhabited since prehistoric times and was first recorded as the main settlement of the Celtic tribe, the Cantiaci, which inhabited most of modern day Kent. In the first century AD, the Romans captured the settlement and named it Durovernum Cantiacorum, meaning stronghold of the Cantiaci by the alder grove. The Romans rebuilt the town with new streets in a grid pattern, a theatre, a temple, a forum, public baths and later a wall, enclosing an area of 130 acres (53ha), with seven gates. After the Romans left, in 410 AD, Durovernum Cantiacorum was abandoned and gradually decayed. Over the next 100 years, an Anglo-Saxon community formed within the city walls, with Jutish (from Jutland)

refugees arriving and possibly intermarrying with the locals. The Jutes named the town Cantwaraburh, meaning Kent people's stronghold. In 597 AD, Pope Gregory the Great sent Augustine to convert King Æthelberht of Kent to Christianity. After the conversion, Canterbury was chosen by Augustine as the centre for an episcopal See (the official seat of a bishop) in Kent and an abbey and cathedral were built. Thus, Augustine became the first Archbishop of Canterbury. The town's new importance led to its revival and trades developed in pottery, textiles and leather. By 630, gold coins were being struck at the Canterbury mint and in 672 the Synod of Hertford gave the See of Canterbury authority over the entire English Church. In 842 and 851, Canterbury suffered great loss of life as a result of Danish raids and during a second wave of attacks in 1011 the cathedral was burnt and Archbishop Alphege was killed. Later, in 1066, the inhabitants of Canterbury remembered the destruction caused by the Danes and chose not to resist William the Conqueror's invasion. William immediately ordered a wooden motte-and-bailey (a form of castle situated on a raised earthwork and surrounded by a protective fence) castle to be built by the Roman city wall and in the early 12th century, the castle was rebuilt in stone. After the murder of Archbishop Thomas Becket at the cathedral in 1170, Canterbury became one of the most notable towns in Europe, as pilgrims from all parts of Christendom came to visit his shrine. A pilgrimage that provided the framework for Geoffrey Chaucer's 14th-century collection of stories, The Canterbury Tales.

Canterbury is also associated with several other saints from this period:

Æthelberht (also Æthelbert, Aethelberht, Aethelbert, or Ethelbert, c.560 - February 616) was King of Kent from about 580 or 590 until his death. In his Ecclesiastical History of the English People, the monk Bede lists Aethelberht as the third king to hold imperium over other Anglo-Saxon kingdoms. In the late ninth century Anglo-Saxon Chronicle Æthelberht is referred to as a bretwalda, or "Britain-ruler". He was the first English king to convert to Christianity. Æthelberht married Bertha, the Christian daughter of Charibert, king of the Franks, thus building an alliance with the most powerful state in contemporary Western Europe; the marriage probably took place before Æthelberht came to the throne. The influence of Bertha may have led to the decision by Pope Gregory I to send Augustine as a missionary from Rome. Augustine landed on the Isle of Thanet in east Kent in 597. Shortly thereafter, Æthelberht was converted to Christianity, churches were established and wider-scale conversion to Christianity began in the kingdom. Æthelberht provided the new church with land in Canterbury, at what came to be known as St Augustine's Abbey. Æthelberht was later canonised for his role in establishing Christianity among the Anglo-Saxons, as were his wife and daughter.

Augustine of Canterbury (c. first third of the 6th century – 26 May 604) was a Benedictine monk who became the first Archbishop of Canterbury in the year 598. Augustine was the

prior of a monastery in Rome when Pope Gregory the Great chose him in 595 to lead a mission (usually known as the Gregorian mission) to Britain to convert the pagan King Æthelberht of the Kingdom of Kent to Christianity. Kent was probably chosen because it was near the Christian kingdoms in Gaul and because Æthelberht had married a Christian princess, Bertha, daughter of Charibert I the King of Paris who was expected to exert some influence over her husband. Before reaching Kent the missionaries had considered turning back but Gregory urged them on and,

in 597, Augustine landed on the Isle of Thanet and proceeded to Æthelberht's main town of Canterbury. King Æthelberht converted to Christianity and also allowed the missionaries to preach freely, giving them land to found a monastery outside the city walls. Augustine was consecrated bishop of the English and converted many of the king's subjects, including thousands during a mass baptism on Christmas Day in 597. Pope Gregory sent more missionaries in 601, along with encouraging letters and gifts for the churches, although attempts to persuade the native Celtic bishops to submit to Augustine's authority failed. Roman Catholic bishops were established in London and Rochester in 604 and a school was founded to train Anglo-Saxon priests and missionaries. Augustine also arranged the consecration of his successor, Laurence of Canterbury. Augustine died in 604 and was soon revered as a saint.

Anselm of Canterbury (c. 1033 – 21 April 1109) was an Italian, a Benedictine monk, a philosopher, theologian and Archbishop of Canterbury from 1093 to 1109. Called the founder of scholasticism, he is famous in the West as the originator of the ontological argument for the existence of God. In 1720, Anselm was recognized as a Doctor of the Church by Pope Clement XI. His family was related to the ascendant House of Savoy and owned considerable property. His father, Gundulf, seems to have been harsh and violent, while Ermenberga, his mother, was considered to be prudent and virtuous. At the age of 15, Anselm wanted to enter a monastery but his father refused to give his consent. Disappointment brought on a psychosomatic illness and he gave up his studies to lead an apparently disreputable existence. During this period, his mother died and his father's harshness became so unbearable that Anselm left home when he was 23, crossed the Alps and wandered through Burgundy and France. Attracted by the fame of his countryman Lanfranc (then prior of the Benedictine Abbey of Bec), Anselm arrived in Normandy in 1059. The *following year, after some time at Avranches, he entered the abbey as a novice at the age of 27 and submitted himself to the Rule of Saint Benedict, a decision that was to change his life.*

Mellitus *was exiled from London by the pagan successors to his patron, King Sæberht of Essex, following the latter's death around 616. King Æthelberht of Kent, Mellitus' other patron, died at about the same time, forcing him to take refuge in Gaul. Mellitus returned to England the following year, after Æthelberht's successor had been converted to Christianity, but he was unable to return to London, whose inhabitants remained pagan. Mellitus was consecrated as Archbishop of Canterbury in 619. During his tenure, he was alleged to have miraculously saved the cathedral and much of the town of Canterbury from a fire. After his death in 624, Mellitus was revered as a saint.*

Theodore *(602 – 19 September 690) was the seventh Archbishop of Canterbury, best known for his reform of the English Church and establishment of a school in Canterbury with major scholarly achievements. He is commemorated as a saint in the Calendar of Saints of the Eastern Orthodox Church on September 19. As Archbishop, Theodore conducted a survey of the English church, appointed various bishops to Sees that had been vacant for some time and then called*

the Synod of Hertford to institute reforms concerning the proper celebration of Easter, episcopal authority, itinerant monks, the regular convening of subsequent synods, marriage and prohibitions of consanguinity. He also proposed dividing the large diocese of Northumbria into smaller sections, a policy which brought him into conflict with Bishop Wilfrid, whom Theodore himself had appointed to the See of York. Theodore deposed and expelled Wilfrid in 678, dividing his dioceses in the aftermath. The conflict with Wilfrid was not finally settled until 686–687. In 679, Aelfwine, the brother of King Ecgfrith of Northumbria, was killed in battle against the Mercians. Theodore's intervention prevented the escalation of the war and resulted in peace between the two kingdoms, with King Æthelred of Mercia paying compensation for Aelfwine's death. Theodore and Hadrian established a school in Canterbury resulting in a "golden age" of Anglo-Saxon scholarship. Theodore also taught sacred music, introduced various texts, knowledge of Eastern saints and may even have been responsible for the introduction of the Litany of the Saints, a major liturgical innovation, into the West. Theodore died at the remarkable age of 88, having held the archbishopric for twenty-two years and was buried in St. Peter's church, Canterbury.

Dunstan *(c. 909 – 19 May 988) was an Abbot of Glastonbury, a Bishop of Worcester, a Bishop of London and an Archbishop of Canterbury, later canonised as a saint. His work restored monastic life in England and reformed the English Church. His 11th-century biographer, Osbern, himself an artist and scribe, states that Dunstan was skilled in "making a picture and forming letters", as were other clergy of his age who reached senior rank. Dunstan served as an important minister of state to several English*

kings. He was the most popular saint in England for nearly two centuries, having gained fame for the many stories of his greatness, including Dunstan's legendary cunning in dealing with the Devil.

*An African by birth, **Adrian** became Abbot of Nerida, a Benedictine monastery near Naples,*

when he was very young. Pope Vitalian intended to appoint him Archbishop of Canterbury to succeed St. Deusdedit, who had died in 664, but Adrian considered himself unworthy and begged the Pope to appoint Theodore, a Greek monk, in his place. The Pope yielded, on condition that Adrian accompany Theodore to England and be his adviser in the administration of the Diocese of Canterbury. They left Rome in 668, but Adrian was detained in France by Ebroin, the Mayor of the Palace who suspected that he had a secret mission from the Eastern Emperor, Constans II. After two years Ebroin found that his suspicion had been groundless and allowed Adrian to proceed to England, where Archbishop Theodore appointed him Abbot of St. Peter in Canterbury, a monastery which had been founded by St. Augustine. Adrian assisted the Archbishop in his work to unify the customs and practices of the Anglo-Saxon Church with those of the Church of Rome. Under his direction the School of Canterbury became the centre of English learning. After spending thirty-nine years in England Adrian died in the year 710 and was buried at Canterbury.

*Archbishop and the "First Martyr of Canterbury", **Alphege** was born in 953 and became a monk in the Deerhurst Monastery in Gloucester. A few years later he received permission to become a hermit and retired to a small hut near Somerset, England. In 984 Alphege assumed the role of abbot of the abbey of Bath, founded by St. Dunstan and in that same year, Alphege succeeded Ethelwold as bishop of Winchester. He served there for two decades and became well known for his care of the poor and for his own austere life. In 994, King Aethelred the Unready sent him to mediate with invading Danes and as a result, the Danish chieftain Anlaf converted to Christianity, although he and the other chief, Swein, demanded tribute from the Anglo-Saxons of the region. Anlaf vowed never to lead his troops against Britain again. In 1005 Alphege became the successor to Aleric as the archbishop of Canterbury, receiving the pallium in Rome from Pope John XVIII. He returned to England in time to be captured by the Danes pillaging the southern regions. The Danes besieged Canterbury and took Alphege captive. The ransom for his release was three thousand pounds, but it was unpaid and Alphege was beaten to death. Revered as a martyr, Alphege's remains were placed in St. Paul's Church in London and then moved to Canterbury in 1023.*

Notable dates:
At 10,000, Canterbury had the 10th largest population in England, but the Black Death hit the town in 1348 and by the early 16th century, the population had fallen to 3,000.
In 1363, during the Hundred Years' War, a Commission of Inquiry found that disrepair, stone-robbing and ditch-filling had led to the Roman wall becoming eroded. Between 1378 and 1402,

the wall was virtually rebuilt and new wall towers were added. In 1381, during the Peasants' Revolt, the castle and Archbishop's Palace were sacked and Archbishop Sudbury was beheaded in London. Sudbury is still remembered annually by the

St. Augustine's Abbey

Christmas mayoral procession to his tomb at Canterbury Cathedral.

In 1413 Henry IV became the only sovereign to be buried at the cathedral.

In 1448 Canterbury was granted a City Charter, which gave it a mayor and a high sheriff, posts which have endured until today.

In 1504 the cathedral's main tower, the Bell Harry Tower, was completed, ending 400 years of building.

During the Dissolution of the Monasteries, the city's priory, nunnery and three friaries were closed. St Augustine's Abbey, the 14th richest in England at the time, was surrendered to the Crown and its church and cloister were levelled. The rest of the abbey was dismantled over the next 15 years, although part of the site was converted to a palace. Thomas Becket's shrine in the Cathedral was demolished and all the gold, silver and jewels were removed to the Tower of London and Becket's images, name and feasts were obliterated throughout the kingdom, ending the pilgrimages.

By the 17th century, Canterbury's population was 5,000; of whom 2,000 were French-speaking Protestant Huguenots, who had begun fleeing persecution and war in the Spanish Netherlands in the mid-16th century. The Huguenots introduced silk weaving into the city, which by 1676 had outstripped wool weaving.

In 1620 Robert Cushman negotiated the lease of the Mayflower at 59 Palace Street for the purpose of transporting the Pilgrims to America.

During the Second World War (1939-45), 10,445 bombs dropped during 135 separate raids destroyed 731 homes and 296 other buildings in the city, including the Simon Langton Grammar Schools where 115 people were killed. The most devastating raid was on 1 June 1942 during the Baedecker Blitz.

Canterbury Cathedral

St Augustine, the first Archbishop of Canterbury, arrived on the coast of Kent as a missionary to England in 597 AD. He was given a church in Canterbury by King Ethelbert whose Queen, Bertha, was already a Christian. Augustine established his seat within the Roman city walls (cathedra – Latin word for seat) and built the first cathedral there, becoming the first Archbishop of Canterbury. Until the 10th century the Cathedral community lived as the household of the Archbishop, but it subsequently became a formal community of Benedictine monks, which continued until the monastery was dissolved by King Henry VIII in 1540. Augustine's original building lies beneath the floor of the nave, because the Cathedral was completely rebuilt by the Normans in 1070, following a major fire. There have been many additions to the building over the last nine hundred years, but some of the windows and their stained glass date from the 12th century. By 1077, Archbishop Lanfranc had rebuilt the cathedral as a Norman church. A staircase and parts of the North Wall - in the area of the

North West transept also called the Martyrdom - remain from that building. Though the Cathedral's role as a monastery came to an end its role as a place of prayer continued. The responsibility for the services and upkeep was given to a group of clergy known as the Dean and Chapter and today, the Cathedral is still governed by the Dean and four Canons, together (in recent years) with four lay people and the Archdeacon of Maidstone. During the Civil War of the 1640s, the Cathedral suffered damage at the hands of the Puritans; much of the medieval stained glass was smashed and horses were stabled in the nave. After the Restoration in 1660, several years were spent in repairing the building. In the early 19th Century, the North West tower, dating from Lanfranc's time, was found to be dangerous and was demolished and replaced by a copy of the South West tower, thus giving a symmetrical appearance to the west end of the Cathedral. During the Second World War, the Precincts were heavily damaged by enemy action. The Cathedral's Library was destroyed, but the Cathedral itself was not seriously damaged.

Canterbury Cathedral

Jannina Veit Teuten, born in London in 1939, gained the National Diploma in Design at Twickenham Art College (1960). She then moved to Florence, Italy (1970) and studied painting and sculpture at the Accademia delle Belle Arte in Florence (1971 to 1980). She is primarily a painter of portraits in oils, but her first water colour exhibition, on request, was of Settignano (1980). Many more followed in England, France and Italy. One, of major importance was to commemorate the 80th Anniversary of the battle of the Somme in Picardy and 30 views of recent urban restoration in Amiens. Work for the via Francigena project began in 1993 - 23 exhibitions of paintings staged from Canterbury to Rome. From 2002, Jannina has exhibited paintings of interiors and portraits, in oils, in Tuscany, and has had repeat showings of the via Francigena Project in Italy. In 2006, she was Commended at ministerial level for her work to promote the project. Work in progress: water colours and drawings of the via Francigena south of Rome for a permanent exhibition due to be launched in 2010.
Tel: 0039 349 17 06 874   veitteuten@hotmail.it

The North Downs Way

On leaving Canterbury, pilgrims join the North Downs way, which follows the legendary Pilgrims Way, an historic route used by pilgrims travelling to holy shrines. Originally they would have travelled from Canterbury to Winchester to pray for St Swithun who was buried

at the cathedral. Later, this route was used in reverse as pilgrims journeyed from Winchester to Canterbury Cathedral in order to pray at the shrine of Thomas Becket. From Canterbury, the North Downs Way traces a large part of the route taken by pilgrims travelling along the via Francigena to Rome.

On the way to Sheperdswell look out for:

Waldershare House - a very elegant Palladian mansion of the Georgian era surrounded by attractive parkland complete with an avenue of limes, spreading chestnut and beech. The ornate square folly is typical of the period.

Coldred Court - located east of Sheperdswell. The motte and the manor house, part of **Coldred Court Farm**, are visible from the road.

Shepherdswell

Also known as Sibertswold, this village is notable for the Shepherdswell memorial (a Celtic Cross) and the Green Man in the church (a sculpture, drawing or other representation of a face surrounded by or made from leaves, frequently found on carvings in churches and other buildings).

Dover

Looming high above the dark waters of the channel, the seven white chalk cliffs of Dover are

one of the most recognizable British sights in the world. For many hundreds of years, the Straits of Dover have been both Britain's frontline and gateway and their history reflects this dramatic and sometimes bloody past. Dover controls the English Channel and is known as the 'Lock and Key of England'. Julius Caesar tried to land here during the Roman Invasion of 55 BC and it was the prime objective of the invasion plans of William the Conqueror, Napoleon and Hitler. As well as the massive castle, Dover's history as a military and garrison town can be seen in the extensive remains of its Roman forts, Napoleonic forts and defences from both the World Wars when Dover was Britain's Frontline Town. Today, Dover still relies on the harbour for its prosperity. It is the busiest passenger ferry terminal in the world, the busiest cruise liner terminal in Britain and a major port for freight.

Dover Castle

After the Battle of Hastings in October 1066, William the Conqueror and his forces marched to Westminster Abbey for his coronation. They took a roundabout route, via Romney, Dover, Canterbury, Surrey and Berkshire. From the inception of the Cinque Ports's foundation* in 1050, Dover has always been a chief member. It was during the reign of Henry II that the castle began to take recognisable shape. The inner and outer baileys and the great Keep belong to this time. In 1216, a group of rebel barons invited Louis VIII of France to come and take the English crown. He had some success breaching the walls but was unable ultimately to take the castle. The vulnerable north gate that had been breached in the siege was converted into an underground forward-defence complex (including St John's Tower) and new gates were built into the outer curtain wall on the western (Fitzwilliam's Gate) and eastern (Constable's Gate) sides. During the siege, the English defenders tunnelled outwards and attacked the French, thus creating the only counter tunnel in the world. This can still be seen in the medieval works. By the Tudor age, the defences themselves had been superseded by gunpowder. During the English Civil War the castle was held for the king but then taken by a parliamentarian trick without a shot being fired. Massive rebuilding took place at the end of the eighteenth century and during the Napoleonic Wars. With Dover becoming a garrison town, there was a need for barracks and storerooms for the additional troops and their equipment. The solution adopted by the Royal Engineers was to create a complex of barracks tunnels about 15 metres below the cliff top. The first troops were accommodated in 1803 and at the height of the Napoleonic Wars the tunnels housed more than 2000 men. To date, they are the only underground barracks ever built in Britain. At the end of the Napoleonic Wars,  the tunnels were partly converted and used by the Coast Blockade Service to combat smuggling. This was a short term endeavour, however and in 1826 the headquarters were moved closer to shore. The tunnels then remained abandoned for more than a century, until World War II, when they were converted first into an air-raid shelter and then later into a military command centre and underground hospital. In May 1940, Admiral Sir Bertram Ramsay directed the evacuation of French and British soldiers from Dunkirk (code-named Operation Dynamo) from his headquarters in the cliff tunnels. Later the tunnels were to be used as a shelter for the Regional Seats of Government in the event of a nuclear attack, but this plan was abandoned for various reasons, including the realisation that the chalk of the cliffs would not provide significant protection from radiation and because of the inconvenient form of the tunnels and their generally poor condition. A statue of Admiral Sir Bertram Ramsay was erected in November 2000 outside the tunnels in honour of his work on the Dunkirk evacuation and protection of Dover.

* Cinque Ports - a historic series of coastal towns in Kent and Sussex, at the eastern end of the English Channel where the crossing to the continent is narrowest. It was originally formed for military and trade purposes, but is now entirely ceremonial.

To be a Pilgrim

Who would true valour see,
Let him come hither;
One here will constant be,
Come wind, come weather.
There's no discouragement
Shall make him once relent
His first avowed intent,
To be a pilgrim.

Whoso beset him round
With dismal stories
Do but themselves confound;
His strength the more is.
No lion can him fright,
He'll with a giant fight,
But he will have a right
To be a pilgrim.

Hobgoblin, nor foul fiend,
Can daunt his spirit:
He knows, he at the end
Shall life inherit.
Then fancies fly away,
He'll fear not what men say,
He'll labour night and day
To be a pilgrim.

John Bunyan

*Before leaving British shores, mention has to be made of **John Bunyan**, Britain's famed author of '**The Pilgrim's Progress**'.*

John Bunyan was born near Bedford, in 1628. Thomas Bunyan, his father, was a brazier, or tinker, and John was brought up to follow his father's trade. When he was 16, Bunyan lost his mother and two sisters who died within months of each other. His father married for the third time and it may have been the arrival of his stepmother that precipitated his estrangement and subsequent enlistment in the parliamentary army. After the civil war was won by The Parliamentarians, Bunyan returned to his former trade and married in 1649 (he was about 21). His wife, Mary, was an orphan and their life was modest to say the least. Bunyan wrote that they were "as poor as poor might be", not even "a dish or spoon between them".

In his autobiographical book, 'Grace Abounding', Bunyan describes himself as having led an abandoned life in his youth and as having been morally reprehensible, though there appears to be no evidence that he was outwardly worse than the average of his neighbours - examples of sins to which he confesses are profanity, dancing and bell-ringing. The increasing awareness of his, apparently, un-Biblical life led him to contemplate acts of impiety and profanity and he was tortured by the fear that he was guilty of what he described as the "unpardonable sin". As he struggled with his newfound faith, Bunyan became increasingly despondent and fell into mental as well as physical turmoil - increasingly identifying himself with St. Paul, who had characterized himself as "the chief of sinners". He also claimed to have heard voices and have visions similar to St. Theresa's and William Blake's religious experiences. As a result of these experiences, he was received into the Congregational church in Bedford in 1653, but remained open to all who had biblical faith in Jesus Christ and was opposed to those who caused divisions over the form and time of baptism. While still in Elstow, Mary gave birth to a blind daughter, also named Mary and a second daughter, Elizabeth, shortly followed by two more children, John and Thomas. In 1655, after moving his family to Bedford, both Bunyan's wife and his mentor, John Gifford, died. Bunyan was utterly grief-stricken and his health declined, but in spite of this he went onto become a deacon of St. Paul's Church, Bedford and began preaching, with marked. As his popularity and notoriety grew, Bunyan increasingly became a target for slander and libel. He was accused of being a witch, a Jesuit, a highwayman and was said to have mistresses and multiple wives. In 1658, aged 30, he was arrested for preaching at Eaton Socon and in 1658, Bunyan was indicted for preaching without a license and finally in November 1660, he was taken to the county gaol in Silver Street, Bedford. Initially, he was confined for three months, but when he refused to conform or stop preaching, his confinement was extended for a period of nearly 12 years. His prosecutor, Mr. Justice Wingate, was not inclined to incarcerate Bunyan, but his stark statement that "If you release me today, I will preach tomorrow", left Wingate with no choice. It was during this time that he conceived his allegorical novel: 'The Pilgrim's Progress'. In 1666, he was briefly released for a few weeks before he was arrested again for preaching and sent back to Bedford gaol for another six years. During this time he wove shoelaces and preached to an imprisoned congregation of about sixty parishioners to support his family. In his possession were two books, John Foxe's Book of Martyrs and the Bible, a violin he made out of tin, a flute he made from a chair leg and an unlimited supply of pen and paper. He was released in January 1672, (when Charles II issued the Declaration of Religious Indulgence) and became pastor of St. Paul's Church in the same month. Bunyan was the recipient of one of the first licences to preach under the new law. He built a new meeting-house and formed a nonconformist sect from his surviving parishioners and increased his congregation to as many as four thousand Christians in Bedfordshire. In addition, he established over thirty new congregations and was given the affectionate title of "Bishop Bunyan" by his parishioners. In March 1675, he was again imprisoned for preaching (when Charles II withdrew the Declaration of Religious Indulgence), but ironically it was the Quakers who helped secure his release. When the King asked for a list of names to pardon, they gave Bunyan's name as well as those of their members. In six months, he was free and, as a result of his popularity, he was not arrested again. In 1688, he served as chaplain to Sir John Shorter, the lord mayor of London, but as he was riding to London from Reading to resolve a disagreement (between a father and a son), he caught a cold, developed a fever and died at the house of his friend, John Strudwick. He was buried in the cemetery at Bunhill Fields in London and many Puritans (for whom worship of tombs or relics is considered most sinful) made it their dying wish that their coffins be placed as close to Bunyan's as possible. In 1862 a recumbent statue was created to adorn his grave. He lies among other historic nonconformists, George Fox, William Blake and Daniel Defoe.

The Pilgrim's Progress *from This World to That Which Is to Come - A Christian allegory, written in February, 1678. The Pilgrim's Progress is regarded as one of the most significant works of English literature. It has been translated into more than 200 languages and has never gone out of print. Pilgrim's Progress catalogs the journey of Christian, a man who is seeking his salvation on a pilgrimage to Heaven. Along the way, Christian encounters many obstacles that test his faith as well as many characters that are useful in showing him the difference between right and wrong, from the perspective of Christian religious faith. After Christian attains his heavenly reward, his family completes a pilgrimage to join him. Told as a dream, this seventeenth century religious classic uses Bible verses mixed with allegorical characters to preach its evangelist message. Christian sets out on a journey, leaving behind his friends and family in the City of Destruction and following the advice of his spiritual guide, Evangelist, in order to reach the Celestial City. His first obstacle is the Slough of Despair, which he manages to overcome with the help of a kind stranger. Christian is admitted into the Wicket Gate, the official starting point of his journey to the Celestial City. Only those who are invited through this gate are eligible for entrance into the Celestial City. He then mounts the Hill of Difficulty and reaches the house called Beautiful, where a group of four sisters examine his conscience and give him supplies for his journey. On his way down the hill, Christian faces more obstacles; battles with Apollyon in the Valley of Humiliation and on through the Valley of the Shadow of Death before being reunited with his old friend, Faithful. Evangelist warns Christian and Faithful about entering the town of Vanity, which hosts a year-long carnival designed to tempt pilgrims to abandon their journeys. In this town, Christian and Faithful are beaten and imprisoned. They stand trial for their religious faith and their rejection of the legal and moral*

codes of the town. Faithful is tortured and killed, sending him directly to the Celestial City as a martyr. Christian manages to escape from prison and is joined by Hopeful as he continues his journey. Christian and Hopeful choose to take a shortcut that lands them in the dungeons of Doubting Castle where they are beaten and starved by the Giant Despair and urged to commit suicide. Finally, they use a magic key called Promise to escape from the Castle. The two pilgrims continue on their journey until they reach the Delectable Mountains. Here, a group of shepherds give them a map to avoid traps along the way. The two meet Ignorance, who has joined the path by a shortcut and believes that he will be admitted to Heaven without any invitation. The three of them continue on the journey until they reach a fork in the road. Instead of looking at the map given to them by the shepherds, the group follows a bad man who leads them into a trap. They manage to get out and walk through the Enchanted Ground, where they have been warned not to fall asleep. To entertain themselves, they discuss their religious visions. Christian and Hopeful have both had visions of Jesus Christ, while Ignorance relies on his own heart as a reason why he should be allowed to enter Heaven. Christian and Hopeful reach the River of Death, where the depth of the river changes to reflect the doubt or faith of the person who enters it. At first Christian is overwhelmed by doubt and almost drowns in the river. Hopeful rescues him and helps him until they are confident enough that the river has become shallow enough to allow them to cross. They are received into the Celestial City and carried off into the clouds. Ignorance also approaches the gates, but is denied entry because he has no invitation or Biblical revelation to make him worthy of Heaven. The second part of the allegory relates the story of the pilgrimage undertaken by Christian's wife, Christiana and their four sons. The family is joined by a neighbour, Mercy, who is hopeful of finding salvation by accompanying the family on the pilgrimage. Her wish is granted when she is admitted at the Wicket Gate. The group is attacked on the first leg of the journey but rescued just in time. They receive one of their first warnings to bring a conductor to guide and protect them on their journey. The group meets the Interpreter and is shown another series of moral images to interpret and learn from. They are given a guide, Great Heart, to conduct them to the next stage of their journey. Great Heart brings them to the house called Beautiful, where the group is shown all the things that Christian once was. One of the sisters who live in the house quizzes the boys on their religious education. Great Heart reappears to lead the group on the rest of the journey. They pass through the Valley of Humiliation and the Valley of the Shadow of Death, where Great Heart protects them from all the dangers and shows them the spots where Christian had his adventures. On their way out, they meet Honest, who accompanies them on their journey. Their travels take them to Vanity, where all the sons are married off. The eldest son marries Mercy. More monsters are defeated and new members join the group. The journey continues to Doubting Castle, where the men of the group fight a battle that destroys the castle and the giant that lives in it. The group is reminded at various points about the fate of Christian during his pilgrimage. Finally the group arrives at the River of Death. The members of the group each receive a letter welcoming them into the Celestial City. The children of Christian and their wives remain on the living side to have children to continue Christian's legacy.

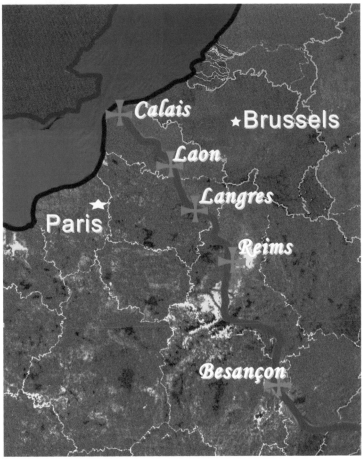

Broke to every known mischance, lifted over all
By the light sane joy of life, the buckler of the Gaul;
Furious in luxury, merciless in toil,
Terrible with strength renewed from her tireless soil;
Strictest judge of her own soul, gentlest of man's mind,
First to follow the Truth and last to leave old Truths behind -
France, beloved of every soul that loves or serves mankind.

Rudyard Kipling

Calais

Calais is the closest French town to England and overlooks the Straits of Dover, the narrowest point in the English Channel, which is only 34 km (21 miles) wide at this point. On a clear day, the white cliffs of Dover can easily be seen from Calais. The old part of the town, Calais-Nord, is situated on an artificial island surrounded by canals and harbours. The modern part of the town, St-Pierre, lies to the south and southeast. Virtually the entire town was destroyed

by heavy bombardments during World War II, so little in Calais pre-dates the war. For most visitors, the town is simply a place to pass through on their way to other destinations. The town centre is dominated by its distinctive city hall, built in the Flemish Renaissance style and directly in front of the statue 'Les Bourgeois de Calais', by Auguste Rodin. The German wartime military headquarters, situated near the train station in a small park, is now open to the public as a war museum.

From Calais, *the route leads along the Cote d'Opale, where long sandy beaches are exposed by huge tidal flows against a backdrop of high chalk cliffs. Within this section it skirts the Cap Blanc-Nez and offers some spectacular views both over the sea and surrounding countryside. On the way,* **look out for** *the statue in memory of Louis Blériot, the celebrated aviator.*

Louis Blériot

Born in Cambrai, France, on July 1, 1872, Louis Blériot, was an inventor, aircraft designer and pilot. During 1903, Blériot teamed up with Gabriel Voisin, another aircraft designer, to form the Blériot-Voison Company. The company built a floatplane glider, which flew during 1905.

They also developed a biplane powered by an Antoinette motor. The company broke up in 1906 and Blériot began to build and fly aircraft of his own design. As lightweight engines became available, he developed planes with various configurations ranging from box-kite biplanes to a canard (tail-first) monoplane. The Blériot V was the world's first successful monoplane. This plane got off the ground in 1907 but soon

crashed and was abandoned. Louis Bleriot is best known for his flight over the English Channel on July 25, 1909, the world's first flight over a large body of water in a heavier-than-air craft. After setting a European endurance record of 36 minutes 55 seconds and winning a cross-country prize, Blériot felt confident and made the trip over the Channel in 37 minutes, delighting the French and worrying the British, who felt that they had suddenly become vulnerable to air attack.

Guines LXXVIII Gisne

A pretty, but unremarkable town, except for its association with the Field of the Cloth of Gold (You can enjoy an account of the event depicted in the Chateau Guines open April to October).

The Field of the Cloth of Gold

The route takes you past the site of one of the most famous Summit Meetings, though it

would not have been recognised as such at the time. After seeing his kingdom divided by splits in the French royal family and royal marriages which latterly put Flanders under Spanish rule, the new King of France, François I, feared being surrounded on both sides by Spain and started to consider an alliance with England. Though a tiny country compared with France, England had (under Henry VII and Henry VIII) built up Europe's

most modern navy and as a growing sea power was potentially a good ally for France against Spain. With this aim in mind, Francis persuaded Henry to attend a meeting arranged between the two monarchs at a location within travelling distance of Calais. Henry and Francis were personal as well as political rivals and each king prided himself on the magnificence of his court. Huge pavilions were erected to serve as halls and chapels and great silken tents were decorated with gems and cloth of gold. It is this ostentatious display of wealth and power that earned the meeting-place the sobriquet 'The Field of the Cloth of Gold'. It lasted for three weeks (June 7-June 24, 1520), during which time each court strove to outdo the other in offering splendid entertainments and making grandiose gestures. Feasts and jousts were held, including a tilt between Henry and Francis themselves. Balls, masques, fireworks and military sports were just some of the activities on offer. The expense incurred by both monarchs was enormous and put tremendous strain on the finances of each country, but in spite of all the trouble and expense, the results of the meeting were negligible. Though Henry and Francis agreed in principle to an alliance, over the next several years the alliances were broken and reformed in an ever-shifting attempt to gain ascendance in Europe, with no-one gaining any permanent advantage.

Almis Simans has journeyed along many of the historic trails of Europe, including the Spanish Camino, the Way of St. James in France, Offa's Dyke in Wales, the Coast to Coast Walk in England and the via Francigena. He teaches a number of travel and history courses at Sydney University's Centre for Continuing Education and Sydney's WEA and is interested in making walking journeys accessible to people, especially to those who have the desire but haven't yet ventured out upon a longer journey. A journey to Santiago de Compostela in 1997 inspired his interest in traditional and contemporary pilgrimages. He has self-published four books about history and personal travel. www.travelsignposts.com/walking-holidays

 www.goodwalkingbooks.com

The Pilgrim's Quest

The Pilgrim set off in search of her quest.

 Travelling the Road to Santiago de Compostela, where the remains of St James are said to be buried, is one of the oldest and most interesting journeys in Europe. The idea of pilgrimage seems to touch a chord in many of us and the journey on the road to Compostela is as important as the destination.

The first inkling we receive of the journey ahead of us is a nudge or a resonance with an exotic destination. This is our first decision point – to take up the challenge or forgo the opportunity.

He accepted the challenge and made preparations for the journey, still unsure of what he would experience along the way.

It was time to leave the familiar and set forth past the threshold. Trials and delights presented themselves.

The journey presented challenges such as tired and sore muscles; sometimes little sleep;

coping with the blistering sun and the colder temperatures of the Galician heights. As if in compensation for these challenges, most villages and tabernas offered a rich and earthy selection of delicious regional cuisines, including wonderful local red wines. As she continued along the path she often thought about the mystery of what would happen to her when she reached Santiago.

The freshness of travel – where one is reborn every morning, ready to follow the sun westwards as a simple pilgrim, carrying two loads – a visible pack and an unseen (but felt) emotional weight. As he continued his walk across the varied landscapes of Northern Spain he spent time looking back at his recent life, the frustrations and hurdles and also the good fortune he had encountered or had let into his life.

Don Juan, the Yanqui Indian once said, "You can follow any path you like, but make sure it is a path with a heart."

After twenty five days of walking, she arrived in Santiago. In the superbly appointed cathedral she experienced a sense of awe at its size and its imposing, yet friendly atmosphere. There were small chapels where one could sit and be quiet. A large statue of the Apostle stood overlooking the central altar with stairs allowing the pilgrim to climb up to touch Santiago (St. James) himself. Here she felt able to lay down her burdens as she hugged the Apostle.

Once at the destination, a number of things can occur – disappointment, elation or a sense of puzzlement. This is part of the mystery. Walt Whitman wrote, "Not I, not anyone else, can travel that road for you. You must travel it for yourself. It is not far, it is within reach. Perhaps you have been on it since you were born and did not know."
The experience of the journey enabled him to grasp the Treasure and return home.

So it is in the spirit of such journeys that you can set out on your own quest along one of Europe's oldest and most interesting journeys – following the Way of St. James. This is a journey that may be right for you now.

Wissant

Located at the eastern end of an ancient lagoon, Wissant has long been a fishing village (the last fishing village in France to use a traditional method of fishing off a wooden boat called  a flobart) and was once the major port for access to England. Many historians think that Wissant is where Julius Caesar embarked for the conquest of England in 55 BC and from here it became an important Channel port, long before Calais was  developed by the English (1347 – 1558). Pilgrims flocking to or from England used to file through Wissant and the plaque shown on a wall of the church reminds everyone of Thomas Beckett's last return journey to England, where he met his death 28 days later (1170). At the end of the 19th century the coastal dunes of Wissant began to cover the seaside villas, but in the 20th century, an entrepreneur, Mr. Létendart from Calais, extracted sand and gravel from the dunes to the west of Wissant and resolved the problem. The subsequent excavations now form lakes and a nature reserve.

Thomas Beckett

Son of a wealthy Norman merchant living in London, Thomas Beckett was born in 1118. After being educated in England, France and Italy, he joined the staff of Theobald, the Archbishop of Canterbury. When Henry II became king in 1154, he appointed Thomas Becket as his chancellor. When Theobald died in 1162, Henry chose Becket as his next Archbishop of Canterbury. The decision angered many leading churchmen. They pointed out that Becket had never been a priest, had a reputation as a cruel military commander and was very materialistic (Becket loved expensive food, wine and clothes). They also feared that as Becket was a close  friend of Henry II, he would not be an independent leader of the church. After being appointed, Thomas Becket began to defy their criticism and showed great concern for the poor. Every morning thirteen poor people were brought to his home and, after washing their feet, Becket served them a meal and gave each one four silver pennies. In addition, he exchanged his expensive clothes for a simple monastic habit, slept on a cold stone floor, wore a tight-fitting hairshirt that was infested with fleas and was whipped daily by his monks. Thomas Becket came into conflict with Roger of Clare when he argued that some of the manors in Kent should come under the control of the Archbishop of Canterbury. Roger disagreed and refused to give up this land. Becket sent a messenger to Roger asking for a meeting. Roger responded by forcing the messenger to eat the letter. In 1163, after a long spell in France, Henry arrived back in England and was told that there had been a dramatic increase in serious crime while he had been away. The king's officials claimed that over a hundred murderers had escaped their proper punishment because they had claimed their right to be tried in church courts. There were several examples of clergy found guilty of murder or robbery who only received "spiritual punishments", such as suspension from office or banishment from the altar. The king decided that clergymen found guilty of serious crimes should be handed over to his courts and initially Thomas Becket agreed with Henry, but after talking to other clergy he asserted that the church should retain control of punishing its own members. The king believed that Becket had betrayed him and was determined to obtain revenge. In 1164, the Archbishop of Canterbury was involved in a dispute over land and Henry ordered Becket to appear before his courts, but when Becket refused, the king confiscated his property. Henry also claimed that Becket had stolen £300 from government funds when he had been Chancellor. Becket denied the charge but, so that the matter could be settled quickly, he offered to repay the money. Henry refused to accept Becket's offer and insisted that the Archbishop should stand trial. When Henry mentioned other charges, including treason, Becket decided to run away to France. Under the protection of Henry's old enemy, King Louis VII, Becket organised a propaganda campaign against Henry. Becket eventually agreed to return to England, but as soon as he arrived on English soil, he excommunicated the Archbishop of York and other leading churchmen who had supported Henry while he was away. Henry, who was in Normandy at the time, was furious when he heard the news and supposedly shouted out: "Will no one rid me of this turbulent priest?". Four of Henry's knights, Hugh de Morville, William de Tracy, Reginald Fitz Urse and Richard le Bret, who heard Henry's angry outburst decided to travel to England and fulfil his wish. When the knights arrived in Canterbury Cathedral on 29th December 1170, they demanded that Becket pardon the men he had excommunicated. When Becket refused, they hacked him to death with their swords. Canterbury Cathedral became a major centre of pilgrimage when the martyr was canonized as St Thomas.

Licques

Today the small town of Licques is famous for the delicious turkeys it rears in time for Christmas every year. The birds are paraded through the streets during its Fête de la Dinde - preceded by the Confrerie de Licques (the town's VIPs) - before being slaughtered and stuffed with chestnuts on Christmas Day. The 'hen of India' was introduced to Licques by the Prémontrés monks and was raised on an excellent free range diet of roots, seeds and the worms living in the damp valley grasslands. Sales to the Licques villagers started when the birds began to reproduce faster than they could be eaten and before long the local farmers were getting in on the act and breeding their own stock. As a consequence the entire region became famous for the tender and tasty meat, which is now sold throughout the year.

Whilst travelling through the **Pas-de-Calais** region it is worthwhile reflecting that it has been inhabited since prehistoric times, by the Celtic Belgae, the Romans, the Germanic Franks and the Alemanni. During the 4th and 5th centuries, the Roman practice of co-opting Germanic tribes to provide military and defence services along the route from Boulogne to Cologne created a Germanic-Romance linguistic border that persisted until the 8th century. Saxon colonization into the region from the 5th to the 8th centuries extended the linguistic border south and west, so that by the 9th century most inhabitants north of the line between Béthune and Berck spoke a dialect of Middle Dutch, while the inhabitants to the south spoke Picard, a variety of Romance dialects. This linguistic border is still evident today in the place names and family names of the region. Pas-de-Calais is also one of the original 83 departments created during the French Revolution. Later some of the heaviest battles of World War I were fought here and in World War II, Pas-de-Calais was the target of Operation Fortitude, an Allied plan to deceive the Germans that the invasion of Europe was to occur here, rather than in Normandy.

Wisques

The little village of Wisques is deceptive, in that despite its size it is home to two monasteries belonging to the order of Saint Benedict : Notre Dame (convent) and Saint Paul (monastery). **Saint Paul's Abbey** was built at the end of the 15th century by the Saint-Aldegonde family, but has undergone many changes over the centuries. First housed in the 'Petit Château', a fine 18th century mansion house situated opposite the present-day cemetery, the monks later moved to the 'Grand Château' which they still occupy today. The most noteworthy parts of the buildings are the bell-tower, the keep (built at the end of the middle ages) and parts renovated by Dom Bellot (Parisian, born into a family of architects and latterly a monk). An additional bell-tower was built in 1945 to house Bertine, the only bell from the old Saint-Bertin's abbey to withstand the ravages of the French revolution. Dating from 1470, it weighs 7.5 tons and is a listed monument. The tower of the present-day chapel was built in 1957 and the abbey was further extended in 1968, when the reception building was fully renovated and redecorated, with retreat accommodation provided in a modern building. Saint-Paul's Abbey's monastic workshops have been producing ceramic tiles for almost 50 years. The design is screen printed before enamel pigments are applied and fired at a high temperature to make them practically inalterable. Mass with Gregorian chants is sung every day at 9.45am.

Notre Dame - founded in 1889 by the nuns of Saint Cécile of Solesmes is the older of the two abbeys. The nuns were originally lodged in part of the buildings of the Grand Château, which was later to become the Abbey of Saint Paul, but the Abbey of Notre Dame was built in 1891. They chose the Lille architect Paul Vilain, who was considered to be the most eminent representative of the neo-gothic school in the north of France. The weather vane was installed at the peak of the tower around 1893 and in 1894 the nuns moved into the abbey, which was only completed in 1898. Although a cloistered order, the chapel is open to the public and there is a shop selling monastic products.

Therouanne LXXVII Teranburh

At the time of the Gauls, Tarwanna or Tervanna was the capital of the Belgian tribe of the Morini. After the Romans conquered Gaul, they too made the city the capital of the Civitas Morinorum district. In the 7th century, probably around 639, Saint-Audomare (Omer) established the bishopric of Terwaan or Terenburg, which, during the Middle Ages, controlled a large part of the left bank of the river Scheldt. Territorially it was part of the county of Artois which belonged to the county of Flanders. Thanks to the ecclesiastical control of some of the most prosperous cities north of the Alps, like Arras and Ypres, the bishopric was able to build a cathedral which was at the time the largest in France. In 1553 Charles V besieged Thérouanne in revenge for a defeat by the French at Metz. After he captured the city he ordered it to be razed to the ground, leaving only a small commune which lay outside the city walls, then named Saint-Martin-Outre-Eaux and later taking over the name Thérouanne.

Look out for:

The **church of Saint Martin**, dating from the nineteenth century. Archaeological site - **remains of the medieval city**.

Saint Audomar better known as Saint Omer, was a Burgundy-born bishop of Thérouanne, after whom nearby Saint-Omer was named. He was born of a distinguished family in Switzerland, but after the death of his mother, he entered (with his father) the abbey of Luxeuil in the Diocese of Besançon. Under the direction of Eustachius, Omer studied the Scriptures and displayed remarkable proficiency. When King Dagobert requested the appointment of a bishop for the important city of Terouenne, the capital of the ancient territory of the Morini in Neustria, Audomar was appointed and consecrated in 637. Though the Morini had received Christianity from Saint Fuscian and Saint Victoricus and later Antmund and Adelbert, nearly every vestige of it had disappeared. In 654 he founded the Abbey of Saint Peter (now Saint Bertin's) in Sithiu, soon to equal if not surpass the old monastery of Luxeuil for the number of learned and zealous men educated there. Several years later he erected the Church of Our Lady of Sithiu, with a small monastery adjoining. The exact date of his death is unknown, but he is believed to have died about the year 670 and probably laid to rest in the church of Our Lady which is now the Cathédrale Notre-Dame de Saint-Omer.

Amettes

Best known as being the birth place of Saint Benedict Joseph Labre (1748 -1783), Amettes is a typical farming village for the region. The church of St.Sulpice, dating from the sixteenth century, is also typical of its kind, but well worth taking some time-out to visit.

Saint Benedict Joseph Labre (1748 – 1783) was a French mendicant and latterly a Roman Catholic saint. He was born in Amettes, the eldest of fifteen children of a prosperous shopkeeper and religious from a very early age. He was noted for performing public acts of penance for his sins, even minor sins. At the age of sixteen, he attempted to join the Trappists, Carthusians and Cistercians, but each order rejected him as unsuitable for communal life. TheThe abbots of these orders suspected some form of mental illness that would make Labre unable to fulfil the vow of obedience necessary for any cloistered religious. Labre took this as a sign that it was God's will that he should abandon his country, his parents to lead a new sort of life: "A life most painful, most penitential, not in a wilderness nor in a cloister, but in the midst of the world, devoutly visiting as a pilgrim the famous places of Christian devotion". Saint Benedict first travelled to Rome on foot, subsisting on what he could receive by begging. He then travelled to most of the major shrines of Europe, often multiple times. He visited Loreto, Assisi, Naples and Bari in Italy, Einsiedeln in Switzerland, Paray-le-Monial in France and Compostela in Spain. During these trips he would always travel on foot, sleep in the open or in a corner of a room, with his clothes muddy and ragged. He lived on what little he was given and often shared the little he did receive with others. He is

reported to have talked rarely, prayed often and accepted the abuse he received quietly. In so doing, Labre was following in the role of the mendicant, the "Fool-for-Christ", found more often in the Eastern Church. In the last years of his life (his thirties), he lived in Rome, for a time, living in the walls of the ruins of the Colosseum. In his final weeks, he collapsed in church and was taken into a house out of charity, despite his protestations. He died of malnutrition on April 16, during Holy Week, in 1783. The 15th century Saint-Sulpice church in the centre of Amettes holds the saint's kneecaps and the straw-mattress he is supposed to have died on. On the walls, 14 scenes retrace the path of the saint's life and in the choir, contemporary stained-glass windows (fitted in 1975) depict the most important stages.

Wizerne

Though a relatively unremarkable, if pleasant town, Wizerne is memorable for one thing: **the Cupola** (La Coupole), a Second World War V-2 rocket base constructed by Nazi Germany at Wizernes, south west of Saint-Omer. Set in a former limestone quarry close to Helfaut, the complex was intended to be an impregnable underground production and launch facility for the

rockets. Work on the site was begun in October 1943 using forced labour under the direction of the Todt Organisation with the intention of quickly building a site that could threaten London. More than 6 km of galleries were dug by the Soviet prisoners in order to store the rockets 42 m underground. A liquid oxygen fuel plant was also built to supplement the supply from the now redeployed Eperleques site and underground barracks and administrative areas were dug out and lined with concrete. In January 1944 a huge concrete dome (71 m in diameter, 5m thick), or cupola, was built over the top. Directly beneath this structure a vast hexagonal room, 21 m high, housed the rocket production facility. Once assembled and fuelled the rockets were to be moved outside and fired, at a rate of 40-50 per day. On November 5, 1943, the Allied Central Interpretation Unit (CIU) reported photographs of the Wizernes rocket project, but attempts to destroy it did not start until March 1944, by which time the protective dome had already been finished. Over the five months, 3,000 tonnes of Allied bombs were dropped on La Coupole but failed to make any impact. However, the Tallboy bombing in June 1944 succeeded in damaging the area and the site was closed down in July 1944 before it was completed and before it had fired a single rocket. The site has a History and Remembrance Centre open to the public as a museum

St Omer

Refined and old fashioned, St Omer seems to have escaped the wholesale destruction of World War II. Pilasters (a slightly-projecting column built into or applied to the face of a wall) adorn the elegant 17th and 18th century houses that line the cobbled streets. In the first part of the 12th century, the River Aa was channelled out, making it possible for sea going vessels to bring their wares right into the city. The water around the town has been responsible for the development of various activities from  the extraction of peat to breweries, mills and 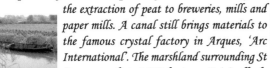 paper mills. A canal still brings materials to the famous crystal factory in Arques, 'Arc International'. The marshland surrounding St

St Omer Town Hall

Omer extends to 3,500 hectares. Originally dug out by the monks in the 7th century, part of the area is still farmed - the farmers using a 'bacove' or flat bottomed boat to transport crops and farming equipment.

Look out for: the Town Hall, begun in 1834 and finished in 1841 by Pierre Bernard Lefranc. **Notre Dame Cathedral.** Widely recognised as being the most beautiful intact example of gothic architecture to be found north of Paris, it houses a famous Rubens painting of Christ being removed from the cross as well as an astrological clock, said to be one of the oldest in France, dating from 1558 and showing days, months, signs of the Zodiac and, of course, the time. The impressive vast organ was built in 1717 by local sculptors and carpenters.

Bruay la Buissière LXXVI Bruwaei

The name of this town has undergone a number of changes before becoming what it is today. The source is in the French old word 'buissy', meaning a wooden box. From here it evolved

to become Bruxeria, then to Boesère, Bouchière, Buissière and then finally in 1725 became Bruay La Buissière. A number of Roman archaeological discoveries have been made and can be seen in Bruay la Buissèrie - principally a statuette of Venus along with evidence of clay-making and a furnace for the firing of clay pots. Bruay la Buissèrie and the surrounding area bear the scars of two world wars. In the First World War, British pilots Watt (27) and Howlett (26) lost their lives during an aerial battle with the infamous 'Red Baron'. They were buried near Bruay, alongside their French and Canadian allies. During the Second World War a number of

'Bruaysienne' became members of the resistance and were latterly recognised for their bravery. Like the rest of France, the people struggled with rationing and the oppression of living in an occupied country. Liberation came on September 4, 1944, with the arrival of the Canadians, but not before 33 people had died. Coal was discovered near Bruay la Buissèrie in 1720, with ultimately 8 shafts operating right up until 1976, after which the entire pit complex was closed. During the 1920s, an increase in the population of Bruay la Buissèrie was needed to meet the labour needs of the mines, with the result that a large Polish immigrant community was established and still remains today. Houses had to be rapidly built to accommodate the new residents and from 1938 to 1968, the city grew from 5,803 houses to 9,559. Marles les Minies is well worth taking a detour to visit.

Arras LXXV Atherats

Flemish culture still holds sway along the border with Belgium. During the approach and leaving of Arras you will find yourself meandering through an unfamiliar France of windmills and canals, where the local taste is for beer, savory stews and festivals with gallivanting giants. The grace of Flemish architecture is handsomely displayed in the central, cobbled squares, enclosed by 17th century Flemish-style façades. For many centuries, Arras was on the border

between France and the Low Countries and frequently changed hands before firmly becoming French in the late 17th century - the fortifications upgraded by Vauban helping to keep it in French hands. The town was closely linked to the trade of Flanders and later became an important centre for sugar beet farming and processing as well as a prosperous market centre. In the 14th and 15th centuries, Arras was a thriving textile town, specialising in fine wool tapestries that were sold to decorate palaces and castles all over Europe. Few of these tapestries survived the French Revolution when hundreds were burnt to recover the gold thread that was often woven into them. Nevertheless, the term 'arras' is still used to refer to a rich tapestry no matter where it was woven. The Union of Atrecht (the Dutch name for Arras) was signed here in January 1579 by the Catholic

Arras Town Hall

principalities of the Low Countries, which remained loyal to King Phillip II of Habsburg; provoking the declaration of the Union of Utrecht in the same month. During the First World War, Arras was near the front and the long series of battles fought nearby are known as the Battle of Arras. A series of medieval tunnels beneath the city, unknown to the Germans, became a decisive factor in the British forces holding of Arras (guided tours available). Nevertheless, the city, was heavily damaged and had to be rebuilt after the war. In the Second World War, during the invasion of France in May 1940, the town was the focus of a major British counter attack. The town was occupied by the Germans and 240 suspected French Resistance members were executed in the Arras citadel.

Look out for: the Grand Place and the smaller Place des Héroes, triumphs of postwar reconstruction, with each residence displaying a slightly varying design and some still visible shop signs.

Hôtel de Ville, rebuilt in the Flamboyant Gothic style at the west end of Place des Héroes and housing statues of Colas and Jacqueline, two giants whose replicas swagger round the town during local festivals. Many of Arras's most notable structures, including the museum and several government buildings, occupy the site of the old Abbaye de Saint-Vaast. The abbey's church was demolished and rebuilt in fashionable classical style in 1833. It now serves as the town's cathedral. There is a fine collection of statuary within the church and a number of religious relics.

Bapaume

This small country town is on a crossing point between Artois and the plains of Flanders on the one hand and the valley of the Somme and the Paris basin on the other - a position that made it the focal point for wars throughout its history. In 1335, Bapaume was fortified outside the castle walls, but unfortunately they were ineffective and the city was repeatedly taken. In 1540, Charles Quint ordered a fortified palace to be built, with thick walls and bastions, including defensive systems such as tunnels and galleries. These fortifications were later reinforced by Vauban. By the 19th century, Bapaume was no longer regarded as a fortified

Le Beffroi

town, with the result that the walls and bastions were blown-up and the moats filled in. Only the tower and part of the bastion of Dauphin are still visible. Work has been done recently to restore and make accessible the underground galleries used as underground shelters during both world wars.

Péronne

Though Péronne was a well-fortified settlement during the early middle ages (the ramparts were built in the 9th century), all that remains today is the Porte de Bretagne. Few towns have been destroyed so often. Burned and pillaged in the time of the Normans, gravely damaged during the time of the Spanish occupation, devastated by the Germans in 1870, totally destroyed in 1917 and finally bombarded and burned by the German airforce in May 1940. In tune with this rather sad history, Péronne is also equally well known for its Monument to the Dead, the work of the architect Louis Faille, representing a Picardy woman with clenched fist raised above the body of her son or

The Historial de la Grande Guerre

husband killed by the war. Within the walls of the ancient château the "Historial de la Grande Guerre" museum is a 'must visit' for those with an interest in the Great Wars. Created in 1992, by architect Henri Ciriani, it illustrates the development of the conflict. The building is characterised by the stark whiteness of the cement, inset with small cylinders, symbolic of military graves.

While travelling through the centre of Péronne, *Look out for:* the statue of Marie Fouré, a local heroine who apparently surprised and then speared one of Count Nassau's officers in 1536, with the result that his siege on the city was abandoned.

The Pilgrimage

Give me my scallop-shell of quiet,
My staff of faith to walk upon,
My scrip of joy, immortal diet,
My bottle of salvation,
My gown of glory, hope's true gage;
And thus I'll take my pilgrimage.

Blood must be my body's balmer;
No other balm will there be given:
Whilst my soul, like quiet palmer,
Travelleth towards the land of heaven;
Over the silver mountains,
Where spring the nectar fountains;
There will I kiss
The bowl of bliss;
And drink mine everlasting fill
Upon every milken hill.
My soul will be a-dry before;
But, after, it will thirst no more.

Sir Walter Raleigh

Somme

The Somme department is named after the Somme river and Amiens is its capital. The bay of Somme is the biggest estuary of the North of France, extending over 70 km² between the headland of Hourdel in the South and the headland of Saint-Quentin-en-Tourmont in the North. Le Crotoy, on the Somme's coastline has played host to several famous names over the centuries including Joan of Arc (who was imprisoned here), Jacques-Francois Conseil (first physician of the French colony of Guyana and physician to King Cayenne (1736 to 1771) and more recently, Jules Verne (French author who helped pioneer the science-fiction genre). Slightly further down the coast, in St-Valery-sur-Somme, William the Conqueror set off for England in 1066.

The many cemetries that cover the Somme region serve as poignant reminders of the mass slaughter that took place on the Western Front in World War 1 (which ended with the Armistice on November 21, 1918). Between July 1 and November 21, 1916, the Allied forces lost more than 600,000 men and the Germans at least 465,000. The Battle of the Somme, a series of campaigns conducted by British and French armies, against fortified positions held by the Germans, relieved the hard-pressed French at Verdun, but hopes of the breakthrough never materialised and the Allies only managed to advance 16km (10 miles). One German officer, General D. Swaha, famously described the campaign as "the muddy grave of the German field army." By the end of the battle, the British had learned many lessons in modern warfare while the Germans had suffered irreplaceable losses. British historian Sir James Edmonds stated, "It is not too much to claim that the foundations of the final victory on the Western Front were laid by the Somme offensive of 1916."

Doingt LXXIV Duin

A small village on the eastern outskirts of Peronne, Doingt is best known for its role in World War 2. Doingt was captured by the 5th Australian Division on 5 September

1918 and the village was completely destroyed in the fighting. Also noteworthy is the Menhir of Doingt, one of the

largest and best preserved Megaliths in the north of France. Two local legends are related to the menhir. The first tells the story of two fairies from the forest of Rocogne who came down to dance around it, while the second describes the moment when the giant Gargantua found a stone in his shoe that he removed and then threw with such strength that it landed on the banks of the river Cologne.

The Life of Gargantua and of Pantagruel is a connected series of five novels written in the 16th century by François Rabelais. It is the story of two giants, a father (Gargantua) and his son (Pantagruel) and their adventures, written in an amusing, extravagant, satirical vein. There is much crudity and scatological humor as well as a large amount of violence. Long lists of vulgar insults fill several chapters. At the same time he gives this definition of what he names Pantagruelism (the philosophy of his giant Pantagruel): "a certain gaiety of mind pickled in the scorn of fortuitous things".

The introduction to the series, in an English translation is as follows:

Readers, friends, if you turn these pages
Put your prejudice aside,
For, really, there's nothing here that's outrageous,
Nothing sick, or bad — or contagious.
Not that I sit here glowing with pride
For my book: all you'll find is laughter:
That's all the glory my heart is after,
Seeing how sorrow eats you, defeats you.
I'd rather write about laughing than crying,
For laughter makes men human and courageous.
BE HAPPY!

Petra Wolf and Mike Metras walked the Camino de Santiago in 2003, Petra from Constance, Germany and Mike from Roncesvalles, Spain. They met on that pilgrimage and were later married. Since then they have walked major portions of the Camino again, once walking back towards Europe from Santiago and following the via de la Plata Camino from Seville to Santiago. They have have also completed a 1200-plus-kilometre (775-mile) pilgrimage to Rome from their doorstep in Kisslegg, Germany. At the time of writing Mike and Petra on a new journey, starting in California and ending in Jerusalem.

Walking with awareness is about being aware of everything around you at all times. Walking with awareness is about physical walking, yes, but it is also about all aspects of our life. It is about our walk through life.

When we walk with awareness we are often walking with more purpose and life often takes on a more sacred character.

We walk with more heart and spirit.

We more easily hear and follow the calls of the Spirit and from deep within our heart.

We seek to find out our deepest truths to define our sacred path.

We learn more from life's daily lessons.

We more readily walk with joy and acceptance of all the variety that comes along our path.

We're calling our walk to Rome a "pilgrimage". What's this thing called pilgrimage? For a long time I have fought with the distinction between "pilgrimage" and a plain old walk because my walks always have been more important than "just" walks. Pilgrimage is a subset of walk; it's a special kind of walk. On a pilgrimage one walks with purpose and asks what's happening to me just now? What am I here? A walker goes from place to place and experiences what's along the way. A pilgrim does the same but tries to learn more about him/her self and his/her place in the Universe. And beyond our aims, a traditional pilgrim walked for the grace available upon arriving at the destination. Our pilgrimage to Rome has specific goals: (for both of us) to decide what to do and where to go next; to feel the Alps, the Po, Tuscany, Rome, the spirit and place of Italy; and to be open and seek out whatever other lessons we can integrate into our life pilgrimage; (for me); to face my fear of heights; and (for Petra) to find Peter's keys to heaven.

45

Aisne

Aisne is one of the original 83 departments created during the French Revolution on March 4, 1790, created from parts of the former provinces of Île-de-France, Picardie and Champagne. Most of the old growth forests in the area were destroyed during battles in World War I. The French offensive against the Chemin des Dames in spring 1917 is sometimes referred to as the Second Battle of the Aisne. The Aisne River crosses the area from east to west, where it joins the Oise River and the landscape is dominated by masses of rock which often have steep flanks. These rocks appear all over the region, but the most impressive examples are at Laon and the Chemin des Dames ridge, so make sure you look out for them. Agriculture dominates the economy, especially cereal crops, with the result that vast tracts of the area are featureless and all too reminiscent of the dust bowl prairies. Nevertheless, silk, cotton and wool weaving still flourish in Saint-Quentin and other towns, which offers some variation and interest. During World War I a number of significant architectural monuments were sadly destroyed, but the medieval churches in Laon, Braine and Urcel survived and are well worth visiting.

Serancourt-le-Grand LXXIII Martinwaeth
Laon LXXII Mundlothuin

As the capital of Aisne department, Laon occupies a dramatic site on top of a long ridge surrounded by wide plains. At the end of the 5th century, Remigius, Archbishop of Reims,

instituted the bishopric of Laon. As a result, Laon became a principal town in the kingdom of the Franks, though possession of it was often disputed. Early in the 12th century the communes of France set about emancipating themselves and as a result the history of the commune of Laon is one of the richest and most varied. The citizens had profited by Bishop Gaudry's temporary absence and failure to secure a communal charter, but on his return he purchased the revocation of this document from the king of France and recommenced his oppressions. The consequence was a revolt, in which the episcopal palace was burnt and the bishop and

Laon Cathedral

several of his partisans were put to death on 25 April 1112. The fire spread to the cathedral and reduced it to ashes. Uneasy at the result of their victory, the rioters went into hiding outside the town, which was then pillaged by the people of the neighborhood, who were eager to avenge the death of their bishop. Later, during the Hundred Years' War, Laon was attacked and taken over by the Burgundians, who then gave it up to the English, only for it to be retaken by the French after the consecration of Charles VII. Finally, in 1870, an engineer

46

blew up the powder magazine of the citadel when the German troops were entering the town. Many lives were lost and the cathedral and the old episcopal palace were damaged. Today, the old town is best approached by Poma, the only fully automated municipal cable car system in the world, which links the upper town (the historical) with the lower town.

Look out for:
Laon's splendid **Cathédrale de Notre-Dame**. Completed in 1235, the cathedral lost two of its original seven towers in the Revolution, but remains an impressive monument to the early Gothic style.

The rest of medieval Laon deserves some casual strolling: a promenade circles the 16th century Citadelle to the east and to the south you can follow the ramparts past the **Porte d'Ardon** and the **Porte des Chenizelles** to **Eglise St Martin**.

Brunhilde (whose route namesake you will have been following more or less since St Omer), was raised as an Arian Christian, but converted to Roman Catholicism after her marriage to Sigebert. From here she took a keen personal interest in the bishoprics and monasteries within her dominion and incidentally commissioned the building of several churches and the abbey of St. Vincent in Laon (580). Unfortunately the rest of her history is less positive and it appears she became embroiled in a number of unsavory assassinations. Ultimately this behaviour led to her own death, when, according to the Liber Historiae Francorum: "The army of Franks and Burgundians joined into one, all *together that death would be most fitting for the very wicked Brunhilda. Then King Clotaire ordered that she be lifted on to a camel and led through the entire army. Then she was tied to the feet of wild horses and torn apart limb from limb. Finally she died. Her final grave was the fire. Her bones were burnt."*

Corbeny LXXI Corbunei

This small town intersects with the Chemin des Dames (Ladies' Way), which is 30 kilometres long and runs along a ridge between the valleys of the rivers Aisne and Ailette. The name dates back to the 18th century when Louis XV's daughters, Adelaide and Victoire travelled to

Château de La Bove, near Bouconville-Vauclair, on the far side of the Ailette. The château belonged to Françoise de Châlus, former mistress of Louis XV, Countess of Narbonne-Lara and former Lady of Honour to Adelaide, whom the two ladies visited frequently. In an unusually magnanimous move for a cuckolded husband, the Count had the road surfaced to make their journey less arduous, which is when it gained its name. The ridge's strategic importance first became

evident in 1814 when Napoleon's young recruits beat an army of Prussians and Russians at the Battle of Craonne. Then, during World War I, the Chemin Des Dames lay in the part of the Western Front held by French armies, a position that led to several bloody battles between 1914 and 1918. There are numerous war memorials and cemeteries all along the route, German, French and British and beneath the ridge there is The Dragon's Lair (La Caverne du Dragon), an almost one kilometre-square cave network, some 20-40 metres below the surface. These subterranean caverns were originally the result of limestone excavations for building purposes in the 17th century, but during World War I, they were used by both French and German forces as field hospitals and command posts, sometimes even simultaneously, though one suspects they were not aware of it at the time. Guided tours are available for visitors, but if you find all this too depressing and prefer something more light-hearted, you could try the Living Bee museum in the centre of Corbeny or the Abbey of Vauclair with its botanic gardens.

 Aube

After Laon and the Chemin des Dames, the via Francigena takes you into the department of Aube, one of the original 83 departments created during the French Revolution on March 4, 1790 and created from part of the former province of Champagne. Aube is perhaps best known for the 1932 visit of the late Turkish president Mustafa Kemal Ataturk, who signed a friendship treaty with France there. Named after one of the Seine's tributaries, Aube is predominantly an agricultural department with arable land covering around a third of its surface. The northern and western parts are fairly mountainous while the south and east contain fertile woodland. It is here that some of the finest wines are produced, such as Les Riceys, Bar-sur-Aube, Bouilly and Laines-aux-Bois. Aube has its own regional park called

Foret d'Orient, a vast land of deep forests and secluded lakes. Local legend says that the knights of the crusades hid the treasure that they brought back with them in this area.

Champagne

As your route meanders through the vineyards of the Champagne region, it is worth remembering that these grapes will be producing an elite French wine - the exceptional nature of the soil determining their unique flavour. Most vineyards are situated halfway up the hillside and the roots of the vine grow deep down into chalky depths covered by a thin layer of nutritious substances.

The climate of the Champagne area also plays a major role as far as the formation of top quality grapes is concerned. The young vines must adapt to the dangers of frost in springtime and poor weather during the flowering period. Grape picking begins towards the end of September, about 100 days after the flowering of the vine and involves a wealth of special precautionary measures found only in this area. Picking is by hand, the grape bunches are examined one by one and the green or damaged grapes are discarded. The initial two or three rapid pressings of the grapes produce the 'cuvée' juice, subsequent pressings give the 'premier taille' and then the 'deuxieme taille'. After

this any further juice is of insufficient quality to become Champagne. To produce its characteristic bubbles, Champagne has to undergo a process of double fermentation. During the first fermentation the base wine, made from rather acidic grapes, is fermented at 68-72° F in either stainless steel or, more traditionally, oak barrels. It is then siphoned off from the sediment and kept at colder temperatures to clear completely, before being drawn off and blended with wines from other areas and years (except in the case of a vintage champagne). The wine is bottled and the 'liqueur de tirage' (sugar, wine and yeast) is added. In the second fermentation the bottles are stored for a year or more in cool, chalky cellars. The yeast converts the sugar to alcohol and carbondioxide, which produces the sparkle and the yeast cells die leaving a deposit.

To remove this the inverted bottles are turned and tapped daily to shift the deposit into the neck. Finally, the deposits are expelled by the process known as 'dégorgement' and sugar is added to adjust the sweetness before the final cork is inserted.

Reims LXX Rems

Renowned the world over from countless champagne labels, Reims is home to some of the best known 'grandes marques', but the city has another, much earlier, claim to fame. Since the crowning of Clovis in 496 AD, most of the French monarchs have also been crowned in the remarkable Cathedrale Notre Dame. A cathedral has stood on this site since 401, but the present building was begun in 1211 and has survived the French Revolution and Two World Wars. Since then, twenty years of major restoration have taken place and continue to this day. Christianity was established in Reims by the middle of the 3rd century, during which Saint Sixtus of Reims founded the Reims bishopric. In 496, ten years after Clovis, King of the Salian Franks, won his victory at Soissons (486) and Remigius, the bishop of Reims, baptized him with oil taken from the sacred phial (believed to have been brought from heaven by a dove for the baptism of Clovis). By the 10th century Reims had become a centre of intellectual culture thanks to Archbishop Adalberon (in office 969 to 988), seconded by the monk Gerbert, who founded schools teaching the 'liberal arts. In 1139, Louis VII granted the town a communal charter, but the Treaty of Troyes (1420) ceded it to the English, who had made a futile attempt to take it by siege in 1360. They were expelled on the approach of Joan of Arc, who in 1429 caused Charles VII to be consecrated in the cathedral. More recently, during World War Two, General Eisenhower and the Allies received the unconditional surrender of the Wehrmacht in Reims. The outskirts of Reims are industrial and unattractive, but it is well worth working one's way through this to reach the relatively compact historical area around the cathedral.

Look out for:

The Great Rose window. Best seen at sunset, the 13th century window depicts the virgin surrounded by apostles and angel muscians.

The Nave, favourably compared with the nave in Chartres, is renowned for its elegant capitals, decorated with naturalistic flower motifs.

The Smiling Angel, the most celebrated of the many that adorn the building.

The Gallery of the Kings, a harmonius west façade decorated with over 2,300 statues, including 56 stone effigies of the French kings.

Notre-Dame

Place Royale, with a statue of Louis XV and the *Place Cardinal-Luçon*, with an equestrian statue of Joan of Arc.

Porte de Mars. The oldest monument in Reims, a triumphal arch consisting of three archways flanked by columns. The Mars Gate was one of 4 Roman gates to the city walls, restored at the time of the Norman Invasion of northern France in the 9th century. Look out for the mosaic displaying thirty-five medallions representing animals and gladiators.

The Palace of Tau - The archbishop's palace, adjoining the cathedral is named after the T-shaped design based on early episcopal crosses (Tau is Greek for T). The palace, built in 1690 by Mansart and Robert de Coute, encloses a Gothic chapel, the 15th century Salle du Tau and rooms associated with French coronations. On the eve of the coronation, the future king spent

the night in the palace. After being crowned in the cathedral, he held a banquet in the Salle de Tau, with its magnificent barrel-vaulted ceiling and walls hung with 15th century Arras tapestries. The palace now houses a museum of statuary and tapestries from the cathedral, including a 15th century tapestry of the baptism of Clovis, the first Christian king.

The Surrender Museum standing on the spot where on May 7, 1945 General Eisenhower and the Allies received the unconditional surrender of the Wehrmacht.

Finally, having visited the monuments and worked up a good thirst, this writer also recommends stopping off at one of the **Champagne houses**, les grandes marques, which have their headquarters in Reims. Most are open for tasting and will often involve a trip down into the limestone caves (originally dug by the Romans) where the champagne is stored.

Châlons-sur-Marne LXIX Chateluns

In 20 BC, Emperor Auguste ordered the establishment of a road network in ancient France (Gaule), which included via Agrippa, one of the main roads connecting Milan to Boulogne-sur-Mer and cutting straight through Châlons (now Rue de la Marne). In 313 AD, the arrival of Saint-Memmie, first bishop of Châlons, transformed the rural settlement into an important cultural and trade centre. A development that continued into the 12 and 13th centuries, when the prosperity of the city was based on the manufacture of high quality woollen sheets, sold throughout Europe. Later, after a series of economic downturns, the two world wars changed the shape of the city considerably with the addition of garrisons, but also wide-scale damage during the second world war. Several districts were completely destroyed. Today, Châlons-sur-Marne's sleepy, bourgeois charm is in its half-timbered houses and gardens reflected again by the canals. From quai de Notre-Dame there are views of a number of old bridges and the towers of **Notre-Dame-en-Vaux** , built between 1157 and 1217 and a masterpiece of Romanesque-Gothic architecture.

Look out for:

Musée du Cloître de Notre-Dame-en-Vaux, containing the original collegiate cloister, a place of pilgrimage in the 12th century.

Cathédrale St-Etienne, Gothic, with a Baroque portal, Romanesque crypt and medieval windows.

Saint-Alpi, perhaps the oldest church of the city.

Porte Sainte-Croix , one of the entries into the city and dedicated to Marie-Antoinette when she came via Chalons on her way to Paris to marry king Louis XVI of France.

Le Cirque - the old town circus, completed in 1899 and housing the Centre National des Arts du Cirque.

Le Petit Jard, a riverside garden overlooking the Château du Marché with a turreted tollgate built by Henri IV.

Fontaine-sur-Coole LXVIII Funtaine

Donnement LXVII Domaniant

Brienne-le-Chateau LXVI Breone

Spread along the right bank of the Aube, Brienne-le-Chateau is overlooked by an imposing château. Built during the latter half of the 18th century by the cardinal of Brienne, it houses an important collection of paintings, many of them historical portraits of the 17th and 18th centuries. The church dates from the 16th century and is best known for its impressive stained glass. A statue of Napoleon commemorates his sojourn at Brienne from 1779 to 1784, when he was studying at  the military school. It was a fairly Spartan existence with students being locked in their cells by ten o'clock every evening. No servants were permitted. Linen was changed twice a week, but only one rug was permitted on the bed, except in cases of illness. Their level of academic achievement would make today's worst student appear to be a genius, but only because the teachers were of poor calibre and sometimes plain incompetent. Worse still, brutality, social snobbery and racial prejudice were the norm and Napoleon's Corsican background meant that he was the regular victim of all three, which is, perhaps, an excuse for his subsequent behaviour.

Bar-sur-Aube LXV Bar

A pretty little town, with architecture typical of the region, Bar-sur-Aube is most renowned as being the birthplace of Bachelard, a postmaster who went on to study physics before finally becoming interested in philosophy. He was a professor in Dijon from 1930 to 1940 and then became the inaugural chair in history and philosophy of the sciences at the Sorbonne. Bachelard's studies of the history and philosophy of

The mill of Marcasselles, Bar-sur-Aube

science in such works as "Le nouvel esprit scientifique" (The New Scientific Mind, 1934) and "La formation de l'esprit scientifique" (The Formation of the Scientific Mind 1938) were based on his vision of historical epistemology as a kind of psychoanalysis of the scientific mind, or rather of the psychological factors in the development of sciences.

Clairvaux Abbey

This small town is entirely dominated by the remains of the Cistercian monastery, founded in 1115 by St. Bernard. Although the original building is in ruins and a high-security prison now occupies the grounds, there is still enough left to give a good impression of the typical Cistercian monastery layout. Cistercian monasteries were all arranged according to a set plan unless the circumstances of the locality forbade it. A strong wall, furnished at intervals with watchtowers and other defenses, surrounded the abbey precincts. Beyond the wall, a moat, artificially diverted from tributaries which flow through the precincts, completely or partially encircled the wall. This water furnished the monastery with an abundant supply of water for irrigation, sanitation and for the use of the offices and workshops.

St. Bernard of Clairvaux

Born in 1090, at Fontaines, near Dijon, France, St Bernard died at Clairvaux in 1153. His parents were Tescelin, lord of Fontaines and Aleth of Montbard, both belonging to the highest nobility of Burgundy. Bernard, the third of a family of seven children, six of whom were sons, was educated with particular care, because, while still unborn, a devout man foretold his great destiny. At the age of nine years, Bernard was sent to a renowned school in Chatillon-sur-Seine, kept by the secular canons of Saint-Vorles. He had a great taste for literature and devoted himself for some time to poetry. St. Robert, Abbot of Molesmes, had founded, in 1098, the monastery of Cîteaux, about four leagues from Dijon, with the purpose of restoring the Rule of St. Benedict. Returning to Molesmes, he left the government of the new abbey to St. Alberic, who died in the year 1109. St. Stephen had just succeeded him (1113) as third Abbot of Cîteaux, when Bernard with thirty young noblemen of Burgundy, sought admission into the order. Three years later, St. Stephen sent the young Bernard, at the head of a band of monks to found a new house at Vallée d'Absinthe, or Valley of Bitterness, in the Diocese of Langres. This, Bernard named Claire Vallée of Clairvaux, on the 25th of June, 1115 and as a result the the names of Bernard and Clairvaux became inseparable. During the absence of the Bishop of Langres, Bernard was blessed as abbot

by William of Champeaux, Bishop of Châlons-sur-Marne, who saw in him the predestined man - servum Dei. The beginnings of Clairvaux Abbey were trying and painful. The regime was so austere that Bernard became ill and only the influence of his friend William of Champeaux and the authority of the General Chapter could make him mitigate the austerities. The monastery, however, made rapid progress. Disciples flocked to it in great numbers and put themselves under the direction of Bernard. His father and all his brothers entered Clairvaux, leaving only Humbeline, his sister, in the world and she, with the consent of her husband, soon took the veil in the Benedictine convent of Jully. Gerard of Clairvaux, Bernard's older brother became the cellarer of Citeaux. The abbey rapidly became too small for the number of people flocking there to enter religious life, making it necessary to send out bands to found new houses. As a result, the Monastery of the Three Fountains was founded in the Diocese of Châlons, Fontenay in the Diocese of Autun and Foigny, in the Diocese of Laon.

The first time we travelled as pilgrims, we packed our rucksacks and could not believe that we would be able to survive the next weeks or months with so little. It is hard to make the decision - which T-shirt should I take? Should it be halfway smart or just practical. When we had last packed everything the rucksack was incredibly heavy for the few things that we had put in there. There are some pilgrims who saw off their toothbrush handles or rewrite their address books in a minuscule script, in order to reduce weight, but as we walked we gradually became used to the weight on our backs. It is incredible how one can survive weeks and months with so little and be so happy and satisfied. Along the way the weight of our rucksacks reduced as we left unessential items behind in the hostels, one or two things being forgotten on the washing line or sent back home by post. In the same way, everyday problems we experienced at home became smaller day by day and in time seemed to evaporate into thin air. In some situations we gained from the new spatial and temporal aspects that enabled us to distance ourselves. The equality we shared with the few pilgrims we met on the via Francigena made us feel as if we had known each other for a long time. We all had the same route and aim in front of our eyes. We were all sweaty, had blisters or other problems on our feet or legs. Each one of us had a rucksack, two pairs of trousers, two T-shirts and were all the same. The only things that counted were food, sleep and of course walking.

We found ourselves in a timeless place where a great deal happened. We met people who said exactly the right words at exactly the right time, told stories that moved us and gave us answers to our questions. Day after day nature was often our only constant companion, our senses sharpened and we found inspiration in a tree, in a cornfield, in a flower,...

 Irrespective of whether one is regarded as a pilgrim saint or vagrant, whether one embarks on a pilgrimage for sporting, spiritual or personal reasons, adventure or to leave the everyday routine, every pilgrim experience is unique, full of wonderful, magical moments and encounters, that one will remember for the rest of ones' life. The Pilgrimage is a present to oneself.

The stretch between Aosta and Rome is rural and very varied. One begins in the Alpine pastures in the Aosta valley and wanders through Piedmont, the Apennines, Tuscany and Lazio. The countryside, as with the people, alters from north to south. In the Aosta valley one still does not have the feeling of being in Italy. The most common language here is French. We stayed overnight in a Cappucin monastery, where there are only 8 monks, most of whom are over 60. The cloisters have become increasingly empty and now offer rooms for pilgrims, in return for a small donation. Modesty and the willingness to cope with whatever happens is important. Often one sleeps on tiled floors or on tables. The via Francigena is very hard without sleeping mats, whoever does not have one is missing a fundamental pilgrim item. The daily search for a place to sleep takes one into interesting places. For us friendship developed into a sense of solidarity that still endures today. In order to find accommodation it helps to speak Italian and to use a pilgrim pass that distinguishes the authentic pilgrim from the usual walkers or tourists. People are very interested in pilgrims, they are not so familiar with them as on the St James Way in Spain. Increasingly we were stopped on the street and invited

 to eat, drink, have a coffee or even stay over. In return our hosts only asked for a prayer in Rome – „Una preghiera a Roma" appears to be the common phrase. But everyone was also pleased to receive a postcard when we arrived. Near Parma we started to speak to a woman who finally invited us to lunch – the table bending with all the rich regional dishes and her heartfelt generosity making such a strong impression. We are friends still.

We used hand drawn maps, their accuracy sadly lacking, with the result that some pilgrim days were spent in being seriously lost. Meantime there are some very good maps in which the balance between road and reasonable track is sought. The signing improves year by year, but is still sporadic and varied. Every commune has its own signing style, so it is still better to rely on the maps.

The Piedmont has its own special rice. Endless fields of it and the waysides full of red poppies. The water and rice fields are a breeding ground for mosquitoes that ingest pesticides and make them so poisonous that their bites swell badly. We wandered through sleepy villages reminiscent of Don Camillo and Peppone, but where the people were also curious and warm.

To cross the Po we needed to find the ferryman Danilo. We got his phone number from two pilgrims walking from Rome to Santiago, so in the opposite direction. Danilo didn't only take us over the big river, but also invited us to eat and even offered us a place to sleep. In the evening, we sat together with him and his friends as if we had known each other all our lives.

For us the most beautiful stage, in terms of landscape, was in Tuscany. One appreciates this much better on foot than in a car. The countryside changes again in Lazio, where one finds thermal springs near the rute and then finally one is standing on Monte Mario. After many weeks of wandering this first view is an unbeatable experience. It is for this reason that the ancient pilgrims called this mountain „Mons Gaudi" - Mountain of Joy.

Marie-Charlotte Bertrand
Karin Bumberger

EURO∧VIA

EUROVIA is an association which brings back to life the cultural streets and pilgrim routes of Europe. Under the motto "Ways for People", we set out to show

the positive effects of pilgrimages on peoples' private and working daily lives. Our activities are primarily concerned with promoting European integration as well as bringing to light the special and unique experience of pilgrimages. This time-honoured way of traveling is constantly gaining in popularity (approx. 100 000 pilgrims per year). Such a journey does not require a lot of money - but just time, the most precious commodity of the 21st century. To discover Europe and oneself through walking and experiencing things first-hand is a challenge for the body and the soul.

Our internet site (http://www.eurovia.tv/) serves as a platform made by pilgrims, for pilgrims. Everybody is welcome to share their experiences with others and to contribute their views and opinions. Other pilgrims are always grateful to receive useful tips. Here you find:  DVD´s, Books, Accommodation information, Pilgrims ID, descriptions of Pilgrimways, Experiences of Pilgrims ... We are convinced that only together is it possible to integrate pilgrimages and all the positive effects they bring, into our modern society. It is time for us to set off on this journey and enjoy the benefits of this internationally supported project.

We wish you a good journey.

Your EUROVIA Team

🛡 Haute-Marne

This department is named after the Marne River, whose source is near Langres, your next stop along the via Francigena. Haute-Marne is one of the original 83 departments created during the French Revolution on March 4, 1790 from parts of the former provinces of Champagne, Burgundy, Lorraine and Franche-Comté. In 1814, Chaumont was the unwitting witness to the end of the First Empire. On the 1st of March, Prussia, Russia, England and Austria signed an accord forbidding any individual peace deal with Napoleon the 1st and to fight until his final defeat. During World War II, Haute-Marne was split under the German occupation, the canal which running from the Marne to the Saône serving as a border and dividing the department into west and east. The east was a "reserved zone", intended for the creation of a new German state, whereas to the west would be the traditional "occupied zone". Haute-Marne was finally liberated by the Allies between August an September 1944.

Blessonville LXIV Blaecuile
Humes LXIII Oisma

Langres

A town built to be noticed and worth giving extra time to see. Soaring above the plateau,

with 3.5 kms of ramparts (offering magnificent views - on a clear day you can see as far as the Bernese Alps) seven towers and seven gates. This stronghold was originally occupied by the Gauls, but it was the Romans who later fortified the town. After a period of invasions, the town prospered in the Middle Ages due, in part, to the growing political influence of its bishops. The diocese covered Champagne, the Duchy of Burgundy and Franche-Comté and the bishops gained the right to coin money in the 9th century and to name the military governor of the city in 927. The Bishop of Langres was a duke and peer of France. The troubled 14th and 15th centuries were reason enough for the town to strengthen its fortifications, which still give the old part of the city its fortified character. Virtually the whole town is still enclosed by medieval ramparts and a succession of towers.

Look out for:

Cathédrale Saint-Mammès de Langres, built in the twelfth century and dedicated to the 3rd century martyr Mammes of Caesarea. In the nineteenth century, from 1852, the highest parts of the cathedral were renovated by the architect Alphonse Durand, who also built the sacristy.

Statue of Denis Diderot - French philosopher and writer, best known as a prominent figure during the Enlightenment and chief editor and contributor to the Encyclopédie.

Grenant LXII Grenant

Denis Diderot (1713—1784)

Denis Diderot, the most prominent of the French Encyclopedists, was educated by the Jesuits and, refusing to enter one of the learned professions, was turned adrift by his father and came to Paris, where he lived from hand to mouth for a time. Gradually, however, he became recognized as one of the most powerful writers of the day. His first independent work was the Essai sur le merite et la vertu (1745). As one of the editors of the Dictionnaire de medecine (6 vols., Paris, 1746), he gained valuable experience in encyclopedic system. His Pensees philosophiques (The Hague, 1746), in which he attacked both atheism and the received Christianity, was burned by order of the Parliament of Paris.

In the circle of the leaders of the Enlightenment, Diderot became well-known for his Lettre sur les Aveugles (Letters on the Blind, London, 1749), which supported Locke's theory of knowledge. He attacked the conventional morality of the day, with the result that he was imprisoned at Vincennes for three months. He gained his release with the influence of Voltaire's friend Mme. du Chatelet and remained in close relation with the leaders of revolutionary thought. He had made very little profit out of the Encyclopedie and Grimm appealed on his behalf to Catherine of Russia, who in 1765 bought his library, allowing him the use of the books as long as he lived and assigning him a yearly salary which a little later she paid him for fifty years in advance.

In 1773 she summoned him and Grimm to St. Petersburg t speak with them in person. On his return he lived, until his death, in a house provided by her. It was here, (according to Grimm) that he wrote two-thirds of Raynal's famous Histoire Philosophique and contributed some of the most rhetorical pages to Helvetius's De l'esprit and Holbach's Systeme de la nature Systeme social and Alorale universelle. His numerous works include a variety of literary genre, from licentious tales and comedies which pointed away from the stiff classical style of the French drama, to the most daring ethical and metaphysical speculations. Like his famous contemporary, Samuel Johnson, he is said to have been more effective as a talker than as a writer and his mental qualifications were rather those of a stimulating force than of a reasoned philosopher. His position gradually changed from theism to deism, then to materialism and finally rested in a pantheistic sensualism. In Sainte-Beuve's phrase, he was "the first great writer who belonged wholly and undividedly to modern democratic society and his attacks on the political system of France were among the most potent causes of the Revolution.

Porte Noir, Besan on

Champlitte

An old fortified town set among vineyards and best known for its castle-museum. One part of it contains a display of Folk Art and Traditions, founded in 1954 by Albert Demard, a local shepherd who collected objects and artifacts connected with disappearing local customs. The lifestyle of a 19th century town is recreated through 40 rooms of traditional interiors. In another part of the castle, the Vine and Winepress Museum goes back over the traditions of the Champlitte wine-growing region with its collection of winepresses from the 17th and 18th centuries, its distillery and barrel workshop. And finally there is the turn of the century Art and Techniques Museum, which represents life in a rural village between 1900 and 1920 through two reconstructed streets.

Seveux LXI Sefui
Cussey sur l'Ognon LX Cuscei

Besançon LIX Bysiceon

The town was first recorded in the journals of Julius Caesar and identified as being the largest town of the Sequani, a small Gaulic tribe. Over the centuries, the name permutated to become Besantio, Besontion, Bisanz in Middle High German and eventually the modern French Besançon. As part of the Holy Roman Empire, the city became the Archbishopric of Besançon and was granted the status of Imperial Free City (an autonomous city-state under the

Holy Roman Emperor) in 1184. In the 15th century, Besançon came under the influence of the dukes of Burgundy. After the marriage of Mary of Burgundy to Maximilian I, Holy Roman Emperor, the city was in effect a Habsburg fief, which took it from Austrian to Spanish influence. In 1526 the city obtained the right to mint coins and continued to strike coins until 1673. Built on a mountaintop, bounded by sheer cliffs on one side and the Doubs river on the other, the city centre has a fantastic defensive stance. It was on this hilltop that Vauban built the largest of his structures in the region - the Citadelle, with its outer and inner court and dual dry moat. Today, Besançon has one of the most beautiful historic centres of any major town

in France. The historic centre presents a remarkable ensemble of classic stone buildings, some dating back to the Middle Ages.

Look out for:

Palais Granvelle (16th century), built by Cardinal Granvelle, chancellor to Habsburg emperor Charles V.

Vauban's citadel

St. Jean cathedral (12th century) - notable for the massive Virgin and saints altarpiece by the Italian Renaissance painter Fra Bartolomeo.

Roman remains - notably the Porte Noire, a triumphal arch and the Square Castan.

Musée des Beaux Arts, housing a collection built up since 1694 and expanded over time by a

remarkable series of bequests. The building itself was totally rebuilt in the 1960s by the architect Miquel, a pupil of Le Corbusier, its interior taking the form of a gently rising concrete walkway that takes visitors up from classical antiquity to the modern age. Among its treasures are a fine collection of classical antiquities and ancient Egyptian artefacts, as well as a very rich collection of paintings including works by Bellini, Bronzino, Tintoretto, Titian, Rubens, Jordaens, Ruysdael, Cranach, Zurbarán, Goya, Philippe de Champaigne, Fragonard, Boucher, David, Ingres, Géricault, Courbet, Constable, Bonnard, Matisse, Picasso and many others.

Nods LVIII Nos

Pontarlier LVII Punterlin

Briefly mentioned in Victor Hugo's Les Misérables, Pontarlier is where convict Jean Valjean was to report for his parole after being released from the galleys. Aside from this Pontarlier was famous for the production of absinthe until its ban in 1915. The distilleries switched over to producing pastis. Apart from this you would think that it has little left to offer, but in fact it was also a pioneer city of aviation. On October 29, 1910, Auguste Junod flew his 50cc Farman biplane and the following year was marked by the first air meeting of Franche-Comté, attracting approximately 10.000 people. The aero club of Pontarlier was created only 20 years later and still exists today.
Look out for:
Triumphal arch of the Porte Saint-Pierre *(18th century)*
Gate of the ancient church of the Annonciades *(18th century)*
Stained glass created in 1976 by painter Alfred Manessier *for Saint-Bénigne Church*

Victor Hugo was born in Besançon on February 26, 1802 He was a poet, novelist, and dramatist and the most important French Romantic writer of the 19th Century. He is best known for his novels "Notre-Dame de Paris" (a.k.a Hunchback of Notre-Dame 1831) and "Les Miserables"(1862). Hugo created poems and novels that integrated political and philosophical questions with stories of his times. Many of his poems addressed the social disquiet of post-revolutionary France. He wrote with simplicity and power about the joys and sorrows of life. Every morning he would write at least 100 lines of verse or 20 pages of prose. A recurring theme in Hugo's work is humanity's ceaseless combat with evil. He eloquently stated the problems of his century and the great eternal human questions. He died in Paris on the 23 of May, 1885 at the age of 83. His state funeral was attended by nearly two million people and it police were brought in to control the crowds. On the first of June, Hugo was laid to rest in the Panthenon alongside Rousseau and Voltaire.

Absinthe is an anise-flavoured spirit derived from herbs, including the flowers and leaves of the herb Artemisia absinthium (wormwood). Absinthe originated in the canton of Neuchâtel in Switzerland and achieved great popularity as an alcoholic drink in late 19th and early 20th century France, Due in part to its association with bohemian culture, absinthe was opposed by social conservatives and prohibitionists. Charles Baudelaire, Paul Verlaine, Arthur Rimbaud, Henri de Toulouse-Lautrec, Amedeo Modigliani, Vincent van Gogh, Oscar Wilde, Aleister Crowley and Alfred Jarry were all notorious "bad men" of the day who were (or were thought to be) devotees of the "Green Fairy". Absinthe has been portrayed as a dangerously addictive psychoactive drug. The chemical thujone, present in small quantities, was singled out and blamed for its alleged harmful effects. By 1915, absinthe had been banned in the United States and in most European countries except the United Kingdom, Sweden, Spain, Portugal, Denmark and the Austro-Hungarian Empire. Although absinthe was vilified, no evidence has shown it to be any more dangerous than ordinary spirits. Its psychoactive properties, apart from those of alcohol, have been much exaggerated.

Pastis , an anise-flavored liqueur was first commercialized by Paul Ricard in 1932, some 17 years following the ban on absinthe. By legal definition, pastis is described as an anise flavored spirit that contains the additional flavor of licorice root and is bottled with sugar (but no more than 100 grams). Pastis is often associated with its historical predecessor absinthe, but the two are in fact very different. Pastis does not contain wormwood. Furthermore, it has the distinct flavor of licorice root (another herb of asian origin), which is not a part of a traditional absinthe. Where bottled strength is concerned, traditional absinthes were bottled at 45-74% ABV (alcohol by volume), while pastis is typically bottled at 45-50% ABV. Finally, unlike a traditional absinthe, pastis is a liqueur, which means it is always bottled with sugar.

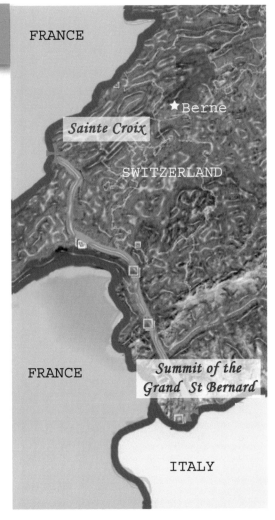

FRANCE

★ Berne

Sainte Croix

SWITZERLAND

FRANCE

Summit of the
Grand St Bernard

ITALY

The Swiss Alps

Yesterday brown was still thy head, as the locks of my loved one,
Whose sweet image so dear silently beckons afar.
Silver-grey is the early snow to-day on thy summit,
Through the tempestuous night streaming fast over thy brow.
Youth, alas, throughout life as closely to age is united
As, in some changeable dream, yesterday blends with to-day.

Johann Wolfgang von Goethe

Vaud is in the French speaking part of Switzerland, one of the 26 cantons of Switzerland and its capital is Lausanne. Vaud was inhabited in prehistoric times and later the Celtic tribe of the Helvetii took over until defeated by Caesar's troops in 58 BC. The towns of Vevey (Latin: Viviscus) and Lausanne (Lausonium or Lausonna) are just two of the many towns established by the Romans. In 27 BC the state of Civitas Helvetiorum was established around the capital of Avenches (Aventicum) - there are still many Roman remains to be found around the town today. Between the 2nd and the 4th century the area was repeatedly invaded by Alemannic tribes and in the 5th century the Burgundians occupied the area. The Merovingian Franks later replaced the Burgundians, but their occupancy did not last long either and in 888 the area of the canton of Vaud was made part of the Carolingian Empire. In 1032 the Zähringens of Germany defeated the Burgundians, but were succeeded in 1218 by the counts of Savoy. It was only under the counts of Savoy that the area was finally given political unity, establishing what is today in greater part known as the canton of Vaud. As the power of the Savoys declined at the beginning of the 15th century the land was occupied by troops from Bern and by 1536 the area was completely annexed. Reformation was started by co-workers of John Calvin like Pierre Viret, including a famous debate at the cathedral of Lausanne; but it was only decisively implemented when Bern put its full force behind it. Nevertheless, the Bernese occupants were not popular. In 1723 Major Abraham Davel led a revolt in protest at what he saw as the denial of political rights for the French-speaking Vaudians by the German-speaking Bernese. He was subsequently beheaded. Undeterred by his cruel fate, the Vaudians drove out the Bernese governor in 1798 and declared the Lemanic Republic. Vaud became the canton of Léman which, in 1803, joined the re-installed Swiss confederation and in spite of Bernese attempts to reclaim Vaud, it has remained a sovereign canton ever since. In the 19th century, the canton of Vaud was an outspoken opponent of the Catholic separatist movement (Sonderbund) which led to intervention in 1847 by 99,000 Swiss

Federal troops under General Henri Dufour against 79,000 separatists in what is called the Sonderbund War. Separation was prevented at the cost of very few lives. The current constitution dates from April 14, 2003, replacing the one from 1885. Today, Vaud is a highly diversified region, offering culture in towns like Lausanne, but also its Chasselas grapes which make it Switzerland's second most important wine canton. The Vaud wine region is distributed across three wine sub-regions: Chablais, La Côte and Lavaux. Here the perpendicular terraced vineyards plunge from hillside villages right down to the edge of Lake Geneva, making this writer wonder how on earth they are harvested.

Yverdon-les-Bains LVI Antifern

The heights nearby Yverdon-les-bains have been settled at least since the Neolithic Age. At that time the town was only a small market place at the crossroads of terrestrial and fluvial communication ways, but gradually people began to settle, first in temporary huts at the water-front, for the fishermen and merchants and then in permanent dwellings. Called Eburodunum and Ebredunum during the Roman era, Yverdon-les-bains' commercial and strategic importance lay in its position which controlled major routes such as Geneva-Avenches, connecting the Rhone and Rhine basins, as well as those of Rhone and Danube. In order to protect this fortuitous location, the Romans built a large military stronghold in 325 BC. The so-called

The stone rows in Yverdon-les-Bains
(3000 B.C.E.)

Castrum (stronghold) Ebredunense covered about 20,000 m2 and was protected by gigantic ramparts and 15 masonry towers. Meanwhile the port served as a naval base for the barges supplying the defensive positions along the Rhine, which marked the North-Eastern border of the Empire. Today Yverdon-les-Bains is best known for its thermal springs. In use at least since the Roman era, but most possibly also before, the spring-site was a sacred place. By 1728, the authorities decided to have a new spa constructed, after which its reputation grew rapidly. The 18th century saw major developments for the town and the spa, but the site subsequently lost its drive and popularity, degrading into a simple political meeting point where the buildings were left unmaintained. Nevertheless, after many years of neglect, the thermal springs were successfully reopened in 1982 and today the spa welcomes more than 1,200 visitors per day.

Look out for:

The Temple - *designed by the Geneva architect Billon, this Protestant church was built in 1757 on the site of Notre-Dame chapel of the 14th century. Its spire was then rebuilt in 1608, on the base of the original one, using huge, sculpted blocks from the ruins of the Roman Castrum.*
The Castle - *the design of the castle followed the geometric characteristics used for castles set in plains and was designed by the young mason and architect Jacques de Saint-Georges (also architect for Caernarvon Castle in the United Kingdom and Saint-Georges d'Espéranches, near Lyon). Yverdon's castle used to be the residence of the castellans of the Savoy dynasty, until 1536, but by 1838 it had been*

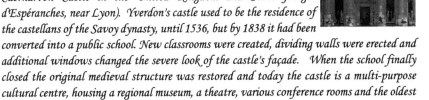

converted into a public school. New classrooms were created, dividing walls were erected and additional windows changed the severe look of the castle's façade. When the school finally closed the original medieval structure was restored and today the castle is a multi-purpose cultural centre, housing a regional museum, a theatre, various conference rooms and the oldest public library in France.

Maison d'Ailleurs *(House of Elsewhere) - museum of science fiction, utopia and extraordinary journeys - the only one of its kind in Europe.*
Swiss Fashion Museum - *a rare and valuable collection of 5000 garments and accessories, illustrating 2 centuries of elegance and clothing.*

Orbe LV Urba

During the Roman times, Orbe - then known as Urba - was a town of Gallia, in the territory of the Helvetii. Located at the crossroads of Roman roads, Urba was subject to regular invasions, to which the still evident fortified walls bear witness. Today the town is best known for the coffee factory owned by Nestlé, a marionette

museum, a late-Gothic church and the Roman mosaics and ruins in the fields of Boscéaz, 2 km outside the town. Nine Roman mosaics were discovered and are now preserved on the site. Well worth setting time aside for these mosaics consist of several hundreds of pieces on the floor of the original site which was once part of an extremely large Roman villa, belonging to a rich but unknown landowner. It is thought to have been built in approximately 160 A.D. and abandoned around the year 270 A.D. Four of the mosaics depict black-and-white or coloured geometrical "trompe l'oeil" (French for trick the eye) motifs . The other mosaics contain figurative portrayals and depict various easily-recognisable scenes, including the Minotaur labyrinth, Theseus abandoning the sleeping Ariadne, Ulysses summoning Achilles to battle and the Roman gods (the symbols of the seven planets and of the seven days of the week).

Lausanne LIV Losanna

When you enter Lausanne, be prepared to indulge in a great deal of hyperbole - permissable when you are surrounded by spectacular natural and architectural beauty. Switzerland's San Francisco, a city of incredibly steep hills, built above the lake on a succession of compact, south-facing terraces. After the Reformation, students flocked to Lausanne's pioneering university and in the eighteenth and nineteenth centuries, restless Romantics sought and found inspiration in the setting and the life of Lausanne, a cult that has been sustained because the municipality has continued to subsidise art and culture of all types. After the fall of the Roman Empire, insecurity forced the transfer of Lausanne to its current centre, a hilly, easier to defend site. The city which emerged from the camp was ruled by the Dukes of Savoy and the Bishop of Lausanne. Then it came under Berne from 1536 to 1798 and a number of its cultural treasures, including the hanging tapestries in the Cathedral, were permanently removed. After the revocation of the Edict of Nantes in 1685, Lausanne became (along with Geneva) a place of refuge for French Huguenots. In 1729 a seminary was opened by Antoine Court and Benjamin Duplan. By 1750 ninety pastors had been sent back to France to work clandestinely; this number would rise to four hundred. Official persecution ended in 1787; a faculty of Protestant theology was established at Montauban in 1808 and the Lausanne seminary was finally closed on 18 April 1812. In 1803, Lausanne became the capital of a newly formed Swiss canton, Vaud, under which it joined the Swiss Federation. The most important geographical feature of the area surrounding Lausanne is Lake Geneva but the centre of the city is also the site of an ancient river, the Flon, which has been covered since the 19th century. The former river forms a gorge running through the middle of the city south of the old city centre, generally following the course of the present Rue Centrale, with several bridges crossing the depression to connect the adjacent neighborhoods. Lausanne suffered from many devastating medieval fires and is the last city in Europe to keep alive the tradition of the nightwatch (le guet). If you install yourself on the cathedral terrace, every night between 22.00 and 02.00, after the bells have struck the hour, you'll hear – and possibly spot – a sonorous-voiced civil servant calling out from all sides of the cathedral tower "C'est le guet; il a sonné l'heure" ("This is the nightwatch; the hour has struck"), assuring the lovers and assorted drunks sprawled under the trees that all is well. Having fulfilled his civic duty, he then retreats to a comfortable little room within the tower for the next 59 minutes. For some years past, this post has been filled by a cartoonist on Lausanne's weekly L'Hebdo, who is reported to appreciate the four hours of peace and quiet each night to concentrate on drawing his strips. As yet, though, he's had no fires to report.

There are too many museums and places of interest to list, but here are a few to **look out for:**

Notre Dame de Lausanne - The old town is dominated by the cathedral, regarded as

Switzerland's most impressive piece of early Gothic architecture. was built in several stages, with the first builder beginning construction work in 1170 with an ambulatory, using Roman materials. Twenty years later, a second erected the present church; this took until 1215. From that point Jean Cotereel, the third builder, continued the work on the site by constructing the western section, giving it a porch and two towers, one with a belfry, the other one remained uncompleted. It was only in 1275 that the cathedral was finally consecrated, by both Emperor Rudolph of Hapsburg and Pope Gregory X. In 1536, during the Reformation, the cathedral underwent significant changes when a new liturgical area was built in the nave. Thereafter, it was restored a number of times in the 18th century and again in the 19th century under the leadership of the famous French architect Eugène-Emmanuel Viollet-le-Duc. The cathedral has a highly significant multi-coloured interior that was covered over during the Reformation and then revealed at the beginning of the 20th century. The paintings are still visible in the Chapel of the Virgin as well as on the statues of the painted doorway, which is unique in all of Europe and has been completely restored since October 2007. The rose window depicts the medieval view of the world arranged around the figure of God the creator.

Olympic Museum - housing permanent and temporary exhibits relating to sport and the Olympic movement - the largest archive of the Olympic Games in the world.

Beaulieu Castle - one of the most majestic private 18th century buildings in the city, as well as one of the most unique. In 1766, the estate was acquired by the pastor Gabriel-Jean-Henry Mingard, who was also the son-in-law of the mayor of Amsterdam. At the time, the chateau had only its western wing (built between 1763 and 1766 by the Lausanne architect Rodolphe de Crousaz in a strictly neoclassical style) and a farm. From 1767 to 1773, Mingard hid the farm by adjoining it with another building that was just one room deep and had a façade that was copied from the first house. He then connected the two façades with a third, imposing building with a Mansard roof* and lots of ornamentation, which was also just a single room deep. Since 1976, the Beaulieu chateau has housed the Collection de l'Art Brut (rough or raw art), which has been built up since the original donation of the personal collection of the French artist Jean Dubuffet. The artists are mainly European, but also from North America, South America, Africa and Asia.

*Mansard refers to a style of roof characterized by two slopes on each of its four sides with the lower slope being much steeper and the upper slope, usually not visible from the ground, is pitched at the minimum needed to shed water.

Musée de l'Elysée photo museum has eight exhibition rooms over four floors, a bookshop, a reading room and more than one hundred thousand original prints. Its international exhibition programme covers a multitude of photographic styles and techniques, both past and present.

Vevey LIII Vivaec

Vevey is a popular holiday resort, wine-trading centre and corporate headquarters of Nestlé. The riviera town has long been popular with British and European celebrities, among them, Charlie Chaplin, who lived for 25 years in the neighboring village of Corsier-sur-Vevey (where he was buried after his death in 1977).

Look out for:

Musée Junisch museum of fine arts

Swiss Camera Museum - covering the history of photography, from the camera obscura and magic lantern to the latest numerical images.

Museum of Food History

If possible (and if you like jazz) try to time your journey to coincide with the nine-day **Cully Jazz Festival**, which takes place on the lakefront in early April. Alternatively you could aim for the **Street Artists Festival** in August, which draws some 1,200 jugglers, mimes, puppeteers and other performers.

Montreux

Château de Chillon

The city's situation on the north east shore of Lake Geneva and at the fork in the Roman road from Italy over the Simplon Pass, made it an important settlement in Roman times. Today, Montreux is a cultural centre for this region and internationally, which means that travellers should be able to include at least one major Montreux event along the way. These include: Freddie Mercury's Montreux Memorial Day - first week-end in September. The Montreux Jazz Festival - annually in July. The Golden Rose Festival - annually in spring. For those of you who are interested in musical facts read on and perhaps guess the predominate interests of your author: Montreux is the home of Mountain Studios, the recording studio used by several artists. In 1978, the band Queen bought the studio and then sold it onto Queen Producer David Richards. In 2002 the Mountain Studios was converted into a bar as part of a complete renovation of the studio. David Richards has left Montreux to settle down somewhere else. Queen also appeared in 1984 and in 1986 at the Golden Rose Festival and Queen guitarist Brian May appeared in 2001 at the Jazz Festival. Montreux was also the subject of the 1995 Queen single A Winter's Tale on the album Made in Heaven, one of Freddie's last songs before his death on November 24, 1991. The album cover features the statue of Mercury beside the lake.

Valais

The Romans called the area Vallis Poenina (Upper Rhône Valley), but from 888 onwards the lands were part of the kingdom of Jurane Burgundy. King Rudolph III of Burgundy gave the lands to the Bishop of Sion in 999, making him Count of the Valais. The count-bishops then struggled to defend their area against the dukes of Savoy, so that the medieval history of the

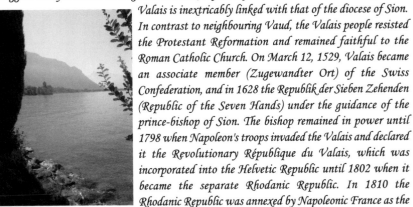

Valais is inextricably linked with that of the diocese of Sion. In contrast to neighbouring Vaud, the Valais people resisted the Protestant Reformation and remained faithful to the Roman Catholic Church. On March 12, 1529, Valais became an associate member (Zugewandter Ort) of the Swiss Confederation, and in 1628 the Republik der Sieben Zehenden (Republic of the Seven Hands) under the guidance of the prince-bishop of Sion. The bishop remained in power until 1798 when Napoleon's troops invaded the Valais and declared it the Revolutionary République du Valais, which was incorporated into the Helvetic Republic until 1802 when it became the separate Rhodanic Republic. In 1810 the Rhodanic Republic was annexed by Napoleonic France as the

département of Simplon. Independence was restored in 1813 and on August 4, 1815 the Valais finally entered the Swiss confederation as a canton. Valais is dominated by the wide, glacial Rhône valley, with many more side valleys branching off it. These vary from narrow and remote to reasonably populous and popular. The Rhône drains almost the entire canton and flows in the main valley from east to west up to Martigny (which the via Francigena runs directly through), then in a right angle north to its mouth in the Lake Geneva. After the small town of Saint-Maurice (also on your route), the northern banks of the river belong to the canton of Vaud. Today, Valais is predominantly French and Arpitan speaking (Franco-Provençal - a Romance language with several distinct dialects), though people in the eastern part of the canton (Upper Valais) speak Walliser German. Apart from tourism, agriculture is still important, particularly cattle breeding in the mountains and dairy farming in the plains. Vines also share the hillsides with a large

number orchards and the saffron crocus, from the flower of which saffron is gathered.

More in keeping with the guidebook theme, the travellers amongst you will be pleased to know that the via Francigena route follows one of the most beautiful walks along the lake, but if you are beginning to feel the strain and would welcome an opportunity to cut a few corners, or simply can't resist the chance of a ride on the paddle steamer 'Montreux', check out the times and sailing options: www.swissitalianpaddlesteamers.com

Versvey LII Burbulei

St Maurice-en-Valais LI Sce Maurici

St. Maurice is best known for its Abbey (Abbaye de Saint-Maurice d'Agaune). Situated against a cliff in a picturesque section of the Simplon Pass between Geneva and northern Italy, the

abbey itself is renowned for its connection to stories of martyrdom of the Theban legions. Built on the ruins of a 1st Century B.C. Roman shrine to the god Mercury in the Roman staging-post of Agaunum, the basilica of St. Maurice of Agaunum became the centre of a monastery under the patronage of King Sigismund of Burgundy, the first ruler in his dynasty to convert from Arian to Trinitarian Christianity. After being a point of contention and serial ownership over the centuries, Pope Gregory XVI finally gave the abbey its title of see of Bethlehem in perpetuity in 1840. The abbey has been built and rebuilt over a period of at least 15 centuries. Excavations on the site have revealed a baptistry dating back to the 4th and 5th centuries, a series of four main churches built over one another dating from the 5th to the 11th century and crypts built

between the 4th and 8th century. The current church was first built in the 17th century, but the tower is 11th century.

St Maurice - commander of the all-christian Theban Legion, revered as the patron saint of the infantry.

Saint Maurice is generally believed to have been a soldier, who lived near Thebes in Egypt in the third century AD. Legend tells us that Maurice was a Christian and a soldier in and later leader of the Thebian Legion. The Legion was composed of some 6,600 Christians recruited in Egypt to fight for the Roman Empire in Gaul, serving under Maximian. Maurice was put to death along with all of his men in the year 287AD, as a punishment for refusing to obey orders to torture and kill fellow Christians in what is now modern-day St

Martyrdom of Maurice

Maurice-en-Valais. Saint Maurice was one of the most well known of the "soldier saints" celebrated in the middle Ages. In 961 his remains and those of the men who perished with him were disinterred and reburied with honors at the Cathedral of Magdeburg where his relics remain to this day.

Martigny

Lying at an elevation of 475 metres, Martigny sits on the crossroads between Italy, France and Switzerland and is the start of the one road over the Great St. Bernard Pass to Aosta in Italy. Martigny's history stretches back two thousand years - Celtic tribes, the Romans and Napoleon's troops have all left their traces. Later, Martigny became the first bishop's seat in Switzerland and is admired for the historical districts of La Bâtiaz and Vieux-Bourg featuring

several churches and secular buildings worth seeing. Martigny is surrounded by vineyards and orchards, because the climate is ideal for growing strawberries, apricots, grapes and asparagus. It is also well known for its famous visitors: Rousseau, Goethe, Stendhal and Liszt. Less seriously and culturally, cow fights are held in the Roman amphitheatre during early autumn - a bizarre spectacle not to be missed if you happen to be there at the right time. King of the beasts these poor milkers may not be, but the most belligerent bovines do win the prized title: "Queen of the Alps." Unlike bullfighting, which exploits the male animal's aggressive instincts by antagonizing him, cows don't kill or seriously hurt anybody, not even one another. Veterinarians file the cows' horns before a fight if they are too sharp, but it is hard to provoke a cow into a fight it doesn't want to. Perhaps the only living beings to get really excited about all of this are the farmers, because the calf of a bell-winner can sell for nearly 10 times the going price of an ordinary calf. So fierce is the competition that a bovine queen, named Samba, was attacked and beaten while grazing in the mountains. Many here suspect rival cow owners.

Martigny Amptheatre

Orsiéres L Ursiores

At an altitude of 900 metres, Orsières is home to a number of architectural treasures, the undisputable jewel in the crown being the church and its bell-tower. Dedicated to Saint Nicolas, it was built in 1895 on the site of two known former churches: the first built between 1177 and 1296, the second devoted in 1497. Orsiéres is also known for the medicinal and aromatic plants grown on its surrounding slopes and used to make herbal and iced teas, or in the manufacture of beauty and healthcare products.

Bourg-st-Pierre XLIX Petrecastel

During the wars of the 1790s, entire armies crossed the pass and, in May 1800, Napoleon led 40,000 troops over the pass into Italy, consuming on the way 21,724 bottles of wine, a tonne and a half of cheese, 800kg of meat and more. The bill came to a staggering Fr.40,000 but though Napoleon sent an IOU promising, "I will reimburse everything", he ultimately dodged payment. When President François Mitterrand visited Switzerland in 1984, the citizens of Bourg-st-Pierre politely reminded him of the outstanding debt, but did not ask for a specific sum. In response, a personal representative of Mitterrand's returned, bearing a commemorative plaque and a handwritten letter from the President, thanking the village for the hospitality shown to Napoleon. Shortly after, Fr.18,500 was offered as a token gesture of account settling with regard to the village's debts and those relating to Napoleon's stay in the hostel on the summit, along with the construction of a swimming pool in Bourg-st-Pierre. French officials said the matter had been resolved "in a warm and friendly way". Mayor Fernand Dorsaz accepted the plaque and letter as symbols of the debt's amicable settlement and declared the matter "closed and settled".

Napoleon Crossing the Alps

"It was high morning and everyone was full of fear and trembling. Through holy prayer we were preparing to face menacing death…" written by a Belgian abbot in 1129, just before beginning his ascent on the Great St Bernard Pass.

The Great Saint Bernard Pass

The Great St Bernard Pass is the most ancient route through the Western Alps, crossing at 2,473 metres and one of the highest of the Alpine frontier passes. Named after Saint Bernard of Menthon, who founded a hospice at its summit in the 11th century, The Grand-St-Bernard Pass has been in use since the Bronze Age - tribes and armies tramping their way to and fro for millennia since. In 390 BC, a Gaulish army crossed to defeat Rome and from the earliest times ordinary people used the pass to trade goods between northern Europe and Italy. Hannibal's famous crossing of the Alps in 217 BC is indelibly associated with the Grand-St-Bernard and (though there's little actual evidence of it actually having taken place) in the 1930s the fabulously eccentric American travel writer, Richard Halliburton, rode his elephant over the pass to re-enact the journey. Sadly, the poor beast suffered from altitude sickness and stalled on the summit.

In 57 BC, Julius Caesar crossed the Summa Poenina (as it was known then) to conquer the pagan peoples of Martigny, who worshipped the Celtic god Poenn (the chain of great peaks on the Swiss–Italian frontier is still called the Pennine Alps). Shortly after, Emperor Augustus built a road across the pass and left a temple to Jupiter on the summit, which subsequently lent

its name to the area (Mons Iovis, or Mont Joux). Unfortunately the temple was sacked with the fall of Rome, but since the great and the good continued to tramp the road, it is assumed that a refuge may well have remained on the pass. Pope Stephen II crossed in November 753 to meet with Pepin the Short (vertically challenged), King of France, while in 800 Charlemagne crossed back following his coronation in Milan. In the early 900s, Huns and Saracens swept through the region, raping, pillaging and destroying churches. In an attempt to keep them quiet, Hugh of Provence, King of Italy, granted them guardianship of the Mont Joux pass, whereupon they just changed their focus to terrorize travellers and demand payment - a prototype for today's muggers. Deeply concerned by the disruption caused to merchants and pilgrims Europe-wide, King Canute of

Roman steps

Denmark took King Rudolf III of Burgundy to one side to have a quiet word. As a result the heathens were ejected and the archdeacon of Aosta, one Bernard of Menthon (who had spent years tending to travellers coming down off the pass stripped of all their belongings), was given permission to oversee the construction of the hospice. Bernard himself travelled around the area, spreading the word of God and was beatified shortly after his death in 1080. Pope Pius XI confirmed him as patron saint of the Alps in 1923. The hospice immediately became a

welcome point of safety on an extremely dangerous route, attracting favours and gifts from royal and noble households. Throughout the Middle Ages, the hospice provided free shelter and food to pilgrims, clerics and travellers, many crossing to and from Rome. By 1817 some 20,000 people were using the road annually. The hospice on the pass is still used by Augustinian monks who, with their St. Bernard dogs, provide services to travellers. When you finally reach

the summit of the Great St Bernard Pass, the first building you will see is the Combe de Morte a 'charnel house' where the corpses of those who never made it over the pass were mummified by the cold, but don't worry it is no longer in use. Next, look out for the sign informing travellers that they are 2473 metres up - an obligatory photo stop. Then, head for the hostel or hotel and a much needed shower. After that, if you still have sufficient energy, visit the St. Bernard Dog

Museum, which is also an important part of the Great St Bernard Pass history. Probably descended from mastiff-like dogs, the St Bernard dogs were brought to the hospice in the late 17th century and remained loyal companions to the monks living there. The name St. Bernard was dedicated to Bernard, the 11th century monk. The most famous dog was Barry, who reportedly saved somewhere between 40 and 100 lives. There is a monument to Barry in the Cimetiére des Chiens and his body is preserved in the Natural History Museum in Berne.

Saint Bernard of Menthon (923 - 1008)

Descended from a rich, noble family and recipient of a thorough education, Bernard refused an honorable marriage proposed by his father and decided to devote himself to the service of the Church. Sneaking away from the chateau the day before the wedding, he fled to Italy and joined the Benedictine order, placing himself under the direction of Peter, Archdeacon of Aosta, under whose guidance he progressed rapidly. Bernard was ordained as a priest and then became the Archdeacon of Aosta (966). Seeing the old pagan ways still prevailing among the people of the Alps, he resolved to devote himself to their conversion. In popular legend it is said that during his flight from Château de Menthon, Bernard cast himself from his window only to be captured by angels and lowered gently to the ground forty feet below.

Richard Halliburton

Writer, Lecturer and World Traveler, Richard Halliburton published numerous books, including The Royal Road to Romance (1925), Glorious Adventure (1927), New Worlds To Conquer (1929) and The Book of Marvels (1937). During his world travels, he visited the Taj Mahal in India, climbed the Matterhorn, flew across the Sahara desert in a bi-winged plane and swam the entire length of the Panama Canal. In his book, Seven League Boots, he describes his journey in the tracks of Hannibal as he rides his elephant over the Alps, through Great St. Bernard Pass, because he thought it would be amusing. The journey caused a sensation throughout Europe, but unfortunately Halliburton's enjoyment of fame was short-lived. He died in March 1939 as he and his crew attempted to sail a Chinese

junk, the Sea Dragon, from Hong Kong to San Francisco. The vessel was unseaworthy and went down in a storm. His body was never recovered.

Pilgrim

Again I become a wanderer, Lord,
A walker, my God, on your paths.
Again your wind goes through my hair,
Time is gone already.

The lights lost in clouds...
As a leaf, carried by wind
Your wanderer, God,
Walking Your paths.

Lauma Lapa from Latvia

On Pilgrimage

It's not about easy or difficult
Or getting something from a place
It's the going, being present
Then leaving no trace

Contributed by Bamboo in the Wind, a Zen Practice
Group led by Rev. Val Szymanski

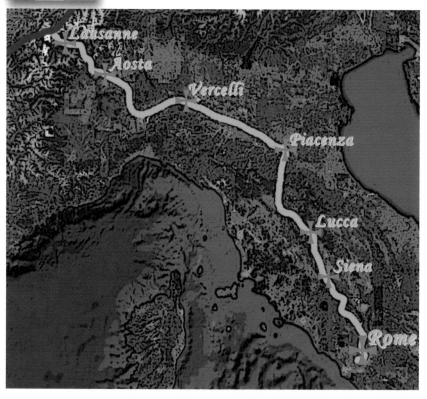

I reached the Alps: the soul within me burned,
Italia, my Italia, at thy name:
And when from out the mountain's heart I came
And saw the land for which my life had yearned,
I laughed as one who some great prize had earned:
And musing on the marvel of thy fame
I watched the day, till marked with wounds of flame
The turquoise sky to burnished gold was turned.
The pine-trees waved as waves a woman's hair,
And in the orchards every twining spray
Was breaking into flakes of blossoming foam:
But when I knew that far away at Rome
In evil bonds a second Peter lay,
I wept to see the land so very fair.

Oscar Wilde

Orfeo walked to Lourdes and then Santiago from his home in Italy. Here he describes his motivation and the reaction of his family and friends.

It was a fresh and luminous morning in 2009. I was working in the garden, preparing the land for seeds when it occurred to me that nearly two years had passed since Laura and Cecilia left us to live in a better place and I had first thought of walking the Way of Santiago. Now, suddenly, like a bolt of lightening the idea came to me again, but this time with the realisation that I must leave from Borgonovo where Laura and Cecilia had lived for most of their seventeen years, sharing school, friends and experiences. I dropped my hoe and went to call Grace, my wife, to tell her about the message I had received. Even though I knew very little about the St James Way at the time, and had only a vague idea of its history and pilgrims, Grace did not express any surprise and simply said, "The idea is beautiful, but can we do it? There are so many kilometres and not much time." I could not give her a sufficient answer, but that same evening I presented the idea to my friends, expecting them to say that it was crazy, madness, but instead they were enthusiastic and offered their help. Samuel, my young son, responded to the brightness in our faces, perhaps not understanding the idea completely, but declaring it to be good and needing organisation. From here, in little more than two months I was ready. Two months of cooperation and satisfaction for all, running as smooth as oil. Incredible! Perhaps proof of a Divine Providence!

From the IIth century to the 18th, both the Valle d'Aosta and Piedmont were part of the French-speaking principality of Savoy and enjoyed the influences of both sides of the Alpine divide. Even today, French and dialectal variants spoken in the remote valleys in much of the Valle d'Aosta. It was only under Duke Emmanuele Filiberto in the 16th century that the region was brought definitively into the Italian sphere of influence; and later it was to play the key role in the Risorgimento, the ambitious movement that united Italy under a king from Piedmont. The vestiges of this history are to be found in the medieval castles and the extraordinary clusters of chapels known as "sacri monti" dotted around the foothills of the Alps. Today, the Aosta Valley is one of the 20 regions of Italy.

Medieval castles and forts in the Valle d'Aosta

The mountains alone provided insufficient protection to the fragmented kingdoms that covered the Valle d'Aosta in the Middle Ages. The medieval lords who ruled ruthlessly over their small domains, built castles to enforce their often fragile power. Of the many built, 70 castles survive in some form to this day. Originally, Aosta castles were designed to be defensive and threatening, but the castles of Fénis (which you will see on the opposite of the valley as you follow the via Francigena out of Nus) and Verrés represent an important shift in the function of the feudal castle. Both Fénis, a splendid 14th century showpiece, and Verrés were not just important military outposts, but also examples of palatial opulence and good living.

Fenis Castle

The castle first appears in a document in 1242 A.D. as a property of the Viscounts of Aosta, the Challant family. At that time it probably was a simple keep surrounded by walls. It was from 1320 A.D. to 1420 A.D., under the lordship of Aimone of Challant and of his son

Bonifacio of Challant, that the castle expanded. Under Aimone's lordship the castle was given its pentagonal layout, the external boundary wall and many of the towers. In 1392 Bonifacio of Challant began a second building campaign to build the staircase and the balconies in the inner courtyard and the prison. He also commissioned Piedmontese painter Giacomo Jaqueiro to paint frescos on the chapel and on the inner courtyard. Under Bonifacio

Fenis Castle

I the castle reached its greatest splendor, with a luxurious centre court surrounded by a vegetable plot, a vineyard and a garden where the lord and his guests could relax. The castle belonged to the lords of Challant until 1716, when Georges François of Challant had to sell it to Count Baldassarre Castellar of Saluzzo Paesana in order to pay his debts. From here it went through a period of neglect, during which it was turned into a rural dwelling and became a stable and barn. In 1895 architect Alfredo d'Andrade purchased it and started a restoration campaign to secure the damaged structures. In 1935 a second campaign by De Vecchi and Mesturino completed the restoration and gave the castle its current appearance. The rooms were also furnished with period wood furniture. Today it is owned by the Regional Council, which has turned it into a museum.

Saint-Rhémy-en-Bosses XLVIII Sce Remei

Aosta XLVII Agusta

For the Romans, Aosta's position at the confluence of two rivers and at the end of the Great

and the Little St Bernard Pass, gave it considerable military importance. Its layout was that of a Roman military camp and today, the ancient town walls of Augusta Praetoria Salassorum are still preserved (6.4 m high and built of concrete faced with small blocks of stone). Towers stand at angles to the 'nceinte' (a French term used to describe the inner ring of fortifications surrounding a town) and others are positioned at intervals, with two at each of the four gates, making twenty towers in total. The east and south gates also exist intact. The latter, a double gate with three arches flanked by two towers known as the Porta Praetoria (1st century AD) was the eastern gate to the city. Apart from the marble covering, the gate is preserved in its original form. The Roman theatre, of which the southern façade remains today, dates from the late reign of Augustus and would have contained up to 4,000 spectators. Not far from this is the amphitheatre, built under Claudius and a marketplace surrounded by storehouses on three sides with a temple in the centre. Outside the town is a triumphal arch in honour of Augustus, built in 35 BC to celebrate the victory of consul Varro Murena over the Salassi.

Also Look out for:
Aosta Cathedral (built in the 4th century and replaced in the 11th century) dedicated to the Madonna.
Sant'Orso - dedicated to Ursus of Aosta and notable for its cloister, which can be entered through a hall on the left of the façade.
Saint-Bénin College, built by the Benedictines and now an exhibition site.

Alfred Van Amelsvoort retired and relocated to Australia from London. He walked the via Francigena in 2008. His project for the Holy Year of 2010 is to walk from Rome to Jerusalem.

Life is a mystery to be lived, not a problem to be solved

It seems reasonable to ask why anyone would want to undertake a long-distance journey such as the via Francigena on foot. The question remains largely unanswered but I'll try. I had experienced the archetypal yearning to practice the type of embodied spirituality that is to be found by going on pilgrimage; in other words, I was gripped by the pilgrim bug. I have a stirring that leads me to want to walk in the footsteps of earlier pilgrims. No matter how weak and far from the Christian religion I may feel before going on pilgrimage, during the time on the road I'm changing and experience lightness and freedom, despite the hardships and ongoing uncertainties and the monotonous routine of repetitive long-distance walking and daily chores. I explore new horizons and I'm in contact with God.

I have little control over what happens when on pilgrimage (or what happens in the world around me, for that matter). So the pilgrimage is my teacher and I learn to accept what the world does to me. I also learn to free myself from anxiety and how much I can do without. I'm also reminded about how much I don't know why I want to undertake these journeys. An old Zen story captures the spirit of going on pilgrimage.

The wandering monk Fa-yen was asked by Ti-ts'ang, "Where are you going?"
"Around on pilgrimage," said Fa-yen.
Ti-ts'ang asked, "What is the purpose of pilgrimage?"
"I don't know," replied Fa-yen.
Ti-ts'ang nodded and said, "Not knowing is nearest."

Paulo Coelho wrote about his pilgrim experience,
"My turning point was my pilgrimage to Santiago de Compostela. It was then that I, who had dedicated most of my life to penetrate the 'secrets' of the universe, realized that there are no secrets. Life is and will always be a mystery."

Bard castle

Far from being a castle, it is in fact a forbidding 19th-century fortress that cascades down the hillside into a gorge. Originally there was another fortress on this spot, guarding the entrance to the entire Valle D'Aosta region. In 1800, 40,000 of Napoleon's troops swooped down across the Alps and besieged it. The garrison held out for 15 days and when they  finally surrendered they were awarded honors by their victors. The local nobility, the House of Savoy, later built the present fortress between 1830 and 1838, since when it has never actually been attacked and remains in a fine state of conservation.

Pont St Martin XLVI Publei

Although a pretty enough town, the main reason for lingering here is the bridge, an impressive testimony to Romanisation in Valle d'Aosta. Its date is uncertain: some say it was built around

120 B.C., while others say 25 B.C. The wooden beam bearings dug into the live rock can be seen at its base, though iron crowns were added at the end of the nineteenth century to strengthen the structure. Legend ascribes the construction of the bridge to the devil. St. Martin, the Bishop of Tours, was returning to his diocese when the Lys River, overflowed and blocked the only footpath. The devil offered to resolve the problem by building a bridge, in one night, but in return he requested the soul of the first to cross the bridge. The saint accepted, but the following morning he threw a piece of bread to the other side of the bridge, ensuring a starving dog was the first to cross. The infuriated devil disappeared into the Lys with bolts of lighting and a sulphur stench, leaving the bridge to the local population.

Ivrea XLV Everi

The town first appears in history as a Roman cavalry station founded in 100 BC and set to guard one of the traditional invasion routes into northern Italy over the Alps. The Latin name of the town, Eporedia (meaning: place to change horses), has long since vanished into the mists of time, but still appears as the root of the name of the town residents, who are known as "porediesi" in Italian and as "Eporedians" in English. After the fall of the Western Roman Empire, Ivrea became the seat of a duchy under the Lombards (6th-8th centuries). Later Ivrea was disputed between the bishops, the marquis of Monferrato and the House of Savoy. In 1356 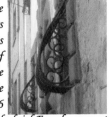 Ivrea was acquired by Amadeus VI of Savoy. With the exception of the brief French conquest at the end of the 16th century, Ivrea remained under Savoy until 1800. On May 26 of that year Napoleon Bonaparte entered the city along with his victorious troops and left in 1814 after his fall.

Look out for:

The Cathedral, probably erected in the 4th century AD over a Pagan temple. The current neo-classical façade is from the 19th century. The main art piece of the interior is the Miraculous

Resurrection of a Child (second half of 15th century), attributed to Nicolas Robert. The sacristy

has two panes by Defendente Ferrari. The cathedral is also seat of the tomb of Blessed Thaddeus McCarthy.

The Capitular Library, not far from the Cathedral, houses an important collection of codices from 7th-15th centuries.

The small Gothic church of **San Bernardino**, houses a notable cycle portraying the Life and Passion of Christ by Giovanni Martino

Spanzotti (1480-1490).

The **Museum Pier Alessandro Garda** has some interesting archaeological findings and a

collection of Japanese art pieces. It is located on the large Piazza Ottinetti.

The Open Air **Museum of Modern Architecture**, inaugurated in 2001 - a show of the main edifices (some by leading architects of the time) built by Olivetti from the 1950s onwards.

The remains of a **Roman theatre** from the first century west of the city centre.

The **Ponte Vecchio**, dating back to 100 AD. Originally built in wood and rebuilt in stone in 1716.

The **St. Stephen Tower** dating back to 11th century. A romanesque bell tower built in 1041 for the Benedictine order, located between Hotel La Serra and Dora Baltea.

Today, Ivrea is best known for its **Battle of the Oranges**, involving thousands of townspeople, divided into nine combat teams, who throw oranges at each other - with considerable violence - during the traditional carnival days, Sunday, Monday and Tuesday and ends with a solemn funeral on the night of Fat

Tuesday. Unfortunately (or fortunately, depending on your point of view), the carnival takes place in February, when most travellers and pilgrims will be at home.

John and Wendy Beecher

We originally became pilgrims in 1998 after one of us had a major operation, walking from Le Puy in France to Santiago de Compostela in NW Spain. This was accomplished over a four year period to fit in with work and other commitments. The most difficult part was breaking away from pilgrimage to return to 'normal life' at the end of each stage. So when we retired in 2007, we were very keen to try a pilgrim route 'end-to-end' or as far as we could, without being time limited. A quieter route which was not well-established seemed appealing and we therefore chose the Via Francigena starting from Canterbury, with its historical links to Sigeric.

After our first month on the pilgrimage route we celebrated and took a step back to review our huge bank of memories and experiences – unusual and charming people we have met in many places, some amazing countryside and towns, tons of wildlife – deer, hares, red squirrels, bats, birds of prey, frogs,... in spite of lots of agricultural spraying and keen hunters and fishers. And of course we've had some highs and lows of emotions: if the weather's good, the route easy going and we've just been to a good town or place to stay, life seems perfect. but rain, route difficulties, or boring/unpleasant towns or hotels can make life seem a real burden (Why are we doing this? Will we manage to finish? How can we feel better?) gradually we learn from this process that we cannot control everything, we can only do what we can and what seems right at the moment we decide but there will be problems, mistakes and disappointments; these are not our fault, so we should not lose confidence. We should accept that there are also unexpected good things that happen, which we can treasure as our good fortune.

The pilgrimage experience provides a great stream of experiences, as if to test us, but in truth this is because we are moving along a path which we do not know, because we are "out of our box", freely taking what the world experience provides. The pilgrimage also gives us some time to reflect on our experiences and our reaction to them and this is a rare opportunity which does not occur so often in "ordinary life".

Piedmont

The via Francigena will take you through Piedmont to Vercelli, after which it proceeds on into the region of Lombardy. The Piedmont region is surrounded by some of the highest mountains in Europe, such as the Gran Paradiso and Monte Rosa, and crossed by the largest river in Italy, the Po. Most of the population live in the plain, especially in the wide metropolitan area of Turin, Novara and Vercelli where a great many mechanical and car industries are located. Thanks to the great abundance of water, agriculture is very important, the main products being rice, wine, maize, potatoes and the precious white truffle.

Piedmont's most ancient inhabitants were the Celts and Liguri, who were succeeded by the Romans. The barbarian invasions of the 5th century completely destroyed the region and it was only under the Lombards that civilized life was re-established. After the Frankish invasion of the late 8th century AD the feudal system was introduced and many monasteries established. Then in the 11th century, as in the rest of Italy, the rise of free Communes began, among them Asti, Chieri, Ivrea, Novara, Torino, Tortona, Cuneo, Mondovì, Vercelli, Alba, Savigliano, which often fought against the powerful Marquises of Monferrato. In the latter half of the 13th century the Communes sided with Charles of Anjou, and the Angevin rule lasted throughout the following century. During the Renaissance the mighty Visconti family ruled over Alba, Alessandria, Asti, Bra, Novara, Tortona, Vercelli, while the Savoy family from Southern France started to spread in the region. In 1559, after a war between France and Spain, the Cateau-Cambrésis Treaty gave part of Piemonte to the Savoy Duke Emanuele Filiberto and to the Marquis of Monferrato, leaving France the cities of Saluzzo, Torino, Chieri, Pinerolo, Chivasso, Asti and Spain the city of Vercelli. In the 18th century, while the European monarchies were all involved in the Succession Wars, the Savoy were able to unify the region. Then in the early 19th century the Italian Risorgimento found fertile ground and the support of the monarchs and of some enlightened ministers, like Camillo Benso Count of Cavour, who was finally able to weave the network of alliances necessary to allow the rise of the Italian State.

Santhià XLIV Sca Agath

Santhià has been inhabited since the Roman period and is thought to have taken its name from Saint Agatha, a Christian martyr. Santhià is an agricultural centre where two branches of the via Francigena join: one towards the Gran San Bernardo Pass and the other one towards the Susa Valley.

Look out for: *the **Church of S.Agata** dating back to the 10th Century.*

St Agatha

Born in Sicily and martyred in approximately 251, St Agatha is one of seven women, excluding the Virgin Mary, commemorated by name in the Canon of the Mass. Rich and noble, she rejected the amorous advances of the low-born Roman prefect, Quintianus and as a result was persecuted by him for her Christian faith. She was given to Aphrodisia, the keeper of a brothel and her nine daughters, but in response to their threats and entreaties to sacrifice to the idols and submit to Quintianus, she responded by saying:

"My courage and my thought be so firmly founded upon the firm stone of Jesus Christ, that for no pain it may not be changed; your words be but wind, your promises be but rain and your menaces be as rivers that pass and how well that all these things hurtle at the foundement of my courage, yet for that it shall not move." Agatha attacked the Roman cult images as idols without philosophical arguments and argued that they were not gods, but devils made of marble and of wood and overgilt. After a number of dramatic confrontations with Quintianus her scorned admirer eventually sentenced her to death by being rolled naked on a bed of live coals.

Vercelli XLIII Vercel

When Sigerico stopped off at Vercelli, it was in a region covered by vast forests with some clearings, fields and marshes. Today, it is the rice capital of Europe, Vercelli is set in a vast plain of paddy fields shimmering into the far distance, but it is also famous for being home to the world's first university funded by public money, established in 1228. Today it has a university of literature and philosophy as a part of the Università del Piemonte Orientale.

Look out for:

*Numerous relics of the Roman period: Amphitheatre, hippodrome, sarcophagi and many important inscriptions, some of which are Christian. There are also two noteworthy towers: the **Torre dell'Angelo** and the **Torre di Città** in via Gioberti.*

The Cathedral, *formerly adorned with precious pillars and mosaics, was erected and enlarged by St Eusebius of Vercelli, to whom it was dedicated* after his death. It was remodelled in the ninth century and radically changed in the sixteenth by Count Alfieri. Like the other churches in the city it contains valuable paintings, especially those of Gaudenzio Ferrari, Gerolamo Giovenone and Lanino, who were natives of Vercelli. The **Vercelli Cathedral Museum** holds the famous **Vercelli Book**, one of the few extant manuscripts of early Anglo-Saxon writings. Although there is still much debate as to how the manuscript wound up in Italy, at least some sources give credence to the theory that **Guala Bicchieri** brought it back with him when he returned from England.

The **Basilica di Sant'Andre**, erected by Cardinal Guala Bicchieri in 1219, is claimed to be one of the most beautiful and best preserved Romanesque monuments in Italy.

Guala Bicchieri was from a prominent family in Vercelli. He trained for law but ultimately entered the clergy. He is first mentioned in 1187 as a canon in the cathedral of Vercelli and by 1205 he had become a cardinal and served as a papal legate in northern Italy before being appointed legate to France in 1208. Innocent III named him legate to England in January 1216, his mission to make peace between the English and the French (the civil war and the threatened invasion by the French in order to depose John from the English throne, were threatening Innocent's plan for a crusade). Guala's position as legate in England was especially influential because the Archbishop of Canterbury, Stephen Langton, was absent from September 1215 to May 1218, during which time Guala Bicchieri was to all intents and purposes in charge of the English church. Guala returned to Italy in 1219 after the final defeat of the English rebel barons and the Treaty of Lambeth. He founded the Abbey of St Andrew in Vercelli, his home town, named after the architecturally imitative of the Abbey of Saint Andrew in Chesterton, which Bicchieri had been given for his services to the church during the difficult period of the civil war. In 1224, he also founded Saint Andrew's hospital in Vercelli.

88

The Basilica of S.Andrea, Vercelli

✤ Lombardy

Lombardy stretches from the Alps, on the the border with Switzerland, down through the lakes of Como and Maggiore to the broad, flat plain of the Po River. It is an area of lakeside villas with azalea-filled gardens, wealthy towns with imposing palazzi and highly decorated churches and modern industry alongside large-scale agriculture. At its centre stands Milan, its style-conscious capital. The region was named after the Lombards or Longobards, a barbarian tribe that invaded Italy in the 6th century AD. During the Middle Ages, Lombardy was part of the Holy Roman Empire, but not always loyal to its German Emperors. The Lombards, who had a talent for banking and commerce and resented outside interference with their prosperity. The 12th century saw the rise of the Lega Lombarda, or Lombard League, a band of forceful separatists founded to counter the brutal imperialism of Frederick Barbarossa. Power was seized by the region's great families, most notably the Visconti and the Sforza of Milan, from the 14th to the early 16th century. These dynasties also became great patrons of the arts, commissioning exquisite palaces, churches and artworks, many of which can still be seen. Ergamo, Mantova and Cremona – not mention Milan itself – contain a remarkably rich array of art treasures. Lombardy is also famous as the birthplace of Virgil, Monteverdi, Stradivari and Donizetti.

Publius Vergilius Maro (also known by the Anglicised forms of his name as **Virgil or Vergil**) (October 15, 70 BCE – September 21, 19 BCE) was a classical Roman poet, best known for three major works—the Eclogues (or Bucolics), the Georgics and the Aeneid—although several minor poems are also attributed to him. The son of a farmer, Virgil came to be regarded as one of Rome's greatest poets. His Aeneid is considered a national epic of Rome and has been extremely popular from its publication to the present day.

Claudio Giovanni Antonio Monteverdi (15 May 1567 (baptized) – 29 November 1643), was an Italian composer, gambist (a musician who performs upon the viola da gamba) and singer. Monteverdi's work, often regarded as revolutionary, marked the transition from the Renaissance style of music to that of the Baroque period. He developed two individual styles of composition: the new basso continuo technique of the Baroque and the heritage of Renaissance polyphony.

Born in Italy in 1644, **Antonio Stradivari** is believed to have been a disciple of Nicolo Amati, of the Amati family of luthiers (someone who makes or repairs stringed instruments) of Cremona. In 1660, Antonio set up shop on his own in Cremona, though his early violins are generally considered inferior to those of his "golden age", between 1698 and 1720.

Domenico Gaetano Maria Donizetti (29 November 1797 – 8 April 1848) was an Italian composer from Bergamo, Lombardy. Donizetti's most famous work is Lucia di Lammermoor (1835) and arguably his most immediately recognizable piece of music is the aria "Una furtiva lagrima" from L'elisir d'amore (1832). Along with Vincenzo Bellini and Gioachino Rossini, he was a leading composer of bel canto (beautiful singing) opera.

Mortara

Originally named *Pulchra Silva* by the Romans, the settlement became Mortara after the bloody battle during which Charlemagne defeated the Longobard King Desiderius in 773.

Quivi cader de' Longobardi tanti,
e tanta fu quivi la strage loro,
che 'l loco de la pugna gli abitanti Mortara dapoi
sempre nominoro.

Ludovico Ariosto, I cinque canti - canto II, 88

Here several Longobards died and the slaughter of them was so great that, from then on, the inhabitants gave the place of the battle the name of Mortara.

Set in the centre of flat, featureless rice fields, the town actually has a great deal to offer.

Look out for:

San Lorenzo - Gothic basilica with a brick facade built by Bartolino da Novara between 1375 and 1380 and restored in 1840 and in 1916. The portrait of SS. Albin, Amicus and Amelius are nineteenth-century copies from a fifteenth-century polyptych by Paolo da Brescia, a work first presented in the Church of San Albin and now conserved in the Savoy picture-gallery of Turin. The Church has several artistic masterpieces inside. From the right of the entrance, in the first span there is a fifteenth-century fresco representing the 'Virgin with Her Child'. In the second span there is 'The Lady between St. Roch and St. Sebastian', which some critics attribute to Gaudenzio Ferrari.
San Croce founded in 1080, originally built outside the town walls, under the patronage of Pope Gregorius VII and re-built inside the city walls in 1596 (based on designs by Pellegrino Tibaldi).

San Albino - during the Middle Ages San Albino was a compulsory halting-place for via Francigena pilgrims and is experiencing a renaissance with the revived interest today. Just outside Mortara, San Albino is one of the Christian mother-churches of the 5th century Lomellina and was re-used by Charlemagne as a burial ground for the soldiers fallen in the battle between the Longobard and Frank armies. The architectural style is developed from a blend of the Romanic and Renaissance styles. Against the Southern side of the porch there is a building, perhaps a part of the ancient monastery and beside the church are the cloister ruins

- an open brick gallery with wooden architraves and fourteenth-century Gothic window decorated with rural motifs. Inside, on the right wall there are three frescoes painted by Giovanni da Milan in 1410 and representing 'Abbott St. Anthony', 'The Baptism of Jesus' and the 'Lady sitting on the throne with St. Albin, St. Jacob, St. Augustine and the client'. Another fresco, by an unknown painter working during the first half of the fifteenth century, can be seen under the triptych and represents St. Laurent with the symbol of his martyrdom in his hand. Next to this fresco there are some visible marks carved in the bricks by the pilgrims to remember their passage. The most ancient readable date is the year 1100. Another anonymous fresco is on the left part of the presbytery and represents a 'Lady with Child and Saints'.

Tremello XLII Tremel

Pavia XLI Pamphica

Dating back to pre-Roman times, the town of Pavia (then known as Ticinum) was a municipality and an important military site under the Roman Empire. Later the city became known as, Papia (probably as a reference to the Pope), which evolved to the Italian name Pavia. During Pavia's golden age, the city was the Lombard's capital and later witnessed coronations of Charlemagne and Frederick Barbarossa. Even after it lost its status to Milan in 1359, Pavia remained an important city and great Romanesque churches, tall towers and other monuments still reflect this.

Look out for:

Duomo di Pavia, begun in 1488. The central dome, (97 m high) is the third largest in Italy.

San Michele Maggiore - an outstanding example of Lombard-Romanesque church architecture and located on the site of a pre-existing Lombard church. Destroyed in 1004, the church was rebuilt from around the end of the 11th century (including the crypt, the transept and the choir) and finished in 1155. Emperor Frederick Barbarossa was crowned here in 1155.

San Pietro in Ciel d'Oro – burial site of Saint Augustine, Boethius and the Lombard king Liutprand. The arch which holds the relics of St. Augustine was built in 1362 by artists from Campione and is decorated by some 150 statues and reliefs. The church is mentioned by Dante Alighieri in the X canto of his Divine Comedy.

San Teodoro (1117), dedicated to Theodore of Pavia, a medieval bishop of the Diocese of Pavia, is situated on the slopes leading down to the Ticino river and served the fishermen. Inside are two outstanding bird's-eye-view frescoes of the city (1525) attributed to the painter Bernardino Lanzani.

Castello Visconteo (1360-1365) built by Galeazzo II Visconti. In spite of its fortifications, it was actually used as a private residence. The poet Francesco Petrarca spent some time there, when Gian Galeazzo Visconti called him to take charge of the magnificent library (over a thousand books and manuscripts), which was subsequently lost. The Castle is now home to the Musei Civici.

Santa Maria del Carmine - one of the best known examples of Gothic brickwork architecture in northern Italy and second largest church in the city.

University of Pavia, founded in 1361 and one of the most ancient universities in Europe.

The medieval towers still shape the town skyline. The main clusters situated in Piazza Leonardo da Vinci, via Luigi Porta and Piazza Collegio Borromeo.

Sante Cristine XL Sce Cristine
Corte Sant'Andrea XXXIX Sce Andrea

Emilia-Romagna

You will be crossing a corner of Emilia-Romagna, a broad corridor through the hills and plains of the Po Valley that marks the watershed between the cold northern Alps and the hot Mediterranean south. With its rich agricultural land, historical cities and thriving industry, it is one of the most prosperous areas in Italy. Most of the major towns in Emilia-Romagna lie near the via Aemilia, a Roman road built in 187 BC that linked Rimini on the Adriatic coast with the garrison town of Piacenza. Prior to the Romans, the Etruscans had ruled from their capital, Felsina, located on the site of present-day Bologna. After the fall of Rome, the region's focus moved to Ravenna, which became a principal part of the Byzantine Empire administered from Constantinople. Today, the region is probably best known for being home to Ferrari, Lamborghini and Maserati, but it also has a reputation as a great gastronomic centre. Piacenza and its province are renowned for the production of seasoned and salted pork products. The main specialities are pancetta (rolled seasoned pork belly), coppa (seasoned pork neck) and salame (chopped pork meat flavoured with spices and wine and made into sausages). Bortellina (salted pancakes) and chisulén (flour, milk and animal fats mixed together and then fried) are also good with fat cheese, particularly Gorgonzola and Robiola. The hills surrounding Piacenza are well known for their vineyards. The wine produced in this area is qualified with a D.o.c. (Denominazione di origine controllata) called "Colli piacentini" (Hills of Piacenza). Main wines are Gutturnio (red wine, both sparkling and still), Bonarda (a red wine, often sparkling and foamy, made from Croatina grapes), Ortrugo (a dry white wine) and Malvasia (a sweet white wine).

Piacenza XXXVIII Placentia

Before its settlement by the Romans, the area was populated by Celtic and Ligurian tribes. The Etruscans were well known for the practice of divining the future by using the entrails of sheep. A bronze sculpture called the "Liver of Piacenza" was discovered in 1877 near Piacenza,

Piazza dei Cavalli

complete with the name of regions marked on it, which were assigned to various gods. It has been connected to the practice of haruspicy (the inspection of the entrails of sacrificed animals). Piacenza, (formerly called Placentia in both Latin and English) was founded in 218 BC and was the first of the Roman military colonies. In the following years the city's territory was drained and a port was constructed along the Po River. Placentia flourished as a production centre for grain, barley, millet and wool. The era of Late Antiquity in Piacenza was marked by the expansion of Christianity. The current patron saint, Antoninus, was a former legionnaire who Christianized the area and who was killed during the reign of Diocletian. Piacenza was sacked during the course of the Gothic Wars (535–552) and after a
short period as a Byzantine Empire city, it was conquered by the Lombards, who made it a duchy seat. After the Frank conquest (9th century) the city began to recover, aided by its location along the via Francigena. In 1095 the city was the site of the Council of Piacenza, in which the First Crusade was proclaimed. From 1126 Piacenza was a free commune and an important member of the Lombard League. In this role it took part in the war against the emperor Frederick Barbarossa and in the subsequent battle of Legnano (1176). It also successfully fought the neighbouring communes of Cremona, Pavia and Parma, expanding its possessions and captured control of the trading routes with Genoa, where the first Piacentini bankers had already settled. In the 13th century, despite unsuccessful wars against emperor Frederick II, Piacenza managed to gain strongholds on the Lombardy shore of the Po River.

The preliminaries of the Peace of Constance were signed in 1183 in the Saint Antoninus church. Agriculture and trade flourished in these centuries and Piacenza became one of the richest cities in Europe. This is reflected in the construction of many important buildings and in the general revision of the urban plan. Struggles for control were commonplace in the second half of the 13th century. The Scotti family, Pallavicino family and Alberto Scoto (1290-1313) held power in that order during the period. Scoto's government ended when the Visconti of Milan captured Piacenza, which they would hold until 1447. Duke Gian Galeazzo rewrote Piacenza's statutes and relocated the University of Pavia to the city. A coin from the 16th century features the motto: Placentia floret (Piacenza flourishes) on one of its sides. The city was

Duomo di Piacenza

progressing economically, chiefly due to the expansion of agriculture in the countryside surrounding the city, but underwent some of its most difficult years during the rule of Duke Odoardo (1622-1646), when between 6,000 and 13,000 Piacentini (out of the population of 30,000) died from famine and plague. In 1802, Napoleon's army annexed Piacenza to the French Empire and young Piacentini recruits were sent to fight in Russia, Spain and Germany, while the city was plundered of a great number of artworks, which are currently exhibited in many French museums. The Habsburg government of Maria Luisa 1816-1847 is remembered fondly as one of the best in the history of Piacenza; the duchess drained land, built several bridges across the Trebbia river and the Nure stream and created educational and artistic activities. Much later, during World War II the city was heavily bombed, the railway bridge across the Po River, railway station and historical centre being destroyed. On the hills and the Appenine mountains, partisan bands were active and in 1996 president Oscar Luigi Scalfaro honoured Piacenza with the Gold Medal for Valour in Battle. Today, Piacenza is one of the most renowned cities in Italy for the arts, boasting a number of historical palaces, often characterized by splendid gardens.

Look out for:

Palazzo Comunale, also known as il Gotico, (1281), government seat and one of the best preserved examples of the kind of Medieval civic building in northern Italy known as the Broletto.

Piazza Cavalli - main square of the town, named after the two bronze equestrian monuments of Alessandro Farnese (Duke of Parma and Piacenza from 1586, nephew and valiant general of Philip II of Spain) and his son Ranuccio, who succeeded him to the dukedom. The statues are masterpieces of Francesco Mochi, a Mannerist sculptor.

Duomo di Piacenza - Romanesque cathedral of the diocese of Piacenza-Bobbio (1122 to 1233), housing frescoes, made in the 14th-16th centuries by Camillo Procaccini and Ludovico Carracci, Morazzone and Guercino. The main gate is enriched by a big lunette of the 15th century representing the Ecstasy of St. Francis. The interior, two aisles divided by low and strong brick pillars that support high Gothic arches, has a Latin Cross scheme. The nave, higher than the aisles, has a pentahedric apse in which the aisle apses meet; decorations include 15th-16th centuries frescoes.

Basilica of Sant'Antonino - example of Romanesque architecture, characterized by a large octagonal tower.

Basilica of San Savino - dedicated to St. Victor's successor, was begun in 903 but consecrated only in 1107. The façade and the portico are from the 17th-18th centuries.

Bronze Liver of Piacenza - Etruscan bronze model of a sheep's liver housed in Piacenza's Archaeological Museum, part of the Musei Civici di Palazzo Farnese. Containing writing on its surface delineating the various parts of the liver and their significance, it was probably used as an educational tool for students studying haruspicy, or divination.

Ricci Oddi Gallery - an art-gallery dedicated to modern Italian painters.

Note: Many inhabitants of Piacenza and the surrounding province still use the Piacentine (or Piacentino) dialect, which is quite different from standard (Florentine) Italian as it is a variety of Emiliano-Romagnolo minority language. The different grammar rules and the dissimilar pronunciation of even similar words make it largely unintelligible to those who speak standard Italian, with many regular vowels being replaced with umlauts or eliminated altogether.

Saint Conrad

The saint's date of birth is uncertain, but it is known that he belonged to one of the noblest families of Piacenza. Having married when he was quite young, he then led a virtuous and God-fearing life until one day, while he was hunting in brushwood, he accidentally started a fire. The prevailing wind caused the flames to spread rapidly and the surrounding fields and forest were soon engulfed. A mendicant, who happened to be found near the place where the fire had originated, was accused of being the source. He was imprisoned, tried and condemned to death. As the poor man was being led to execution, Conrad, stricken with remorse, confessed his guilt and in order to repair the damage, sold all of his possessions. Reduced to poverty, Conrad retired to a lonely hermitage some distance from Piacenza, while his wife entered the Order of Poor Clares. Later he went to Rome and then to Sicily, where for thirty years he lived a most austere life and worked numerous miracles until he died in 1351. Though bearing the title of saint, Conrad was never formally canonized. His liturgical feast day is kept in the Franciscan Order on the day of his death, 19 February.

Fiorenzuola d'Arda XXXVII Floricum

The name is derived from Florentia, meaning prosperous and d'Arda, which refers to the River Arda flowing from the Apennine Mountains into the valley where Fiorenzuola is situated. The most important monument in the town is the **Collegiata of S. Fiorenzo**, built in 1300 and reconstructed by the end of 1400. Other historic landmarks are the church of **Beata Vergine di Caravaggio**, the **Oratorio della Beata Vergine**, the **Verdi Theatre** and the church of **St Francis**.

Burgo Santo Donnino XXXVI Sce Domnine
Medesano XXXV Metane
Fornovo di Taro XXXIV Phi<lemangenur

Fidenza

For a considerable number of years, Fidenza was known as Borgo San Donninore, but it was

renamed Fidenza in 1927, recalling its Roman name of Fidentia. The town's most famous monument is its 12th century cathedral dedicated to Domninus of Fidenza, who was martyred under Maximian in AD 304. The cathedral is one of the finest and best preserved Lombard-Romanesque churches of the 11th to 13th centuries in northern Italy. The upper part of the façade is incomplete, but the lower, with its three portals and sculptures, is a fine example of Romanesque architecture, including two statues by Benedetto Antelami and bas-reliefs with the Histories of San Donnino. The statue erected on the front of the cathedral of the apostle Simon Peter is famous for its fingers which point in the direction of the city of Rome. On the left hand there is a card reading "I show you the way to Rome"- one of the world's first road signs. Fidenza was a major staging post on the via Francigena. The tomb of St Donnino in the Cathedral was a point of reference for pilgrims to Rome and carvings depict them, as well as more domestic subjects.

Cisa Pass

The pass runs along the border between the Duchy of Parma and the Grand Duchy of Tuscany, while also offering stunning views. Dominated by the chapel of Nostra Signora della Guardia, built in 1921, the pass is part of the via Francigena, but also one of the favourite itineraries followed by motorbike lovers in the province of Parma.

Berceto XXXIII Sce Moderanne

The origins of this stopping place on the via Francigena, either before or after crossing the

Appennines, are linked to a Benedictine abbey founded in the 8th century by the longobard King Liutprand, following a request by Moderanus, the bishop of Rennes. The medieval atmosphere that pervades the village come from its old stone houses, small and rustic buildings and the remains of a 12th century castle which dominates the town. The Cathedral is devoted to St. Moderanno, who was abbot here since 719. Rebuilt between the 12th and the 13th century, the church still shows Romanesque features despite alterations undergone during the 16th and 19th century. The façade in sandstone dates back to the restoration of the 19th century, but nevertheless preserves the precious 12th century portal with fanlight and reliefs lintel. The severe interior, divided into three aisles, is rich with works of art. In the third chapel on the right is
the entrance to the treasure of the Cathedral, preserving precious pieces of furniture and liturgical objects.

Look out for: St. Moderanno's green silk vestment dating back to the 8th-9th century, a wine glass (1517) chiseled with vine tendril and leaves of acanthus motives and a wine glass origin found in a grave inside the church.

The baroque sanctuary of the **Madonna delle Grazie**, *built in the early 16th century on the remains of a medieval pilgrims' hospice, lies slightly outside the town.*

Montelugo XXXII Sce Benedicte

Pontremoli XXXI Puntremel

Literally translated, **Pontremoli** *means 'Trembling Bridge' (from the Italian tremare - to tremble), with the commune having been named after a prominent bridge across the Magra, which one presumes, trembled. Pontremoli is believed to have been first settled around a thousand years before Christ and was known in Roman times as Apua. The large number of churches in Pontremoli provide the main cultural sights of the city, but more modern attractions of Pontremoli include Il Bar Moderno (a local*

café), winner of a gold award in the Milanese Ice Cream and Coffee competition.

San Nicolò which houses a wooden cross, dating back several centuries.

Chiesa Cattedrale S. Maria Assunta *(Il Duomo)*, built in the 17th century and dedicated to SaintGeminianus, it also contains many valuable sculptures and paintings. The dome of this cathedral, along with Il Campanone (the bell tower), dominates the city skyline. The church of the **SS. Annunziata** with its Augustinian monastery and painted mural.

There are also several buildings of interest, connected with Pontremoli's noble families. The major site is the **Castello del Piagnaro**, one of the largest castles in Lunigiana. Several palaces, such as those of the houses of Malaspina and Dosi, are also located within the commune.

Aulla XXX Aguilla

The name Aulla probably comes from the Latin words 'lacus' or 'lacuna', meaning lake. Traces of Roman and Etruscan civilizations found in the Church of Saint Caprisio indicate that there

were settlements in Aulla long before the eighth century, when Adalberto of Tuscany founded a village and castle to accommodate pilgrims travelling the via Francigena. During the Middle Ages the Abbey became one of the most influential religious centres in the Lunigiana region and in 1522 the village of Aulla was bought by the commander Giovanni delle Bande Nere, who built the imposing Fortress of Brunella. In 1943 the historic centre of Aulla was destroyed by Anglo-American bombings aimed at German troups stationed there during the Second World War.

Santo Stefano di Magra XXIX Sce Stephane

Located near the confluence of the Vara with the Magra river, Santo Stefano di Magra is in the Montemarcello-Magra Natural Regional Park. Founded before 1000 AD, the settlement was described as a marketplace in 981 by Emperor Otto II and in 1185 by Emperor Frederick . Today the town is divided into two parts by the old central road and enclosed by powerful late Renaissance walls. The church, dedicated to St. Stephen was built in the 18th century over a medieval 'pieve' (a term defining rural churches with a baptistery).

Sarzana

The first mention of the city is found in 983, but owing to its militarily strategic position, it changed masters more than once, belonging first to Pisa, then to Florence, then to the Banco di S. Giorgio of Genoa and from 1572 to Genoa itself. **Look out for:**

The former citadel - built by the Pisans, then demolished and re-erected by Lorenzo de Medici.

Fortezza Firmafede - built by the condottiero Castruccio Castracani

Palazzo del Capitano - designed by Giuliano da Maiano (1472), but now entirely altered.

Eric Sylvers. a journalist by training and a walker by nature.

Making the World Better One Step at a Time

25 September 2009, Milan – When we try to improve something in this world whether it be by recycling, going to work by bike rather than car or getting people to notice the potential of the via Francigena it's because we want a better world to live in, but it's above all because we want to

 leave the world a bit better than when we arrived. I've got an extra stake now because this month I became a father for the first time with the birth of Luca on 09-09-09. Lucky day for

sure and let's hope that luck means that sometime before he turns 95 he'll be able to enjoy a wonderful walk on a via Francigena that has finally been sign posted and moved almost entirely onto dirt trails. (And here's hoping it doesn't take so long before those markers and dirt trails become a reality so that his father is not too old to join him on the pilgrimage.)

Tuscany

Renowned for its art, history and evocative landscape, with hill towns encircled by Etruscan walls and slender cypress trees, Tuscany is a region where the past and present merge in pleasant harmony. But even without these the landscape - rolling hills so soft and continuous that this writer has the sense of walking over a recently petrified sea - is enough to make one want to add at least another week to the schedule. Tuscany must be seen at leisure and preferably on foot. Like all of Italy, Tuscany has its Etruscan and Roman past, with the scars and treasures associated with each. Today, as you walk through the countryside, among the vineyards and olive groves, you will encounter hamlets and farmhouses as well as fortified villas and castles symbolizing the violence and intercommunal strife that tore Tuscany apart during the Middle Ages. Several imposing castles and villas were built for the Medici family, the great patrons of the Renaissance who supported eminent scientists, such as Galileo. Northern Tuscany and the heavily populated plain between Florence and Lucca, which the via Francigena will take you through, is dominated by industry, with intensively cultivated land between the cities and the wild mountainous areas. At the heart of central Tuscany lies Siena, also a town on your route, which was involved in a long feud with Florence. Its finest hour came with its victory in the Battle of Montaperti in 1260, but it was devastated by the Black Death in the 14th century and finally suffered a crushing defeat in the siege of 1554-5. Northeastern Tuscany, with its mountain peaks and woodland, provided refuge for hermits and saints, while the east was home to Piero della Farncesca the early Renaissance painter. Along with its great artists, Tuscany is also know for its cuisine. Olive groves and wild herbs that grow everywhere. Many of the best oils are reserved for use as a condiment at the table, rather than as an ingredient for cooking. It is often pointed out that Tuscan cooking has its roots in "cucina povera" (peasant cooking) and it is indeed very simple. No fancy sauces, no elaborate creations or heavy seasoning. Meat and fish tends to be grilled simply over a fire, vegetables served raw, steamed or sautéed. Pasta plays a small role in the diet, but certainly not as much as it does in other parts of Italy, because salads and a variety of bean dishes, predominate.

Luni XXV!II Luna

The site is located on the border between Liguria and Tuscany, on the bank of the river Magra, though today there are only the ruins left. Founded by the Romans in 177 BC, it was a military stronghold for the campaigns against the Ligures. In 109 BC it was connected to Rome by the via Aemilia Scauri which became the via Aurelia in the second century AD. Luni achieved prosperity based on the exploitation of white marble quarries in the nearby Alpi Apuane mountains and remained wealthy until it was taken over by the Lombards in 642. The Lombards damaged the city's economy by favouring the trade routes passing through the nearby port of Lucca to the south. Luni, now reduced to a small village, was repeatedly attacked by pirates and its citizens finally moved to Sarzana in 1058 in order to escape malaria and the declining economy that had been exacerbated by the silting up of the port.
Main sights: *The remains of the elliptical Roman amphitheatre (first century AD).*

Camaiore XXVII Campmaior

The name is derived from the Latin Campus Majo, or wide level space. Around 190 B.C., in this vast area at the foot of the mountain Prana, the Romans constructed fortifications known as the Colonia Lucensis. Later, in 1300 Camaiore was the capital of the Republic of Lucca and its defense systems were put in place. From 1374 the village was provided with city walls, including thirteen towers and a stronghold. Just outside the town centre, is St. Peter's Abbey, founded by the Benedictin monks in the 17th century. In the Middle Ages, the town grew considerably, thanks to the via Francigena, and was identified as Campmaior by Sigeric as he passed through.
Look out for:
Collegiate Church of Santa Maria Assunta - *built in 1260*
Church of San Lazzaro
Archaeological Museum - *located inside the Palazzo Tori Masons*

Pietrasanta

Straddling the last foothills of the Apuan Alps, Pietrasanta has Roman origins and part of

San Antonio Abate

the Roman wall still exists. The medieval town was founded in 1255 upon the preexisting 'Rocca di Sala' fortress of the Lombards by Luca Guiscardo da Pietrasanta. At its height, Pietrasanta was a part of the Genova city-state (1316 - 1328). Then, in 1494, Charles VIII of France took control of the town and it remained so until Pope Leo X gave Pietrasanta back to the Medici family. The town suffered a long period of decline during the seventeenth and eighteenth centuries, partially due to malaria, but in 1841, the Grand Duke of Tuscany, Leopold II di Lorena, promoted several reconstruction projects (including the building of schools specially created to teach carving skills and the reopening of the once famous quarries), which brought back much of the town's former glory. Throughout history and even to this day, artists have appreciated the mellowness of Tuscany and have been inspired to capture the beauty of this unchanged landscape on canvas. Pietrasanta grew in importance during the 15th century, mainly due to its connection with marble. Michelangelo was the first sculptor to recognize the beauty of the local stone. Today's artists and sculptors are drawn to Pietrasanta from all over the world. The Colombian painter and sculptor Fernando Botero as well as the Polish sculptor Igor Mitoraj have residences in the comune.

Look out for:

Cathedral of St. Martin Duomo (13th-14th centuries).

Church of Saint Augustine (15th century), Romanesque style and now used for exhibitions.

Gothic Civic Tower

Column and Fountain of the Marzocco (16th century).

Palazzo Panichi Carli (16th century).

Palazzo Moroni (16th century), home to the local Archaeological Museum.

Lucca XXVI Luca

Situated to the left of the river Serchio, Lucca was founded by the Etruscans and became a Roman colony in 180 BC. The rectangular grid of its historical centre preserves the Roman

Duomo di Lucca

street plan and the Piazza San Michele is on the site of the ancient forum. Traces of the amphitheatre can still be seen in the Piazza dell'Anfiteatro. The medieval walls around the old town remain intact, which is unusual for cities in the region. As the walls lost their military importance, they became a pedestrian promenade which encircled the old town, although they for a number of years they were used for racing cars. Each of the four principal sides is lined with a different tree species. Lucca is the birthplace of composers Francesco Geminiani, Gioseffo Guami, Luigi Boccherini, Giacomo Puccini and Alfredo Catalani.

There is a great deal to see in Lucca, but ensure that you **Look out for:**

San Michele in Foro – notable for its 13th century façade, with a large series of sculptures. The highest part of the church features a 4 metre statue of St. Michael the Archangel flanked by two other angels. On the lower right corner of the façade is a statue (1480) of the Madonna salutis portus, sculpted by Matteo Civitali to celebrate the end of the 1476 plague. Amongst the artworks in the interior, are a Madonna with Child terracotta by Luca della Robbia and a panel with Four Saints by Filippino Lippi.

Cattedrale di San Martino (Italian Duomo) - begun in 1063 by Bishop Anselm (later Pope Alexander II) and notable for the Labyrinth on the portico of the cathedral. In the nave a little octagonal temple or chapel shrine contains the most precious relic in Lucca, the Volto Santo di Lucca or Sacred Countenance. According to the legend, this cedar-wood crucifix and image of Christ was carved by his contemporary Nicodemus and miraculously conveyed to Lucca in 782. Christ is clothed in the colobium, a long sleeveless garment. The chapel was built in 1484 by Matteo Civitali, the most famous Luccan sculptor of the early Renaissance. Additionally the cathedral contains a Ghirlandaio Madonna and Child with Saints Peter, Clement, Paul and Sebastian; a Federico Zuccari Adoration of Magi, a Jacopo Tintoretto Last Supper and finally a Fra Bartolomeo Madonna and Child (1509).

Museo della Cattedrale – best known for its Romanesque stone heads, human and equine.

Fonta Lustrale – a huge 12th century font executed by three unknown craftsmen. Behind this is Annunciation by Andrea della Robbia.

Piazza Anfiteatro - built on the foundations of the Roman amphitheatre, the arches and columns of which can still be seen.

Torre Guinigi - (15th century) home of Lucca's leading family and notable for its battlemented tower, surmounted (44 metre up) by a holm oak, the roots of which have grown into the room below.

Museo Nazionale di Villa Guinigi - notable for its Romanesque works by della Quercia and Matteo Civitali and Renaissance works by Fra Bartolomeo.

Porcari XXV Forcri

Ponte a Cappiano XXIII Aqua Nigra

On entering the town, the first thing one sees is the bridge. This and its complex system of sluice gates, was commissioned by Cosimo dei Medici during the 1530s, in order to regulate the waters and increase the numbers of fish. The construction is huge and more accurately described as an elongated building suspended over the waters of what used to be the greatest inner marsh in Italy. Interestingly, in terms of the via Francigena, the Medici bridge was put in place when the area was little more than a system of waterways, which means that though Sigerac listed the area as number XXIII, it is likely that there was no settlement and he travelled past by boat.

Fucecchio XXIII Arne Blanca

Situated half way between Florence and Pisa, Fucecchio lies on the right bank of the Arno near the natural basin of the Padule, or Wetlands, from which it has taken its name. Its origins date back to the 10th century and its development was helped by the Bonfiglio bridge (which allowed travellers along the via Francigena to cross the river) and by the presence of the Castle of Salamarzana, seat of the Cadolingi Counts, one of the most powerful feudal noble families of Tuscany. The current street plan of this small town dates back to the second half of the 13th century and the early 14th century, when the increasing population required a second city wall. The 14th century towers of the Florentine Fortress, which have recently been restored, are in the park of the ex- Palazzo Corsini - a green oasis in the heart of the old town.

Also look out for:

Salamarzana Castle *- dominating the historical centre of the town on a hill from where the Cadolingi controlled the underlying ford and wooden bridge where the via Francigena originally crossed the Arno.*

Towers of the Rocca Fiorentina *- erected in 1322, during the war against Castruccio Castracani, lord of Lucca. Consisting of two large towers, Torre Grossa' and Torre di Mezzo' and another smaller one known as Pagliaiola. Bombardments during World War 2 left the complex in ruins.*

Borgo Santo Genesio XXII Sce Dionisii
Colanno XXI Sce Peter Currant.

Gambassi Terme XX Sce Maria Glan

The territory around Gambassi Terme was densely populated from the 7th century BC until the late-Roman age in the 3rd century AD. Its history is heavily influenced by its position and

it features as a transit route for the Etruscans and later the Romans on the via Clodia, which linked Lucca with Rome. The town was also used as a stopping place for pilgrims on the via Francigena and the establishment of a hospice was recorded in the 13th century. Between the 12th and 13th centuries the inhabitants of Gambassi Terme enjoyed relative autonomy and prosperity, but this ended when the town was absorbed into the district of San Gimignano. A harsh conflict took place as a result, with considerable loss of life and property. Eventually, the castle of Gambassi was annexed to the territories under the powerful jusdiction of Florence. Today, Gambassi Terme is primarily known as a spa resort.

Look out for:

*The **church of San Giovanni Battista**, which houses a replica of Andrea del Sarto's Madonna with Child and Saints.*

In the entrance of the town, a 14th century fresco depicting a Madonna with child St. Michele and saints.

Church of St. Jacob and Saint Stefano - 13th century
Church of the Misericordia, famous for its terracotta statues and its 14th century role as a glass handicraft centre.

San Gimignano XIX Sce Gemiane

The story behind the founding of San Gimignano has been lost in the mists of time. Legend attributes it to two young noblemen, Muzio and Silvio, who were on the run after having been

involved in the Catalina conspiracy. In AD 63 the two brothers took refuge in Valdelsa and built two castles there, one was named Mucchio and the other Silvio. The 13 towers that dominate San Gimignano's majestic skyline were built by noble families (Ardinghelli and the Salvucci) in the 12th and 13 centuries, when the town's position on the via Francigena brought it great prosperity. The plague of 1348 and the diversion of the pilgrim route, led to its decline as well as its preservation. In its heyday the town walls enclosed five monasteries, four hospitals, public baths and a brothel, but today, only one of the towers, Torre Grossa, is open to the public.

Look out for:

Museo Civico - frescoes in the courtyard of this museum feature the coats of arms of city mayors and magistrates, as well as the 14th century 'Virgin and Child' by Taddeo di Bartolo. The first room is the Sala di Dante, where an inscription recalls a visit by the poet in 1300. The walls are covered with hunting scenes and a huge 'Maesta' fresco (1317) by Lippo Memmi. The floor above has an art collection, which includes excellent works by Pinturicchio, Bartolo de Fredi, Benozzo Gozzoli and Filippino Lippi. The famous 'Wedding Scene' frescoes by Memmo di Filipucci (early 14th century) show a couple sharing a bath and going to bed - an unusual record of life in 14th century Tuscany.

Collegiata - this 12th century Romanesque church contains some magnificent frescoes. In the north aisle they are comprised of 26 episodes from the Old Testament (1367) by Bartolo di Fredi. The opposite wall features scenes from the 'Life of Christ' (1333-41) by Lippo Memmi, while at the back of the church there are scenes from 'The Last Judgement' painted by Taddeo di Bartolo.

Sant' Agosto - Consecrated in 1298, this church has a simple façade, contrasting markedly with the heavily decorated Rococo interior (1740) by Vanvitelli. Above the main altar is the 'Coronation of the Virgin' by Piero del Pollaiuolo, dated 1483. The choir is entirely covered in a cycle of frescoes of the 'Life of St Augustine' (1465) executed by the Florentine artist Benozzo Gozzoli. In the **Capella di San Bartolo,** on the right of the main entrance, there is an elaborate marble altar by Benedetto da Maiano (1495).

Dante Alighieri (1265-1321)

 When a person's name recurs so regularly along a single route, he deserves further examination. Dante is best known for the epic poem La Divina Commedia, which has profoundly affected not only the religious imagination, but all subsequent allegorical creation of imaginary worlds in literature. Dante spent much of his life travelling from one city to another, but this probably had more to do with the restless times than his wandering character or fixation on the Odyssey. He was born into a Florentine family of noble ancestry. His mother, Bella degli Abati, died when he was seven years old. His father, Alighiero II, made his living by money-lending and the renting of property. After the death of his wife he remarried, but died himself in the early 1280s, before the future poet reached manhood. Brunetto Latini, a man of letters and a politician, became a father figure for Dante, but later in his Commedia, Dante placed Latini in Hell, the seventh circle, among those who were guilty of "violence against nature" – sodomy. Dante received a thorough education in both classical and Christian literature. At the age of 12 he was promised to his future wife, Gemma Donati, though he had already fallen in love with another girl called Beatrice. She was 9 years old. The nature of his love had its roots in the medieval concept of courtly love and the idealization of women. In 1289 Dante entered politics and joined the White (Bianchi) Guelphs, one of the rival factions within the Guelph party. In 1295 he entered the Guild of Apothecaries, to which philosophers could belong and which opened for him the doors to public office. Dante served the commune in various councils and was ambassador to San Gimignano in 1300 and then to Rome. In June 1300 he was elected a prior and the following year he was appointed superintendent of roads and road repair. Dante was exiled when the Black (Neri) Guelphs, who had the pope's support, ascended to power. The White Guelphs were condemned to death by burning should they ever be caught again in Florence, but they soon made an alliance with the Ghibelline party and attempted several unsuccessful attacks on Florence. Their hopes ended with the death (1313) of the emperor Henry VII. Dante was charged with financial corruption in January 1302 and some months later he was condemned to death by burning. After 1302 Dante never saw his home town again, but found shelter in various Italian cities and with such rulers as Ordelaffi of Forlì, the Scaligeri of Verona and the Malaspina of Lunigiana. He lived his remaining years in the courts of the northern Italy princes. During his exile, and under the patronage of the Ghibelline leaders, he started to write his Commedia, a long story-poem through the three worlds of the afterlife. In 1320 Dante made his final home in Ravenna, where he died on the night of September 13, 1321. His body was brought to the church of San Francisco. Shortly after he died, Dante was accused of Averroism (the term applied to a philosophical trends among scholastics in the late 13th century) and his book, De Monarchia, was burned by the order of Pope John XXII. In 1519, Franciscan monks hid Dante's remains, when Pope Leo X decided to deliver them in Florence to Michelangelo who planned to construct a glorious tomb. Again in 1677 Dante's remains were moved and in 1865 construction workers rediscovered them accidentally.

"How bitter another's bread is, thou shalt know By tasting it; and how hard to the feet Another's stairs are, up and down to go." (from The Divine Comedy)

Monteriggioni

Sitting on a small natural hillock, this completely walled medieval town was built in the 13th century by the overlords of Siena to command the Cassia Road running through the Val d'Elsa and Val Staggia just to the west of Monteriggioni. Today, its fortified walls and fourteen heavily fortified towers remain intact and create an unforgettable impression. Two gates lead inside - Porta Franca (or Romea) and Porta di san Giovanni - and from here one can proceed into the large piazza, with its a pretty Romanesque church (13th century) dedicated to the Assumption of the Virgin. Less postively, it must also be mentioned that Dante used Monteriggioni as a simile for the deepest abyss at the heart of his 'Inferno', which compares the town's "ring-shaped citadel... crowned with towers" with giants standing in a moat.

Molino XVIII Sce Martin in Fosse

Abbadia dell'Isola XVI Burgenove

Three kilometres west of Monteriggioni, it is impossible to miss the former Cistercian Abbey of Abbadia dell'Isola. This Romanesque church was largely rebuilt in the 18th century, after the cupola fell apart. It contains a renaissance altar and frescoes by Taddeo di Bartolo and Vincenzo Tamagni.

Castelfiorentino

The town was founded on the ruins of a Roman settlement and later developed as a halt for pilgrims on the via Francigena.

Look out for:

Benozzo Gozzoli Museum - home to a number of well-known frescoes by the Florentine painter of the same name.

Siena XV Seocine

Once a capital to rival Florence, Siena is Italy's prettiest medieval town and is still endowed

with the grandeur of the age when it was at its peak (1260-1348). Like other Tuscan hill towns, Siena was first settled by the Etruscans (c. 900 BC to 400 BC), an advanced people who changed the face of central Italy through their use of irrigation to reclaim previously unfarmable land and their custom of building their

settlements in well-defended hill-forts. Later, Emperor Augustus, founded the Roman town, Saena Julia on the same site. An origin that accounts for the town's emblem – a she-wolf suckling the infants Romulus and Remus. According to legend, Siena was founded by Senius, son of Remus, who was in turn the brother of Romulus, after whom Rome was named. Statues and other artwork depicting a she-wolf suckling the young twins Romulus and Remus can be seen all over the city of Siena. Nevertheless, Siena did not prosper under Roman rule. It was not sited near any major roads and therefore missed out on the resulting opportunities for trade. As a consequence, Christianity did not reach the town until the 4th century AD and it was not until the Lombards invaded Siena and the surrounding territory that it became prosperous. Their occupation and the fact that the old Roman roads of Aurelia and the Cassia passed through areas exposed to Byzantine raids, caused the roads between the Lombards' northern possessions and Rome to be re-routed through Siena. The inevitable consequence of this was that Siena prospered as a trading post and the constant streams of pilgrims passing to and from Rome were to prove a valuable source of income in the centuries to come. It was during the early 1200s that the majority of the construction of the Siena Cathedral (Duomo) was completed. It was also during this period that the Piazza del Campo, grew in importance as the centre of secular life. New streets were constructed leading to it and it served as the site for the market and various sporting events . In 1194, a wall was built on the current site of the Palazzo Pubblico to stop soil erosion, an indication of how important the area was becoming as a civic space. Siena's principal sights cluster in the maze of narrow streets and alleys around the fan-shaped Piazza del Campo.

Look out for:

Piazza del Campo - now regarded as one of the most beautiful civic spaces in Europe, the Piazza occupies the site of the old Roman forum and for much of Siena's early history was the city's principal market place. It began to assume its present shape in 1293, when the Council of Nine, Siena's ruling body at the time, began to acquire land with a view to creating a grand civic piazza. The red-brick paving was begun in 1327 and completed in 1349 - its distinctive nine segments designed to reflect the authority of the Council and symbolise the protective folds of the Madonna's cloak. The piazza has been the focus of civc life ever since - a setting for executions, bullfights and the twice-yearly drama of the Palio.

Fonte Gaia - a 19th century copy of an original carved by Jacop della Quercia in 1409. Its relief depicts the 'Virtues', Adam and Eve' and the 'Madonna and Child'. The water still comes from a 500-year-old aqueduct.

Palazzo Pubblico - Although it continues in its ancient role as Siena's town hall, the Palazzo

Pubblico's medieval rooms, some decorated with paintings from the Sienese School, are open to the public. The main council chamber, or Sala del Mappamundo, is named after a map of the world painted by Ambrogio Lorenzetti in the early 14th century. One wall is covered in Simone Martini's recently restored fresco of the 'Maesta' (1315), which depicts the Virgin in Majesty as the Queen of Heaven, attended by the Apostles, saints and angels. Opposite is a fresco of the mercenary Guidoriccio da Fogliano (1330). The walls of the chapel alongside are covered with frescoes of the 'Life of the Virgin' (1407) by Taddeo di Bartolo and the choir stalls are decorated with wooden panels inlaid with biblical scenes. The Sala della Pace contains the famous

'Allegory of Good and Bad Government' (1338-40), a pair of frescoes by Ambrogio Lorernzetti. They form one of the most important series of secular paintings from the Middle Ages. In the 'Good Government' fresco civic life flourishes, while the 'Bad Government' is presided over by a demon and shows rubbish-strewn streets and ruins. The Sala del Risorimento is covered with late 19th century frescoes illustrating the events leading up to the unification of Italy under King Vittorio Emanuele II. In the palace courtyard is the entrance to the **Torre del Mangia**, the palace's bell tower. Rising 102m (330ft) high, the tower was built by the brothers Muccio and Francesco di Rinaldo between 1338 and 1348 and named after the first bellringer, whose idleness led to the nickname 'Mangiaguadagni' (literally - eat the profits). There are 505 steps to the top of the tower, but the incredible view makes the strain worthwhile.

Santuario e Casa di Santa Caterina - Siena's patron saint Catherine Beneincasa (1347-80) was

the daughter of a tradesman. At the age of eight she devoted herself to God and had many visions, as well as later receiving the stigmata. Like her namesake, St Catherine of Alexandria, she was believed to have been betrothed to the Christ Child in a vision - a scene that inspired many artists. Her eloquence persuaded Pope Gregory XI to return the seat of the papacy to Rome in 1376 after 67 years of exile in Avignon. St Catherine died in in Rome and was canonized in 1461. Today, Catherine's house is surrounded by chapels and cloisters. The house itself is decorated with paintings and events from her life by a number of artists, including Francesco Vanni and Pietro Sorn.

Palazzo Piccolomini - Siena's most imposing private palazzo was built for the wealthy Piccolomini family in the 1460's by the Florentine architect and sculptor Bernado Rossalini. It now contains the Sienese state archives, account books and taxation documents dating back to the 13th century. Some of the leading artists of their day were employed to paint the wooden bindings used to enclose the tax and account records. The paintings, now on display in the Sala di Congresso, often show scenes of Siena itself, bristling with towers, or episodes from the city's past.

Pinacotela Nazionale - a gallery, housed in the 14th century Palazzo Buonsignori and containing a collection of paintings by artists of the Sienese school, including: Duccio's 'Madonna dei Francescani' and Simone Martini's 'The Blessed Agostino Novello and Four of his Miracles'.

Siena's **Duomo** - (1136-1382) one of Italy's greatest cathedrals. Among its treasures, one can see sculptural works by Nicola Pisano, Donatello and Michelangelo. You are advised to take time out to see the pulpit panels, carved in 1265 by Nicola Pisano, the Massacre of the Innocents (an inlaid marble floor), the Piccolomini Library, famous for its frecoses depicting the life of the Piccolomini Pope, Pius II.

Museo dell'Opera del Duomo - part of the museum is devoted to items removed from the Duomo, including a tondo of a 'Madonna and Child', probably by Donatello. The highlight is Duccio's 'Maestà (1308-11), one of the Sienese School's finest works.

Fortezza Medicea - a huge red-brick fortress, built for Cosimo I, by Baldassarre Lanci in 1560, following Siena's defeat by the Florentines in the 1554 war. The fortress now houses the Enoteca Italica, a wine shop offering visitors the chance to taste and buy a comprehensive list of wines from all over Italy.

The Palio - The Palio di Siena (Il Palio) is a horse race held twice each year, in which ten horses and riders, riding bareback and dressed in the appropriate colours, represent ten of the seventeen Contrade, or city wards. The Palio, held on July 2, is known as the Palio di Provenzano, in honour of Madonna di Provenzano, whose church is in Siena. The Palio held on August 16 is

named Palio dell'Assunta, in honour of the Assumption of Mary. A magnificent pageant, the Corteo Storico, precedes the race, which attracts visitors and spectators from around the world. The race itself, involves circling the Piazza del Campo three times and usually lasts no more than 90 seconds. It is not uncommon for a few of the jockeys to be thrown off their horses and it is not unusual to see unmounted horses finishing the race . The Palio in fact is won by the horse who represents his contrada and not by the jockeys. The earliest known antecedents of the race are medieval. The town's central piazza was the site of of a range of largely combative public games, but the public races organized by the Contrade only became popular from the 14th century on. Called 'palii alla lunga', they were run across the whole city. When the Grand Duke of Tuscany outlawed bullfighting in 1590, the Contrade took to organising races in the Piazza del Campo. The first such races were on buffalo-back and called 'bufalate'. The 'asinate, races on donkey-back, later took their place, while horse-racing continued elsewhere. The first modern Palio (called palio alla tonda to distinguish it from the earlier palii alla lunga) took place in 1656. At first, one race was held each year, on July 2, a second, on August 16, was added later.

Ritual and Rivalry

The Palio di Siena is more than a simple horse race. It is the culmination of ongoing rivalry and competition between the contrade. The lead-up to and the day of the race are invested with passion and pride. Formal and informal rituals take place as the day proceeds, with each contrada navigating a strategy of horsemanship, alliances and animosities. Prior to the race itself there is the two hour pageant of the Corteo Storico, which is finally crowned by the race, which takes all of about 75 seconds to complete.

*A contrada (plural: contrade) is a district, or a ward, within an Italian city. The most well-known contrade are probably the 17 contrade of Siena that race in the Palio di Siena. Each is named after an animal or symbol and each with its own long history and complicated set of heraldic and semi-mythological associations.

In the summer, as excitement builds, it is customary for members of the various contrade to dress in ceremonial garb and parade through the city. These

districts were set up in the Middle Ages in order to supply troops to the many military companies that were hired to defend Siena as it fought to defend its independence from Florence and other nearby city states. As time has gone by, however, the contrade have lost their administrative and military functions and have instead become simply areas of localised patriotism, held together by the emotions and sense of civic pride of the residents. Their roles have broadened so that every important event - baptisms, deaths, marriages, church holidays, victories at the Palio, even wine or food festivals - is celebrated only within one's own contrada. Every contrada has its own museum, fountain and baptismal font and motto.

Sienese contrad

Aquila (eagle) one of only four nobile (noble) contrade; its title bestowed by the Habsburg emperor Charles V, out of gratitude for the warm reception he received there in 1536. Aquila is situated immediately to the south-west of the Piazza del Campo in the centre of the city and is home to the duomo (cathedral). Traditionally, its residents were notaries. Their last victory was on July 3, 1992 and they have had 24 official victories. The contrada's museum is home to the oldest surviving Palio di Siena banner (also called a palio), which dates from 1719. Aquila's patron Saint is la Vergine (the name of the Most Holy Maria), her titulary festival being celebrated on 8 September. Aquila's are allied to the Civetta (Owl) and Drago (Dragon) contrade. They are opposed to the Pantera (Panther) contrada.

Giraffa (Giraffe) is in an affluent area of the city to the north-east of Piazza del Campo. Traditionally its residents were painters. Giraffa has the title of 'contrada imperiale', bestowed by King Vittorio Amanuele III when it won the palio in 1936, the year the race was dedicated to Italy's empire in East Africa.

Bruco (Caterpillar), *traditionally, its residents worked in the silk trade. Bruco is one of only four nobili contrade; its title was earned in 1369 by its people's bravery in helping to defeat Charles IV and consolidated in 1371 when they led the revolt to replace the Sienese council with a people's government. Its Sede is at via del Comune and its patron Saint is Madonna (Visitation of the Saintest Mary) and the Titulary feast is on 2 July. Bruco's are allied to the Istrice, Nicchio and Torre Contrada and not officially opposed to any other contrade since its animosity with neighbouring Giraffa (giraffe) ended. Last victory- 16 August 2008. It has 37 official Victories.*

Chiocciola - (Snail), *their last victory was on August 16, 1999. Chiocciola is situated in the south-western corner of the city. Traditionally, its residents worked as terracotta makers.*

Civetta (Little Owl), *situated immediately to the north of the Piazza del Campo in the centre of the city. Traditionally, its residents were shoemakers. For years Civetta was considered the Nonna because it hadn't won a palio for 30+ years, but it won in August 2009, thereby getting rid of the name "nonna" (grandmother).*

Drago (Dragon), *situated to the north-west of the Piazza del Campo. Traditionally, its residents were bankers. it won the palio in 1936, the year the race was dedicated to Italy's empire in East Africa.*

Istrice (Crested Porcupine), *occupies the north-westernmost edge of Siena and contains the San Vincenzo e Anastasio church, home of the city's oldest surviving fresco and burial place of Pinturicchio. Istrice has the title of contrada sovrana (sovereign contrada). It was bestowed this title as a result of it headquartering the Sovereign Military Order of Malta during the 14th century. Istrice won the Palio in July 2008.*

Leocorno (Unicorn), *situated to the west of the Piazza del Campo. Traditionally, its residents were goldsmiths. Leocorno won the Palio of August 16th 2007.*

Lupa (She-Wolf), *situated to the north of the Piazza del Campo. Traditionally, the residents of Lupa were bakers. The she-wolf of this contrada refers to the legend that Siena was founded by Senius, the son of Remus who, along with his twin Romulus, was raised by a wolf. Because of this, Lupa's sister city is Rome. Lupa's museum prize exhibit is a photograph of Giuseppe Garibaldi, which he donated to the contrada on its victory in the Palio di Siena of 1867.*

Nicchio (Seashell), *situated in the far eastern corner of the city. Traditionally, its residents worked as potters. Nicchio is one of only four nobile (noble) contrade; it earned its title for bravery shown during the Battle of Montaperti against Florence in 1260, when its soldiers led the attack.*

Oca (Goose), *situated just to the west of the Piazza del Campo. Traditionally, its residents made dyes. Oca is one of only four nobili (noble) contrade, a title in recognition for its people's bravery during many battles fought by the former Sienese Republic. It is the only contrada that has no allies. The most recent palio win for Oca was in the July 2, 2007 race on Fedora Saura.*

Onda (Wave), *describes itself as "The colour of Heaven, the force of the sea". Onda runs south from the Piazza del Campo in the centre of the city. Traditionally, its residents were carpenters. Onda has the title of contrada capitana (captain contrada) because in the past its soldiers mounted guard at the Palazzo Pubblico. One of the famous members of Onda was the sculptor Giovanni Duprè, after whom the main street in Onda is named. Onda's adversary is Torre.*

Pantera (Panther), *situated at the western edge of the city. Traditionally, its residents were grocers and chemists.*

Selva (Forest) *runs west from the Piazza del Campo in the centre of the city. Traditionally, its residents were weavers, but when the contrade were mainly military they had a reputation for being excellent archers. Winner of the Palio, on August 16 2006, with Salasso on Caro Amico.*

Tartuca, *situated at the southern end of the city. Traditionally, its residents were sculptors. Winner of the Palio, on July 2 2009, with Giuseppe Zedda on Già del Menhir. It is opposed to Chiocciola.*

Torre (Tower), *situated just to the south-east of the Piazza del Campo in the centre of the city and Torre is the enemy of both Onda (wave) and of Oca (goose). It is the only contrada to have two enemies, making it the most contentious contrada in Siena. Torre encompasses Siena's Jewish quarter and synagogue. Traditionally, its residents worked as woolcombers.*

Valdimontone (Ram), *situated in the south-east of the city near Porta Romana. Traditionally, its residents were tailors. It is allied with Onda contrada (wave) and opposed to Nicchio (shell), its neighbour.*

Ponte d'Arbia XIV Arbia
San Quirico d'Orcia XIII Turreiner

San Quirico d'Orcia XII Sce Quiric

Though Etruscan in origin, the first explicit reference to San Quirico was when there was a dispute between the diocese of Siena and Arezzo over the possession of some parishes, among which was San Quirico in Osenna. The outcome of this dispute was a decision, confirmed by King Liutprando, in favour of the church of Arezzo. The name "Osenna" was in use until the 17th century and probably referred to a water-course which has now disappeared. It is an Etruscan place-name and perhaps even "Orcia" (water, stream or brook) is pre-Roman. From the beginning of the 11th century, the name of San Quirico in Osenna is mentioned more frequently, especially in connection with travel along the via Francigena.

If you have time in the next section, try a detour to **Abbadia San Salvatore**. The abbey is one

of the oldest monasteries in Tuscany and was an important station in the Middle Ages on the via Francigena. The modern suburb which has developed round the monastery, has become a popular summer and winter resort. The picturesque medieval borgo or village preserves its outer walls and streets intact, with medieval and Renaissance houses of local grey stone. The Benedettine abbey, which was immensely rich and powerful, enjoyed numerous privileges under the protection of popes and emperors and exercised feudal jurisdiction over much of southern Tuscany. It was founded according to tradition, in 743 by the Lombard king, Ratchis, on the spot where he saw a vision. At the peak of its temporal and spiritual powers in 1035 the abbey was rebuilt and reconsecrated by Abbot Winizzo. It was eventually incorporated into the

Medici state in 1559. Other places to look out for include the Chiesa di Santa Croce, the Palazzo Comunale (Municipal Palace) and the Parco Museo Minerario del Monte Amiata (Mineral Park and Museum of the Amiata Mount). The area was once important for the extraction of cinnabar - generally found in a massive, granular or earthy form and bright scarlet to brick-red in colour.

Buonconvento

Today, Buonconvento is an important agricultural centre on the gentler side of the Sienese clay hills and benefits from its site at the confluence of the Arbia and Ombrone rivers on one hand and along the via Francigena on the other. This favourable position brought rich trade, but also raids. Still enclosed in the rectangular form imposed by the walls built by the Sienese in 1371, the town has preserved the monumental northern gate opening towards the capital of the province. Buonconvento was the seat of a podesta fron 1270 onwards and still boasts a fine Town Hall on whose facade one can distinguish the coats-of-arms of 25 podesta of olden days.

Look out for:

The *Sacred Art Museum*, which houses works from local churches including paintings by Sano di Pietro and Matteo di Giovanni, as well as interesting wooden and marble sculptures.

Radicofani XI Abricula

The main landmark of Radicofani is its Rocca (Castle), which is of Carolingian origin and documented from 978. It was the castle of Ghino di Tacco. Occupying the highest point of a hill (896 m), it was restored after sustaining damage during the conquest with the Grand Duchy of Tuscany (1560-1567). The settlement's position on the edge of the Roman Cassia road, then named Francigena or Romea, was crucial for its development and a cause for contention. Initially Radicofani was under the control of the Benedictine Abbey of the Mount Amiata, but in 1081 the counts of the Aldobrandeschi family and shortly after the counts of Chiusi, tried to replace the monks. The Senese control began in 1139, when Count Manente da Pepone gave a sixth part of the castle to the Bishop of Siena, but the monks refused to surrender and with the help of the Roman Church, were granted half of the fortress. Pope Adriano IV, successor of Eugene, reinforced the castle and in 1198 Innocenzo III started new works on the fortification. From this period Radicofani was often at the centre of the continued struggle between Siena and Orvieto and opted to ally with Florence. In 1301-1302, Radicofani was at the centre of a war conducted by Guido of Montfort and Margherita Aldobrandeschi, Ghibelline against the Guelphs Commons allied with the Pope. The Guelphs won the war and the fortress remained in peace for a long time under the control of the papacy. After significant restoration work in 1999, the castle was opened to the public.

Look out for:

The *Romanesque church of San Pietro*, with a nave, housing works by Andrea della Robbia, Benedetto Buglioni and Santi Buglioni. Also by della Robbia is the precious Madonna with Saints at the high altar of the church of Sant'Agata.

Voltole X Sce Petir in Pail

Acquapendente IX Aquapendente

When the via Cassia was still the main connection between Florence and Rome, Acquapendente was the crossroads for both trade and pilgrim traffic. The town was a favourite "statio" or stopping point for pilgrims travelling to Rome and the coasts of Apulia to reach the Holy Land. *I Pugnaloni* - this event originated in 1166 when Acquapendente was ruled by one of Barbarossa's tyrants. Two citizens of the era supposedly said: "It is more likely for an old, dried up cherry tree to blossom than for our town to rid itself of the invaders". The sudden miraculous flowering of the cherry tree was welcomed as a divine sign from Our Lady, giving

the local population the strength and confidence to rebel. To commemorate this ribbons were tied to the "pugnoli"(wooden sticks) that were used used to drive oxen and to fight enemies. Today, these have become "pugnaloni", enormous mosaics composed mainly of flowers and depicting images about freedom. Late in the afternoon on the first Sunday after 15th May, there is a procession to bring them from the cathedral of Santo Sepolcro to the Palazzo Comunale. The "pugnaloni" (about twenty in all), are created the night before by groups of young people.

Look out for:

The **cathedral of Santo Sepolcro**, constructed around the year 1000, consecrated in 1149 and given the title of cathedral in 1649. Following damage during World War II, much of it was rebuilt based on the plans of Vincenzo Fasolo. Inside the cathedral take time out to see the altarpiece in the right transept, a work in enamelled terracotta by Jacopo Beneventano (1522) portraying the Eternal Father worshipped by angels and the wooden choir (1685-1688) in the apse attributed to artist Matteo Tedesco.

The **chapel of St. Hermes** venerates the memory of the patron saint and there is a beautiful 14th century baptismal font under the presbytery, between the two entry stairs. The 10th century crypt was built over the original aedicule of the Holy Sepulchre that is set in the middle and covered by a pyramid with a rectangular base. According to tradition, it holds a stone relic that was bathed in the blood of Christ.

The **tower of Julia di Jacopo**, located near the church, marks the remains of the fortress built by Arrigo IV (currently used as a cultural and welcome centre).

The clock tower (also known as **Barbarossa's tower**) in the uppermost part of town was part of the imperial castle held by the Swabians for many years.

San Lorenzo Nuovo

The town is located on the northern side of Lake Bolsena's crater rim and dominates the lake basin on one side and the valley of the Acquapendente. The old village of San Lorenzo alle Grotte was located in the lowlands closer to Lake Bolsena than the current village. This ancient hamlet was named after the numerous surrounding caves inhabited by the Etruscans. According to local legend, the inhabitants asked for protection from the heavens during the fifth-century invasions of the Vandals and on the feast of Saint Apollinare, a dense fog came down and the invaders spared the town. San Lorenzo alle Grotte had been always of strategic importance, owing to its position along the via Cassia and a point of contention for local noblemen and the Church. In the year 1113 the area was donated to the Church by Matilda of Canossa, countess of Tuscany, but the same area was sacked by the Holy Roman Emperor Henry VI in 1186. The opposition of Pope Celestine III, mediated by the bishop of Sovana, is recorded in a document dated 28 June 1183. The new town was built in the year 1774 because the lower position of San Lorenzo alle Grotte made it rather unhealthy for its inhabitants. People were affected by malaria and other epidemics and as a conseqence trade had ceased. After numerous attempts to decontaminate the area, Cardinal Giovanni Angelo Braschi induced Pope Clement XIV to take the decision to move all homes to a higher and more liveable site.

An area was identified on a wide upland in the vicinity of the old village (in a location named Gabelletta) and mandated with a signed document dated June 3, 1772. Pope Clement XIV commissioned the work of reconstruction to architect Alessandro Dori and then to architect Francesco Navone, who designed an ideal city according to urban planning canons of his time.

Look out for:

Collegiate church of San Lorenzo Martire - parish church of San Lorenzo Martire with a particulary fine, wooden crucifix and two mannerist canvases by Jacopo Zucchi, representing the Ascension and Resurrection.

Church of Capuchin Fathers - a single nave building with three lateral chapels on each side, completed in 1784 and dedicated to a Capuchin friar, Saint Seraphim of Montegranaro. The interiors were decorated by the Sicilian Capuchin friar, painter, Fidelis of San Biagio (1717-1801). He painted: Immaculate Conception with Saint Seraphim of Montegranaro, Saint Francis receiving stigmata, martyrdom of Saint Fidelis of Sigmaringen, ecstasy of Saint Lawrence of Brindisi, Sacred Family with Saint Felix of Cantalice, martyrdom of Saint Joseph of Leonessa. The painting representing the blessed Bernard of Corleone was lost during World War II. Built in the early 18th century, it was part of a convent of the Capuchin Fathers until 1810, when all religious orders were suppressed by Napoleon I.

The Brigands' path

During the 19th century the area across Latium, Umbria and Tuscany marked the southern border of the Grand Duchy of Tuscany and, since 1861, the Kingdom of Italy and the States of the Church. The area included woodlands such as Selva del Lamone and Monti di Castro, with isolated caves and small rivers. Several brigands used to live here. Fortunato Ansuini was one of these and known for being extremely cruel. Born in Norcia in 1844 to a family of farmers, Ansuini was forced by his parents to work as a stonemason. He killed a man in a tavern and was sentenced to 11 years in prison in Rome, but in May, 1866, he escaped through a drain with three jail-mates. The fugitives left Rome and chose Maremma as a secure place to hide. Here, their new life began, involving robberies and racketeering, though the authorities forced them to continuously move from one place to another. Eventually, they were caught while banqueting inside a cave. Ansuini was locked up in the fort Filippo II, but he managed to escape again, with other captives. After breaking their chains, they went out through the window with the help of bed sheets. The next night the brigands stormed a shepherd 's house near Capalbio, tied up the shepherds and stole their food, money and guns. Anecdotes about Ansuini are numerous. He liked to mock the authorities, leaving signed letters in the restaurants where he used to eat. Once he went elegantly dressed to Bassano in Teverina and entered the barracks of the carabinieri in the name of a tradesman travelling from Milan. On his request, he received an escort of two gendarmes for personal protection during his journey. At the end he asked the two men to deliver a letter to their commander explaining how he had been duped. The Brigands' Path is an historical 120 km hiking trail that follows in the footsteps of some of Italy's infamous figures. It links the Tyrrhenian Sea (area of Vulci) to the Apennine mountains of central Italy. A trail is marked in the area across Onano, Grotte di Castro, Gradoli and San Lorenzo Nuovo where most of the adventures of Ansuini and other brigands are said to have taken place.

Bolsena is best known for a miracle said to have occurred there in 1263, when a Bohemian priest, in doubt about the doctrine of Transubstantiation, reported bleeding from the host he had consecrated at Mass. The Duomo di Orvieto was eventually built to commemorate the miracle and to house the Corporal of Bolsena. The town is also well known for the lake in front of it. Of volcanic origin, it was formed following the collapse of a caldera into a deep aquifer. Roman historic records indicate activity of the Vulsini volcano as recently as 104 BC, since when it has been dormant. The two islands in the southern part of the lake were formed by underwater eruptions following the initial collapse of the caldera. The lake has a long historic tradition. The Romans called it Lacus Volsinii, adapting the Etruscan name, Velzna, of the Etruscan city that had originally existed on its shores. Later, one third of the lake was donated to the Church by the noble family Alberici of Orvieto. In recognition of the donation the Alberici family was honoured with a ceremony three times a year performed by the Bishop

Duomo di Orvieto

of Orvieto. From April to September, excursion boats offer rides to the islands. Both are privately owned and Martana is not open to the public, but Bisentina is an ex-summer residence of the Popes and has a large church on it. There are also seven small chapels built around the island. One of them contains some beautiful frescoes attributed to Benozzo Gozzoli or his school. The chapels were originally built to make it easier to get a plenary indulgence, by giving pilgrims an alternative to having to visit each of the seven major churches in Rome. While it is fairly certain that the town of Bolsena is the successor to the ancient Roman town of Volsinii, scholarly opinion is sharply divided as to whether Volsinii was the same as the ancient Etruscan city of Velzna or Velsuna (sometimes termed Volsinii Veteres – Old Volsinii), the other candidate being Orvieto, 20 kilometres to the northeast. Other historians have pointed out that the town of Bolsena has no Etruscan characteristics; for example, Etruscan cities were built on defensible crags, which the castle is not. The Roman historian Pliny the Elder said that a bolt from Mars fell on Bolsena, "the richest town in Tuscany" and burned it down entirely . As a consequence , he claims, the population moved to another site, which is thought to be Bolsena. **Look out for:**

Rocca Monaldeschi della Cervara *- sitting at the top of the hill, overlooking the medieval quarter of town, the castle was built between the 12th and 14th centuries and has been completely renovated. Today it is home to the Museo Territoriale del Lago di Bolsena (Lake Bolsena Territorial Museum). The museum is well laid out; each of its three floors dedicated to various aspects of Bolsena's history, ranging from its prehistoric volcanic origins to its Etruscan-Roman period. Your guide writer recommends a walk along the ramparts of the castle, which offers a gorgeous view of the entire lake that should not be missed.*

The **Duomo di Orvieto** *- a Romanesque church built in 1078 in a typical basilica style over the catacombs where St. Christine, a young woman martyred during the reign of the Roman Emperor Diocletian, was buried. In reality, the church is a complex composed of three separate segments: early Christian catacombs from the 4th century, the basilica built in the 11th century and the "new" Chapel of the Miracle built in 1693.*

Montefiascone VII Sce Flaviane

Like Bolsena, Montefiascone sits on the shores of Lake Bolsena, but is dominated by the octagonal bulk of its cathedral, Santa Margherita, whose dome was created in the 1670's by Carlo Fontana and is second only in size to the dome of St Peter's.

Viterbo VI Sce Valentine

Although an important Etruscan centre before falling to the Romans in the 4th century,

Viterbo's heyday only came in the 13th century when it briefly became the papal seat. In a period in which the Popes had difficulties asserting their authority over Rome, Viterbo became their favourite residence, beginning with Pope Eugene III (1145-1146). In 1164 Frederick Barbarossa made Viterbo the seat of his Antipope Paschal III and three years later he gave it the title of "city" and used its armies against Rome. Today, in spite of sustaining serious bomb damage during World War II, Viterbo's historic centre is one of the best preserved medieval towns of central Italy. Many of the older buildings (particularly churches) are built on top of ancient ruins, recognizable by their large stones, 50 centimetres to a side.

Look out for:

*In **San Pellegrino**, Viterbo's oldest and best preserved quarter, medieval houses with towers, arches and external staircases line narrow streets running between little piazzas decorated with fountains. On Piazza San Lorenzo the 12th century Duomo boasts an elegant black and white striped bell tower, a solemn 16th century façade and a Romanesque interior.*

*13th century **Palazzo Papale**, with a finely carved loggia, was built for popes on their visits to the city.*

*15th century **Palazzo dei Priori**, frescoed inside by Baldassare Croce with scenes from the town's history and mythological past.*

***Santa Maria della Verità**, outside the the city walls, has wonderful 15th century frescoes by Lorenzo da Viterbo.*

Vetralla V Furcari

Apparently, the mythological origins of Vertralla go back to Noah, who supposedly settled in these parts after the flood to found a village and recover his strength with the wine of Vetralla. Proof of Etruscan settlements can be found in various necropoli in the region (Cerracchio and Grotta Porcina), while evidence of the Roman age are seen in the via Cassia. The present-day town has a medieval layout, along a road that winds its way between the ancient houses where the fortress used to be. Modest remains are still visible (a lavishly restored cylindrical tower), but not a great deal more.

Look out for:

The **cathedral of Sant'Andrea** - known for the Madonna of the Rosary, attributed to Ludovico Mazzanti, Crucifixion of St. Andrew by Domenico Muratori (also responsible for the Immaculate Conception and Our Lady of the Assumption), the Baptist and Saints Giacomo Triga and the Transfiguration by Marco Benefial. There is an outstanding 12th century panel of the Madonna Intercessor (on the reverse, the Head of the Saviour). A small crystal shrine houses several reliquaries, including one in silver gilt by Giovanni Anastasio di Vitale and a small silvered urn with the relics of St. Hippolytus.

The **church of San Francesco**, 11th century, Romanesque, with an elegant Cosmati portal and, most notably, 16th and 17th century frescoes on the walls of the central nave and in the presbytery, with stories on the life of St. Francis by Francesco Villamena 1566-1624.

The **Museo della Città e del Territorio** has been set up in premises in the historic centre, near the castle walls and puts on exhibits dedicated to the historic centres and traditional handicrafts of Tuscia. The town of Vetralla extends for all practical purposes as far as the nearby hamlet of Cura, whose parish church or Maria Santissima del Soccorso contains an eighteenth-century altarpiece of the Visitation and a fifteenth-century fresco depicting the Madonna and Child and Saints.

Santa Maria Rosa - patron saint of Viterbo (1235-1252) was a virgin saint, born in Viterbo, Italy. Rose was remarkable for her holiness and miraculous powers from her earliest years. When only three years old, she raised her maternal aunt from death. At the age of seven, she had already lived the life of a recluse, devoting herself to penances. Her health was poor, but she was reputed to have been cured by the Blessed Virgin Mary, who ordered her to enrol herself in the Third Order of Francis of Assisi and to preach penance to Viterbo, at that time (1247) held by Frederick II, Holy Roman Emperor and a prey to political strife and heresy. Her mission seems to have extended for about two years and such was her success that the prefect of the city decided to banish her. The imperial power was seriously threatened. Accordingly, Rose and her parents were expelled from Viterbo in January 1250 and took refuge in Soriano nel Cimino. On 5 December 1250, Rose foretold the speedy death of the emperor, a prophecy realized on 13 December. Soon afterwards she went to Vitorchiano, whose inhabitants, according to surviving reports, were affected by a supposed sorceress. Rose secured the conversion of all, even of the sorceress, by standing unscathed for three hours in the flames of a burning pyre. With the restoration of the papal power in Viterbo (1251) Rose returned. She wanted to enter the monastery of St. Mary of the Roses, but was refused because of her poverty. She accepted her rejection, but foretold that she would be admitted to the monastery after her death. The remainder of her life was spent in the cell in her father's house, where she died. The process of her canonization was opened in that year by Pope Innocent IV, but was not definitively undertaken until 1457. Her feast is celebrated on 4 September, when her body, believed by the faithful to be still incorrupt, despite the passage of time, is carried in procession through Viterbo.

Capranica

Located at the confluence of two small rivers, Capranica can be accessed only from one side. **Look out for:** the church of Madonna del Piano (approximately 1km outside the gate of Capranica) designed by il Vignola in the second half of the XVIth. The gate was built in the same period and leads to Borgo, one of the two peaks of the hill.

Sutri IlIl Suteria

Ancient Sutrium occupied an important position, commanding as it did the road into Etruria, which was to become the via Cassia. Livy (Titus Livius, 56 BC - AD 17, known as Livy in English, was a Roman historian who wrote a monumental history of Rome and the Roman people) described it as being one of the keys of Etruria, Nepi being the other. The settlement came into the hands of Rome after the fall of Veii and a Latin colony was founded there, then lost again in 386 BC and finally recovered and recolonized around 383. Picturesquely situated on a narrow tuff (a type of rock consisting of consolidated volcanic ash ejected from vents during a volcanic eruption) hill and surrounded by ravines, Sutri is best known for its Roman amphitheatre and Etruscan necropolis with dozens of rock-cut tombs and a Mithraeum* incorporated in the crypt of its church of the Madonna del Parto. The amphitheatre is completely carved out of local tufa stone. Although it is fairly small, it faces the town as it did in ancient times and offers an enchanting, almost mystical atmosphere. Opinions vary as to exactly when it was built, ranging from as early as the Etruscan archaic period to the first decades of the Christian era. Built on a north-south axis, it has two entrances at its farthest extremities and its shape is slightly oval. A tunnel, with five entrances still visible on each side, circles the area at its outer circumference, thus separating it from the spectators' section, the cavea, which was divided into three orders of tiers. A rectangular niche cut into the lowest section on the northwest side had its own private entrance and is believed to be the

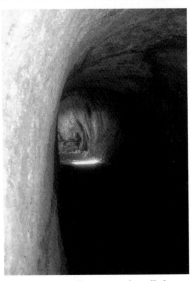

VIP seats, or what we might call the royal box. Sutri's municipal cemetery, alongside the

ampitheatre, dates from the ancient Roman period and features a variety of tombs including the single chamber, double chamber, arched entrance and rectangular niche varieties. Not all are visible, because many were badly damaged when used by local farmers as storage for farm equipment, or even as pig sties. A particulary unusual feature of this necropolis is the way in  which both burial and cremation ceremonies were practised simultaneously. This has led experts to surmise that the tombs were used again and again over successive periods of time. After first belonging to wealthy Etruscans, it was then used by the Romans, later converted into a temple by the Mithraic cult and finally adopted by the Christians. The first of its two rooms is small and square and was probably a vestibule. The second room is long and rectangular, with three naves divided by two rows of pilasters carved of the same rock. At the base of the pilasters are rock benches which would have formed the reclining tables where participants at a Mithraic service consumed the meal that was part of the devotional rite. The whole structure displays many of the characteristics found in Mithraic temples: they were almost always underground, had faux grotto decorations, were poorly lit, and featured reclining benches. Christians frequently built churches over Mithraic shrines (witness Rome's Santa Prisca and San Clemente) or pagan temples (Rome's Santa Francesca Romana was built on the site of Augustus' Temple to Venus and Rome). Thus, in the 6th or 7th century AD, Sutri's Mithraic shrine became a church dedicated to the Madonna del Parto. The earliest frescoes in the church date from this period and are to be found on the two pilasters closest to the altar. The upper part of Sutri is on higher ground (acropoli) and, notwithstanding the fact that it is now occupied by the Cathedral and by Palazzo Vescovile, it still conveys the image of a fortress. The main medieval buildings of Sutri retain something of the Etruscan and Roman times and this applies to the whole town.

Also look out for:

Sutri also has some interesting signs of the Baroque period. For example, a 17th century clock in the centre of the town is still set to indicate the Italian hour, which shows 6 rather than 12 hours and has just one pointer (in this clock a ray of the sun). The pointer reached 6 at sunset in every period of the year, because the clock was reset every two weeks to take care of the changes in the duration of daylight, so that the Italian hour was indicating what was left of the day before sunset.

*Mithraeum - a place of worship for the followers of the religion of Mithraism, often constructed underground or in a cave to resemble the cave where Mithras is said to have slain the sacred bull depicted in the Enkidu seal.

Baccano III Bacane
Monterosi

The region is characterized by a number of lakes of volcanic origin. The smallest ones have been drained at different stages with the exception of the circular pond near the little town of Monterosi. In the past Monterosi was just a handful of houses along the via Cassia, but in spite of this it is home to a large palace built in 1690 by Giovanni Battista Contini for the Altieri family (the palace is currently known as Palazzo Del Drago and is under restoration).

Campagnano di Roma

The first documentation of "Borgo di Campagnano" dates from 1076 when it was defined as a "castellum", having been carved out of the great estate assembled on the Roman pattern by Pope Adrian I (ca. 780) - his Domuscula Caprarorum. It was cited again in 1130 among the properties of the monastery of San Paolo. Campagnano remained relatively autonomous until 1410 when it entered into the possession of the Orsini family. In 1662, the village passed to the Chigi, who between 1600 and 1700, enlarged the medieval centre with the addition of the "Borgo Paolino" who received the rights to the lakes of Bracciano and Stracciacappe. They retained ownership until the first decades of the 19 century. In 1818, Campagnano became a municipality and participated actively in the birth of the Kingdom of Italy to which it was annexed in 1870. The current town is composed of three distinct sectors: the modern sector through which one passes upon arrival from Rome, the Renaissance-Baroque sector created by the Chigi family, extending from the Porta Romana to the Palazzo Comunale Leonelli and the medieval sector which is located at the extremities of the plateau and is rich in towers, palaces and churches. **Look out for:** *S. Giovanni and la Pietà.*

La Storta Il Johannis VIIII

Vision at la Storta *While on his way to Rome in 1537, St Ignatius had a vision in which God the Father and Christ instructed him to establish a religious community in that city. As a result, he became the founder of the Jesuit order, which grew dramatically and helped to spread the influence of the Catholic Church around the world during the late 16 and 17 centuries, the period of the Counter Reformation.*

Montemario Park

The hill was known as Mons Vaticanus or Clivus Cinnae in Roman times. The current name, according to some theories, comes from Mario Mellini, a cardinal who around the middle of 15th century owned a villa and several hamlets in the area. However, in the Middle Ages it was known as Monte Malo (Bad Mountain), due to the murder of patrician Giovanni Crescenzio (998). The eastern part of the hill is a nature reserve, on the west side lies the now upmarket district of the same name. On one hill there is the church and convent of Santa Maria Rosario. On the hilltop, now occupying the site of the 15th century Villa Mellini, is the Rome

Observatory and the Museo Astronomico Copernicano. This location (12°27'8.4"E) was used as the prime meridian (rather than Greenwich) for maps of Italy until the 1960s. The side of the hill was the former site of the Villa Pigneto built by Pietro da Cortona, the ruins of which were razed in the 19th century. Although the highest hill in the modern city of Rome, Monte Mario is not one of the proverbial Seven Hills of Rome, being outside the boundaries of the ancient city.

Tempio di Ercole Vincitore - Roma

Rome I Urbs Roma

According to Roman tradition, the city was founded by the twins Romulus and Remus on 21 April 753 BC. Archaeological evidence supports the view that Rome grew from pastoral settlements on the Palatine Hill built in the area of the future Roman Forum. While some archaeologists argue that Rome was indeed founded in the middle of the 8th century BC, the date is subject to controversy. Nevertheless, the original settlement developed into the capital of the Roman Kingdom (ruled by a succession of seven kings, according to tradition) and then the Roman Republic and finally the Roman Empire. This success depended on military conquest and commercial predominance, as well as selective assimilation of neighbouring civilisations, most notably the Etruscans and Greeks. From its foundation Rome, although losing occasional battles, had been undefeated in war until 386 BC, when it was briefly occupied by the Gauls. According to legend, the Gauls offered to deliver Rome back to its people for a thousand pounds of gold, but the Romans refused, preferring to take back their city by force of arms rather than ever admitting defeat, after which the Romans did indeed recover their city in the same year. Roman dominance expanded over most of Europe and the shores of the Mediterranean Sea, while its population surpassed one million inhabitants. For almost a thousand years, Rome was the most politically important, richest and largest city in the Western world. After the Empire started to decline and split, it lost its capital status to Milan and then to Ravenna and was surpassed in prestige by the Eastern capital Constantinople.

Fall of the Empire and Middle Ages

With the reign of Constantine I, the Bishop of Rome gained political as well as religious importance, eventually becoming known as the Pope

and establishing Rome as the centre of the Catholic Church. After the Sack of Rome in 410 AD by Alaric I and the fall of the Western Roman Empire in 476 AD, Rome alternated between Byzantine and Germanic control. Its population declined to a mere 20,000 during the Early Middle Ages, reducing the sprawling city to groups of inhabited buildings interspersed with large areas of ruins and vegetation. Rome remained nominally part of the Byzantine Empire until 751 AD, when the Lombards finally abolished the Exarchate of Ravenna. In 756, Pepin the Short gave the Pope temporal jurisdiction over Rome and surrounding areas, thus creating the Papal States. In 846, Muslim Arabs invaded Rome and looted St. Peter's Basilica. Rome remained the capital of the Papal States until its annexation by the Kingdom of Italy in 1870. The city became a major pilgrimage site during the Middle Ages and the focus of struggles between the Papacy and the Holy Roman Empire starting with Charlemagne, who was crowned its first emperor in Rome in 800 by Pope Leo III. Apart from brief periods as an independent city during the Middle Ages, Rome kept its status as Papal capital and "holy city" for centuries, even when the Papacy briefly relocated to Avignon (1309–1377).

Renaissance Rome

The latter half of the 15th century saw the seat of the Italian Renaissance move to Rome from Florence. The Papacy wanted to equal and surpass the grandeur of other Italian cities and to this end created ever more extravagant churches, bridges and public spaces, including a new Saint Peter's Basilica, the Sistine Chapel, Ponte Sisto (the first bridge to be built across the Tiber since antiquity) and Piazza Navona. The Popes were also patrons of the arts engaging such artists as Michelangelo, Perugino, Raphael, Ghirlandaio, Luca Signorelli, Botticelli and Cosimo Rosselli. The period was also infamous for papal corruption, with many Popes fathering children and engaging in nepotism and simony. The corruption of the Popes and the extravagance of their building projects led, in part, to the Reformation and, in turn, the Counter-Reformation.

The Vatican

Vatican City, the world capital of Catholicism, is the world's smallest state. It occupies 106 acres within high walls watched over by the Vatican guard.

It was the site where St. Peter was martyred (c.AD 64) and buried and became the residence of the popes who succeeded him. The Vatican, a sovereign state since 1929, is ruled by the Pope, Europe's only absolute monarch. About 500 people live in the Vatican, which also has its own post office, banks, currency, radio station, shops, daily newspaper and judicial system. The papal palaces, next to the great basilica of St Peter's, are home to the Sistine Chapel and the eclectic collections housed in the Vatican Museums.

St Peter's Basilica

Catholicism's most sacred shrine, the sumptuous, marble-caked basilica of St Peter's draws

pilgrims and tourists from all over the world. It holds hundreds of precious works of art, some salvaged from the original 4th century basilica built by Constantine, others commissioned from Renaissance and Baroque artists. The dominant tone is set by Bernini, who created the baldacchino twisting up below Michelangelo's huge dome. He also created the cathedra in the apse, with four saints supporting a throne that contains fragments once thought to be relics of the chair from which St. Peter delivered his first sermon.

The Vatican Museums

Home to the Sistine Chapel and Raphael Rooms, as well as one of the world's most important art collections, the Vatican Museums are housed in palaces originally intended for Renaissance popes. Most of the latter additions were made in the 18th century, when priceless works of art accumulated by earlier popes were first put on show. The Vatican's greatest treasures are its Greek and Roman antiquities, together with artifacts excavated from Egyptian and Etruscan tombs during the 19th century. Some of Italy's greatest artists: Raphael, Michelangelo and Leanardo de Vinci are represented in the Pinacoteca and parts of the former palaces, where they were previously used by popes to decorate their apartments and galleries.

The Sistine Chapel

Michelangelo frescoed the ceiling for Pope Julius II between 1508 and 1512, working from specially designed scaffolding. The main panels, which chart the Creation of the World and Fall of Man, are surrounded by subjects from the Old and New Testaments - except for the

Creation of Adam by Michelangelo

Classical Sibyls who are said to have foreseen the birth of Christ. The recent restorers of the Sistine Chapel used computers, photography and spectrum technology to analyze the fresco before cleaning began. They separated Michelangelo's work from that of the later restorers and discovered that they had attempted to clean the ceiling with materials ranging from bread to retsina wine. The new restoration

revealed the familiarly dusky, eggshell -cracked figures to have creamy skins, lustrous hair and brightly-coloured robes. Experts agreed that the new colours probably matched those painted by Michelangelo. The walls of the Sistine Chapel, the main chapel in the Vatican Palace, were frescoed by some of the finest artists of the 15th and 16th centuries. The 12 paintings on the side walls, by artists including Perugino, Ghirlandalo, Botticell and Signorelli, show parallel episodes from the life of Moses and of Christ. Decoration was completed between 1534 and 1541 by Michelangel, who added the great altar wall fresco, the "Last Judgement".

Pilgrim Churches of Rome - the Major Basilicas (excluding St Peter's)

There are traditionally seven churches that have been designated Pilgrim Churches. The two most important of these are Saint Paul Outside the Walls and of course, Saint Peter's Basilica in the Vatican. Praying at the tomb of Peter, the Rock upon which Jesus built his Church is second only perhaps to praying in the Church of the Holy Sepulchre itself. Besides visiting the resting places of the pillars of Christianity, pilgrims to Rome also make stops at the other major and minor basilicas of Rome.

Saint Paul Outside the Walls - San Paolo fuori le Mura

Ravaged by fire, floods and earthquakes, the Basilica dedicated to Saint Paul still retains its ancient layout. The Basilica, enlarged and greatly rebuilt over the centuries, was built on the site of a former graveyard outside the walls of Rome where the martyred Saint Paul was buried.

Much like the tomb of Saint Peter, Saint Paul's grave was also a pilgrimage location marked by centuries of veneration before the church was built. Today, the Benedictine monks of San Paolo fuori le Mura offer services and confessions for pilgrims wishing to venerate Saint Paul and their abbey. The Basilica has a wonderful cloister for contemplation. After a long and turbulent history in which most of the ancient church has been rebuilt, the actual location of Saint Paul was lost somewhere underneath the main altar. At the request of recent pilgrims, excavations by Vatican archaeologists have been carried out at San Paolo fuori le Mura in order to make the relics of Saint Paul more accessible to the faithful.

Saint John Lateran - San Giovanni in Laterano

This is the site of the first church allowed by Constantine and is still considered the "Mother Church" of Roman Catholicism. San Giovanni in Laterano is the Cathedral of Rome and therefore the Church of Rome's Bishop, the Pope. Inspite of being robbed by barbarians, damaged by earthquakes and destroyed by fire, the church has never lost its importance to pilgrims. Although St Peter's has become more important in recent times, many of the Catholic Church's most important events took place here and the Lateran Palace was the official Papal residence for centuries. San Giovanni in Laterano and the surrounding area is home to very important relics including the heads of Saints Peter and Paul housed in the elaborate gothic baldachin of the high altar. The high altar is also said to contain a portion of a table used in masses held by Saint Peter himself. Across the street are the remains of the original Papal palace which houses both the Scala Santa, or Holy Stairs and the Sancta Sanctorum, a series of chapels known for having many holy relics including the Salvatore Acheiropoieton, an icon of Christ supposedly painted by Saint Luke the Evangelist.

Saint Mary Major - Santa Maria Maggiore

The Basilica of Santa Maria Maggiore is the oldest church in Western Europe dedicated to the Virgin Mary. The church was built on the 5th century site of a miraculous snowfall in the height of Roman summer. Unlike the other ancient basilicas of Rome, Santa Maria Maggiore has not been completely rebuilt and a large amount of the ancient church survives, including original mosaics. The church is the final resting place of Saint Jerome, translator of the Vulgate and houses relics belonging  to the Apostle Matthias. Under the high altar lies the Bethlehem Crypt and the relic of the Holy Crib, pieces of wood from the manger of Jesus. Santa Maria Maggiore also houses the Marian icon known as the Salus Populi Romani, another holy image that may have been originally painted by Saint Luke. The image, located in the Borghese Chapel has been the object of veneration for pilgrims, popes, saints and especially the citizens of Rome.

Pilgrim Churches of Rome - the Minor Basilicas

Saint Lawrence Outside the Walls - San Lorenzo fuori le Mura

In the year 258, Lawrence, a Deacon of Rome, was burned to death on the future site of this basilica. The present structure is actually two churches that were combined in the Middle Ages, giving the basilica a slightly uneven floor plan. During World War II San Lorenzo was heavily damaged, but has since been faithfully restored. The church is the final resting place of at least three saints: Saint Lawrence, Pope Saint Hilarius and Christian proto-martyr Saint Stephen, all of whom are buried below the high altar. San Lorenzo fuori le Mura also holds a blood-stained stone, where the body of Saint Lawrence was placed before burial.

Saint Sebastian Outside the Walls - San Sebastiano fuori le Mura

This Basilica is one of the most historically important of the Christian pilgrim sites in Rome. The catacombs under the church were once the temporary resting places of many early Christian martyrs, including Saints Peter and Paul during the Roman persecutions. It was during this time that the saints were interred here and the site became popular with pilgrims. Saint Sebastian was a Roman soldier condemned to death by arrows, a very popular subject for Medieval and Renaissance artists. Pillaged by Saracens in the 9th century, nothing remains of the ancient structure, except the catacombs below. Saint Sebastian's body is buried under the altar, while the Chapel of the Relics houses other holy objects, including one of the arrows said to have pierced Saint Sebastian during his martyrdom.

Basilica of the Holy Cross - Santa Croce in Gerusalemme

Saint Helena, the mother of Emperor Constantine, built this Basilica in the imperial Sessorian palace to house the relics she brought back from the Holy Land. These relics include nails from the Crucifixion, two thorns from the Crown of Thorns, small fragments of the True Cross and the Titulus Crucis, or headboard of the Crucifixion. These relics were once housed in Saint Helena's personal chapel, but since the church has undergone several redesigns over the centuries, the Relics of the Passion are now housed in the Sanctuary of the Cross. Besides these important relics Santa Croce also houses a finger of the Apostle Thomas.

Our Lady of Divine Love - Santuario della Madonna del Divino Amore

This church, the most recent of the pilgrim churches of Rome, was added by Pope John Paul II for the 2000 Jubilee celebration. The Sanctuary houses a Medieval fresco of the Virgin Mary, said to have performed documented miracles since the 18th century. Although the building is very recent, the image of the Virgin has been venerated by the Popes and citizens of Rome for a long time. The new shrine was built in order to give thanks to Mary for her intercession during the dark days of World War II. Pope Pius XII credited the venerated image with saving Rome from destruction in 1944. Since the year 2000 the Sanctuary has officially replaced San Sebastiano fuori le Mura as the seventh Pilgrim Church of Rome, however most pilgrims have simply added the Santuario della Madonna del Divino Amore to their itinerary. Pilgrims to the Santuario della Madonna del Divino Amore should look into the night pilgrimages that are held from Easter to October.

Rome Unvisited

I.

The corn has turned from grey to red,
Since first my spirit wandered forth
From the drear cities of the north,
And to Italia's mountains fled.

And here I set my face towards home,
For all my pilgrimage is done,
Although, methinks, yon blood-red sun
Marshals the way to Holy Rome.

O Blessed Lady, who dost hold
Upon the seven hills thy reign!
O Mother without blot or stain,
Crowned with bright crowns of triple gold!

O Roma, Roma, at thy feet
I lay this barren gift of song!
For, ah! the way is steep and long
That leads unto thy sacred street.

II.

And yet what joy it were for me
To turn my feet unto the south,
And journeying towards the Tiber mouth
To kneel again at Fiesole!

And wandering through the tangled pines
That break the gold of Arno's stream,
To see the purple mist and gleam
Of morning on the Apennines.

By many a vineyard-hidden home,
Orchard and olive-garden grey,
Till from the drear Campagna's way
The seven hills bear up the dome!

III.

A pilgrim from the northern seas—
What joy for me to seek alone
The wondrous Temple and the throne
Of Him who holds the awful keys!

When, bright with purple and with gold,
Come priest and holy Cardinal,
And borne above the heads of all
The gentle Shepherd of the Fold.

O joy to see before I die
The only God-anointed King,
And hear the silver trumpets ring
A triumph as He passes by!

Or at the altar of the shrine
Holds high the mystic sacrifice,
And shows a God to human eyes
Beneath the veil of bread and wine.

IV.

For lo, what changes time can bring!
The cycles of revolving years
May free my heart from all its fears,—
And teach my lips a song to sing.

Before yon field of trembling gold
Is garnered into dusty sheaves,
Or ere the autumn's scarlet leaves
Flutter as birds adown the wold,

I may have run the glorious race,
And caught the torch while yet aflame,
And called upon the holy name
Of Him who now doth hide His face.

Oscar Wilde

Anthology of artists, architects and musicians mentioned in Companion to the via Francigena.

Benedetto Antelami *(c. 1150 – c. 1230) was a leading Italian architect and sculptor of the Romanesque school, whose sculptural style sprang from local north Italian traditions that can*

be traced back to late antiquity. His works are characteristic for their realism, and strong emotion, within the formalist context of their time. Little is known about his life. He was probably originally from Lombardy, perhaps born in Val d'Intelvi. It is believed from the Provençal style of his art that he served as an apprentice in Saint-Trophime d'Arles. In 1178 he worked on a bas-relief of the Deposition from the cross in the Cathedral of Parma. Later, in 1196, he was working with the sculptural decoration of the Baptistry of Parma, a building of which he was probably also the architect. Here, between 1196 and 1214, he made the lunettes of the three

portals: on the outside portraying the Adoration of the Magi, the Last Judgement and an allegory of life. On the inside the Flight into Egypt, the Presentation at the Temple and David Playing the Harp. Benedetto's work can also be seen in the cathedral of Fidenza, formerly Borgo San Donnino, dedicated to Saint Domninus of Fidenza. The main west door of the Basilica di San Marco, Venice, is also attributed by some to Antelami or his school, and the current replacement version of the Holy Face of Lucca (the Volto Santo) is ascribed to his circle.

Taddeo di Bartolo *(1362 or 1363 - August 26, 1422), an Italian painter of the Sienese School and born in Siena. Much of his early work was in Pisa, where he was responsible*

for the frescoes of Paradise and Hell in the Cathedral there and for paintings in the Palazzo Pubblico and the church of San Francesco. At the Collegiata di San Gimignano, Taddeo painted a fresco depicting the Last Judgement and another of Saint Gimignano holding the town in his lap cab be seen at the Museo Civico

Inferno *there. Taddeo died in Siena, aged 60.*

Fra Bartolomeo *(March 28, 1472 - October 6, 1517), an Italian Renaissance painter of religious*

subjects and born in Savignano di Prato, Tuscany. He was apprenticed in the workshop of Cosimo Rosselli, one of the greatest painters of his time. Then in 1490 he began a collaboration with Mariotto Albertinelli. In the late 1490s Baccio was drawn to the teachings of Fra Girolamo Savonarola, who denounced what he viewed as vain and corrupt contemporary art. After completing his famous portrait of Savonarola in 1498 and fresco of the Universal

The Vision of St. Bernard *Judgement for the Ospedale di Santa Maria Nuova he entered the convent of San Marco and renounced painting for several years, not resuming until 1504 when he became the head of the monastery workshop. In that year he began a Vision of St. Bernard for Bernardo Bianco's family chapel in the Badia Fiorentina, finished in 1507. Soon after, Raphael visited Florence and befriended the friar. Bartolomeo learned perspective from the younger artist, while Raphael added skills in colouring and* handling of drapery, which was noticeable in the works he produced after their meeting. He and Raphael remained on the friendliest terms and when he departed from Rome he gave him two unfinished pictures which Raphael completed. At the beginning of 1508 Bartolomeo moved to Venice to paint a Holy Father, St. Mary Magdalene and St. Catherine of Siena for the Dominicans of San Pietro Martire in Murano. As the Dominicans did not pay for the work, he took it back to Lucca, where it can be seen now. Also in Lucca, he painted an altarpiece with Madonna and Child with Saints for the local cathedral. On November 26, 1510 Pier Soderini commissioned an altarpiece for the Sala del Consiglio of Florence, now in the Museum of San Marco. Two years later he finished another altarpiece for the cathedral of Besançon. His last work is a fresco of Noli me tangere also in Pian di Mugnone. He died in Florence in 1517.

Marco Benefial (1684 - 1764) an Italian, proto-Neoclassical painter was born in and died in Rome. His initial training was under Ventura Lamberti da Carpi, a pupil of Carlo Cignani and he helped in the painting of the Chapel of the Sacrament in Saint Peter's Basilica and in the Carmelite Convent of San Alberto. Benefial is best known for his repudiation of 18th century decorative Rococo styles pre-eminent in Rome, dominated by Carlo Maratta and his pupils. His paintings portrayed tangible human figures, with complex treatment of space and luminous, warm colours. Along with the altarpieces and frescoes, he also

Vision of St Philip Neri

painted many portraits. Because he was partnered with some inferior artists some of his paintings have been frequently misidentified. In 1720, he protested against the Accademia di San Luca's decree that only members or those meeting the approval of the painter's guild could teach drawing. His appeal to the councils of Pope Clement XI succeeded in having the ruling revoked and he was finally elected into the Accademia di San Luca at the age of 57. Nevertheless, he soon denounced its members' mediocrity and ignorance and was consequently expelled in 1755.

Pierre Bonnard (3 October 1867 - 23 January 1947) was a French painter and printmaker. He

The Dining Room in the Country

was born in Fontenay-aux-Roses, Hauts-de-Seine. At the insistence of his father, Bonnard studied law, graduating and practising as a barrister briefly. However, he had also attended art classes on the side and soon decided to become an artist. In 1891 he met Toulouse-Lautrec and began showing his work at the annual exhibition of the Société des Artistes Indépendants. His first show was at the Galerie Durand-Ruel in 1896. In his twenties he was a part of Les Nabis, a group of young artists committed to creating work of symbolic and spiritual nature. Other Nabis included Édouard Vuillard and Maurice Denis. He left Paris in 1910 for the south of France. Bonnard is known for his intense use of colour, especially via areas built up . with small brushmarks and close values. His often complex compositions, typically of sunlit interiors of rooms and gardens populated with friends and family members, are both narrative and autobiographical. His wife Marthe was an ever-present subject over the course of several decades. She is seen seated at the kitchen table, with the remnants of a meal or nude, as in a series of paintings where she reclines in the bathtub. He also painted several self-portraits, landscapes and many still lifes which usually depict flowers and fruit. He finished his last usually depict flowers and fruit. He finished his last painting, The Almond Tree in Flower, a week before his death in his cottage on La Route de Serra Capeou near Le Cannet, on the French Riviera, in 1947.

Gian Lorenzo Bernini (7 December 1598 - 28 November 1680) was an Italian artist who worked principally in Rome, but was born in Naples to a Mannerist sculptor, Pietro Bernini. At the age of seven he accompanied his father to Rome, where his father was involved in several high profile projects. There, as a boy, his skill was soon noticed by the painter Annibale Carracci and by Pope Paul V and Bernini gained the patronage of Cardinal Scipione Borghese, the pope's nephew.

Self- Portait

His first works were inspired by antique Hellenistic sculpture. He was the leading sculptor of his age and also a prominent architect. In addition he painted, wrote plays and designed metalwork and stage sets. A student of Classical sculpture, Bernini possessed the unique ability to capture, in marble, the essence of a narrative moment with a dramatic naturalistic realism which was almost shocking. This ensured that he effectively became the successor of Michelangelo, far outshining other sculptors of his generation, including his rival, Alessandro Algardi. His talent extended beyond the confines of his sculpture to consideration of the setting in which it would be situated. His ability to be able to synthesise sculpture, painting and architecture into a coherent conceptual and visual whole has been termed by the art historian, Irving Lavin, the 'unity of the visual arts'. A deeply religious man, working in Counter Reformation Rome, Bernini used light as an important metaphorical device in the perception of his religious settings. Often it was a hidden light source that could intensify the focus of religious worship,or enhance the dramatic moment of a sculptural narrative. Bernini was also a leading figure in the emergence of Roman Baroque architecture along with his contemporaries, the architect, Francesco Borromini and the painter and architect, Pietro da Cortona. At an early age, he came to the attention of the papal nephew, Cardinal Scipione Borghese and in 1621, at the age of only twenty three, he was knighted by Pope Gregory XV. Following his accession to the papacy, Urban VIII is reported to have said, "Your luck is great to see Cardinal Maffeo Barberini Pope, Cavaliere; but ours is much greater to have Cavalier Bernini alive in our pontificate".
The grave of Bernini is in the Basilica di Santa Maria Maggiore. in Rome.

Fernando Botero was born in 1932 in Colombia, South America, where the Catholic church adopted the Baroque style. His work includes still-lifes and landscapes, but Botero tends to primarily focus on situational portraiture. His paintings and sculptures are united by their proportionally exaggerated, or "fat" figures, as he once referred to them. Throughout his childhood, Botero was isolated from traditional art presented in museums and other cultural institutes. He lost his father at the age of 4. In 1944, after going to a Jesuit school, Botero's uncle sent him to a school for matadors for two years. In 1948, at the age of 16, Botero published his first illustrations in the Sunday supplement of the El Colombiano daily paper and used the money he received to pay for his high school education at the Liceo de Marinilla de Antioquia. From 1949 to 1950, Botero worked as a set designer, before moving to Bogotá in 1951. His first one-man show was held in the Galería Leo Matiz in Bogotá, a few months after his arrival. In 1952, he travelled with a group of artists to Barcelona, where he stayed only briefly before moving on to Madrid. In Madrid, Botero studied at the Academia de San Fernando. In 1953, Botero moved to Paris, where he spent most of his time in the Louvre. He lived in Florence, Italy from 1953 to 1954, studying the works of Renaissance masters. More recently, in 2005, he reced considerable attention in 2005 for his Abu Ghraib collection, which began as an idea he had on a plane, finally culminating in more than 85 paintings and 100 drawings.

François Boucher (29 September 1703 - 30 May 1770) was a French painter and a proponent of Rococo taste. Born in Paris, the son of a lace designer, François Boucher was perhaps the most celebrated decorative artist of the 18th century, with most of his work reflecting the Rococo style. At the young age of 17, Boucher was apprenticed by his father to François Lemoyne, but after only three months he went to work for the engraver Jean-François Cars. Within three years Boucher had won the elite Grand Prix de Rome, although he did not take up the consequential opportunity to study in Italy until four years later. On his return from studying in Italy in 1731, he was admitted to the Académie de Peinture. Along with his painting, Boucher also designed theatre costumes and sets and the ardent intrigues of the comic operas of Favart (1710-1792) closely parallel his own style of painting. Additionally, he worked with the Beauvais tapestry workshops for whom he first designed a series of Fêtes italiennes in 1736, which proved to be very successful. During two decades' of collaboration Boucher produced designs for six series of hangings in all. Only his appointment in 1755 as director of the rival Gobelins terminated the association. He was also called upon for designs for court festivities organized by that section of the King's household called the Menus plaisirs du Roi and for the opera and for royal châteaux Versailles, Fontainebleau and Choisy. His designs for all of the aforementioned augmented his earlier reputation, resulting in many engravings from his work and even reproduction of his designs on porcelain and biscuit-ware at the Vincennes and Sèvres factories. Francois Boucher died on 30 May 1770 in Paris. His name, along with that of his patron Madame de Pompadour, had become synonymous with the French Rococo style, leading the Goncourt brothers to write: "Boucher is one of those men who represent the taste of a century, who express, personify and embody it."

Boucher

Luigi Rodolfo Boccherini (February 19, 1743 - May 28, 1805) was an Italian classical era composer and cellist whose music retained a courtly and galante style. He is best known for one particular minuet from his String Quintet in E, Op. 11, No. 5 (G 275) and the Cello Concerto in B flat major (G 482). His music was clearly influenced by the Spanish and Mediterranean style in that he composed several quintets for guitar. Boccherini was born in Lucca, Italy, into a musical family. In 1761 Boccherini went to Madrid, where he was employed by Infante Luis Antonio of Spain, younger brother of King Charles III. There he flourished under royal patronage, until one day when the King expressed his disapproval at a passage in a new trio and ordered Boccherini to change it. The composer, no doubt irritated with this intrusion into his art, doubled the passage instead, leading to his immediate dismissal. Then he accompanied Don Luis to Arenas de San

Pedro, a little town at the Gredos mountains. There, Boccherini wrote many of his most brilliant works. Among his late patrons was the French consul Lucien Bonaparte, as well as King Friedrich Wilhelm II of Prussia, himself an amateur cellist, flautist and avid supporter of the arts. Boccherini fell on hard times following the deaths of his Spanish patron and he died in poverty in Madrid in 1805.

Benedetto Buglioni (1429/30-c. 1510), son of the sculptor Giovanni di Bernardo and possibly a pupil of Andrea Verrocchio. Buglioni probably worked with Andrea della Robbia, whose glazing techniques he learnt. In the early 1480s he opened his own shop, producing works in the style of della Robbia, often with compositions after Verrocchio, Antonia Rossellino or Benedetto da Maiano. From c. 1500 his workshop produced terracottas with naturalistic colourings, such as the Virgin with SS Jerome and Nicholas of Bari.

Il Botticello - meaning the little barrel (1445 - May 17, 1510) - was an Italian painter of the Florentine school during the Early Renaissance. Details of his life are sparse, but we know that he became an apprentice when he was about fourteen years old. By 1462 he was probably apprenticed to Fra Filippo Lippi and many of his early works have been attributed to the elder master. Influenced also by the monumentality of Masaccio's painting, it was from Lippi that Botticelli learned a more intimate and detailed manner. By 1470 Botticelli had his own workshop. Even at this early date his work was characterized by a conception of the figure as if seen in low relief, drawn with clear contours and minimizing strong contrasts of light and shadow which would indicate fully modelled forms. The master works Primavera (c. 1482) and The Birth of Venus (c. 1485) were both seen by Vasari at the villa of Lorenzo di Pierfrancesco de' Medici at Castello in the mid-16th century and, until recently, it was assumed that both works were painted specifically for the villa, though recent research suggests otherwise. In these works, the influence of Gothic realism is tempered by Botticelli's study of the antique. In 1481, Pope Sixtus IV summoned Botticelli and other prominent Florentine and Umbrian artists to fresco the walls of the Sistine Chapel. In addition he painted many frescoes in Florentine churches. In 1502 he was accused of sodomy, though charges were later dropped. Botticelli never married and expressed a strong aversion to the idea, a prospect he claimed gave him nightmares. The popular view is that he suffered from unrequited love for Simonetta Vespucci, a married noblewoman who had served as the model for The Birth of Venus and recurs throughout his paintings. Botticelli's dying request was he be buried at her feet in the Church of Ognissanti in Florence. His wish was carried out.

Self-portrait

Alfredo Catalani (19 June 1854 - 7 August 1893) was an Italian operatic composer, best remembered for his operas Loreley (1890) and La Wally (1892). Catalani was born in Lucca and trained at the Conservatory of Milan under Antonio Bazzini. Despite the growing influence of the verismo style of opera during the 1880s Catalani chose to compose in a more traditional manner. As a result his operas have largely lost their place in the modern repertoire, even compared to those of Massenet and

Puccini, whose style his works most closely resemble. The influence of Amilcare Ponchielli can also be recognized in Catalani's work.

Philippe de Champaigne *(26 May 1602 - 12 August 1674) was a Flemish-born French Baroque era painter and a major exponent of the French school. Born in Brussels of a poor family, Champaigne was a pupil of the landscape painter Jacques Fouquières. In 1621 he moved to Paris, where he worked with Nicolas Poussin on the decoration of the Palais du Luxembourg under the direction of Nicolas Duchesne, whose daughter he married. According to Houbraken, Duchesne was angry with Champaigne for becoming more popular than he was at court, which is thought to be reason for Champaigne's return to Brussels. After the death of his protector Duchesne, Champaigne worked for the Queen Mother, Marie de Medicis and for Cardinal Richelieu, (for whom he decorated the Palais Cardinal), the dome of the Sorbonne and other buildings. He was a founding member of the Académie de peinture et de sculpture in 1648. After his paralysed daughter was allegedly miraculously cured at the nunnery of Port-Royal, he painted the celebrated, but atypical picture Ex-Voto de 1662, now in the Louvre, which represents the artist's daughter with Mother-Superior Agnès Arnauld. Champaigne produced a very large number of paintings, mainly religious works and portraits. Influenced by Rubens at the beginning of his career, his style later became more austere. Champaigne was of significant enough prominence in his time to be mentioned in Cyrano de Bergerac:*
"Truly, I should not look to find his portrait By the grave hand of Philippe de Champagne. He died in Paris in 1674.

Lucas Cranach the Elder *(4 October 1472 – 16 October 1553) was a German Renaissance painter and printmaker in woodcut and engraving. He was court painter to the Electors of Saxony for most of his career and is best known for his portraits, both of German princes and those of the leaders of the Protestant Reformation, whose cause he embraced with enthusiasm, becoming a close friend of Martin Luther. He also painted religious subjects, first in the Catholic tradition and later trying to find new ways of conveying Lutheran religious concerns in art. He continued throughout his career to paint nude subjects drawn from mythology and religion. He had a large workshop and many works exist in different versions. His son Lucas Cranach the Younger and others, continued to produce versions of his father's works for decades after his death. According to Gunderam (the tutor of Cranach's children) Cranach demonstrated his talents as a painter before the close of the 15th century. His work then drew the attention of Duke Friedrich III, Elector of Saxony, known as Frederick the Wise, who attached Cranach to his court in 1504. The records of Wittenberg confirm Gunderam's statement to this extent that Cranach's name appears for the first time in the public accounts on the 24 June 1504, when he drew 50 gulden for the salary of half a year, as pictor ducalis ("the duke's painter"). Cranach was to remain in the service of the Elector and his successors for the rest of his life, although he was able to undertake other work. Early in the days of his official employment he startled his master's courtiers by the realism with which he painted still life, game and antlers on the walls of the country palaces at Coburg and Locha; his pictures of deer and wild boar were considered striking and the duke* fostered his passion for this form of art by taking him out to the hunting field, where he sketched "Duke John sticking a boar". Before 1508 he had painted several altar-pieces for the Castle Church at Wittenberg in competition with Albrecht Dürer, Hans Burgkmair and others. The duke and his brother John were portrayed in various attitudes and a number of his best woodcuts and copper-plates were published. In 1509 Cranach went to the Netherlands and painted the Emperor Maximilian and the boy who afterwards became Emperor Charles V. Until 1508 Cranach signed his works with his initials. In that year the elector gave him the winged snake as a emblem, or Kleinod, which superseded the initials on all his pictures after that date. Cranach, like his patron, was friendly with the Protestant Reformers at a very early stage, yet it is difficult to fix the time of his first meeting with Martin Luther. The oldest reference to Cranach in Luther's correspondence dates from 1520. In a letter written from Worms in 1521, Luther calls him his "gossip", warmly alluding to his "Gevatterin", the artist's wife. Cranach first made an engraving of Luther in 1520, when Luther was an Augustinian friar. Five years later, Luther renounced his religious vows and Cranach was present as a witness at the betrothal festival of Luther and Katharina von Bora. Cranach died agde 81 on October 16 1553, in Weimar, where the house in which he lived still stands in the marketplace. He is commemorated as a saint by the Lutheran Church on April 6, along with Durer and Burgkmair.

John Constable (11 June 1776 - 31 March 1837) was an English Romantic painter known principally for his landscape paintings of Dedham Vale, the area surrounding his home. Although his paintings are now among the most popular and valuable in British art, he was never financially successful and did not become a member of the establishment until he was elected to the Royal Academy at the age of 52. He sold more paintings in France than in his native England. In his youth, Constable

Self-portrait   embarked on amateur sketching trips in the surrounding Suffolk countryside that was to become the subject of a large proportion of his art. These scenes, in his own words, "made me a painter and I am grateful". In 1799, Constable persuaded his father to let him pursue art and Golding even granted him a small allowance. Entering the Royal Academy Schools as a probationer, he attended life classes and anatomical dissections as well as studying and copying Old Masters. His early style has many of the qualities associated with his mature work, including a freshness of light, colour and touch and reveals the compositional influence of the Old Masters he had studied, notably of Claude Lorrain. Constable's usual subjects, scenes of ordinary daily life, were unfashionable in an age that looked for more romantic visions of wild landscapes and ruins. He did, however, make occasional trips further afield. For example, in 1803 he spent almost a month aboard the East Indiaman ship Coutts as it visited south-east coastal ports and in 1806 he undertook a two-month tour of the Lake District. In order to make ends meet, Constable took up portraiture, which he found dull work - though he executed many fine portraits. He also painted occasional religious pictures. From 1809 onwards, his childhood friendship with Maria Bicknell developed into a deep, mutual love. But their engagement in 1816 was opposed by Maria's father and Maria herself pointed out that a penniless marriage would detract from any chances John had of making a career in painting. Golding and Ann Constable, while approving the match, held out no prospect of supporting the marriage until Constable was financially secure, but they died in quick succession and Constable inherited a fifth share in the family business. John and Maria's marriage in October 1816 at St Martin-in-the-Fields was followed by a honeymoon tour of the south coast, where the sea stimulated Constable to develop new techniques of brilliant colour and vivacious brushwork. At the same time, a greater emotional range began to register in his art. Although he had scraped an income from painting, it was not until 1819 that Constable sold his first important canvas, The White Horse, which led to a series of "six footers", as he called his large-scale paintings. After the birth of her seventh child in January 1828, Maria fell ill and died of tuberculosis that November at the age of forty-one. Thereafter, Constable always dressed in black and was "prey to melancholy and anxious thoughts". He cared for his seven children alone for the rest of his life.

Agnolo di Cosimo *(November 17, 1503 - November 23, 1572) was an Italian Mannerist painter* *from Florence. The origin of his nickname, Bronzino is unknown, but could derive from his dark complexion. According to his contemporary, Vasari, Bronzino was a pupil first of Raffaellino del Garbo and then of Pontormo. The latter was ultimately the primary influence on Bronzino's developing style and the young artist remained devoted to his eccentric teacher. Indeed, Pontormo is*

Venus, Cupid, Folly and Time

thought to have introduced a portrait of Bronzino as a child into one of his series on Joseph in Egypt. During the mid 1520s, the two artists worked together on this commission, though Bronzino is believed to have mostly served as an assistant to his teacher on the masterly Annunciation and The Deposition from the Cross frescoes that adorn the main walls of the chapel. Bronzino first received Medici patronage in 1539, when he was one of the many artists chosen to execute the elaborate decorations for the wedding of Cosimo I de' Medici to Eleonora di Toledo, daughter of the Viceroy of Naples. It was not long before he became and remained for most of his career, the official court painter of the Duke and his court. In addition to images of the Florentine elite, Bronzino also painted idealized portraits of the poets Dante and Petrarch. Bronzino's so-called 'allegorical portraits,' such as that of a Genoese admiral, Andrea Doria as Neptune is less typical but possibly even more fascinating due to the peculiarity of placing a publicly recognized personality in the nude as a mythical figure. In addition to being a painter, Bronzino was also a poet and his most personal portraits are perhaps those of other literary figures such as that of his friend Laura Battiferri (right), wife of sculptor/architect Bartolommeo Ammanati. Bronzino's work tends to include sophisticated references to earlier painters, as in The Martyrdom of St. Lawrence (1569), in which almost every one of the extraordinarily contorted poses can be traced back to Raphael or to Michelangelo, who Bronzino idolized. Bronzino's skill with the nude was even more enigmatically deployed in the celebrated Venus, Cupid, Folly and Time, which conveys strong feelings of eroticism under the pretext of a moralizing allegory. His other major works include the design of a series of tapestries on The Story of Joseph, for the Palazzo Vecchio.

Jean Désiré Gustave Courbet *(10 June 1819 - 31 December 1877) was a French painter who led the Realist movement in 19th-century French painting. The Realist movement bridged the Romantic movement (characterized by the paintings of Théodore Géricault and Eugène*

Delacroix), with the Barbizon School and the Impressionists. Courbet occupies an important place in 19th century French painting as an innovator and as an artist willing to make bold social commentary in his work. Courbet was a painter of figurative compositions, landscapes, seascapes and still-lifes. He courted controversy by addressing social issues in his work and by painting subjects that were considered vulgar: the rural bourgeoisie and peasantry and the working conditions of the poor. His work belonged neither to the predominant Romantic nor Neoclassical schools, but became known as Realism. For Courbet realism dealt not with the perfection of line and form, but entailed spontaneous and rough handling of paint, suggesting direct observation by the artist while portraying the irregularities in nature. He depicted the harshness in life and in so doing, challenged contemporary academic ideas of art. Courbet was born in 1819 to Régis and Sylvie Oudot Courbet in Ornans (Doubs). Though a prosperous farming family, anti-monarchical feelings prevailed in the household. (His maternal grandfather fought in the French Revolution.) Courbet's sisters, Zoé, Zélie and Juliette, were his first models for drawing and painting. After moving to Paris he returned home to Ornans often to hunt, fish and find inspiration. He went to Paris in 1839 and worked at the studio of Steuben and Hesse. An independent spirit, he soon left, preferring to develop his own style by studying Spanish, Flemish and French painters and painting copies of their work. His first works were an Odalisque, suggested by the writing of Victor Hugo and a Lélia, illustrating George Sand, but he soon abandoned literary influences for the study of real life. Trips to the Netherlands and Belgium in 1846–1847 strengthened Courbet's belief that painters should portray the life around them, as Rembrandt, Hals and the other Dutch masters had done. By 1848, he had gained supporters among the younger critics, the Neo-romantics and Realists, notably Champfleury. In 1849 Courbet painted Stone-Breakers (destroyed in the British bombing of Dresden in 1945), which was admired by Proudhon as an icon of peasant life and has been called "the first of his great works". Courbet became a celebrity and was spoken of as a genius. He actively encouraged the public perception of him as an unschooled peasant, while his ambition, his bold pronouncements to journalists, gave him a reputation for vanity. In the Salon of 1857 Courbet showed six paintings. These included the scandalous Young Ladies on the Banks of the Seine (Summer), depicting two prostitutes under a tree, as well as the first of many hunting scenes. By the 1870s Courbet had become well established as one of the leading artists in France and in 1870 he created the Fédération des artistes, for the free and uncensored expansion of art. The group's members included André Gill, Honoré Daumier, Jean-Baptiste Camille Corot, Eugène Pottier, Jules Dalou and Édouard Manet.

Baldassare Croce (1558 - 1628) was an Italian painter, active during the late-Mannerist period,

active mainly in and around Rome. Known as a prolific academic painter, he was named director of the Academy of St. Luke. He painted for the Sala Clementina of the Vatican palace, for the Chapel of San Francesco at the Gesù, San Giovanni in Laterano and San Giacomo degli Spagnoli. He painted six large frescoes along the nave of the church of Santa Susanna, depicting the life of the

St. Francis of Assisi

Susanna from the Old Testament.

Donatello *(Donato di Niccolò di Betto Bardi; c. 1386 - December 13, 1466) was a famous early Renaissance Italian artist and sculptor from Florence. He is, in part, known for his work in basso rilievo, a form of shallow relief sculpture that, in Donatello's case, incorporated significant 15th-century developments in perspectival illusionism. Donatello was the son of Niccolo di Betto Bardi and apparently received his early artistic training in a goldsmith's workshop. While undertaking study and excavations with Filippo Brunelleschi in Rome (1404–1407), work that gained the two men the reputation of treasure seekers. Their*

Donatello

Roman sojourn was decisive for the entire development of Italian art in the 15th century, for it was during this period that Brunelleschi undertook his measurements of the Pantheon dome and of other Roman buildings. Brunelleschi's buildings and Donatello's sculptures are both considered supreme expressions of the spirit of this era in architecture and sculpture and they exercised a potent influence upon the painters of the age. In Florence, Donatello assisted Lorenzo Ghiberti with the statues of prophets for the north door of the Florence Baptistery and in 1409–1411 to create the colossal seated figure of Saint John the Evangelist, which until 1588 occupied a niche of the old cathedral facade and is now placed in a dark chapel of the Duomo. This work marks a decisive step forward from late Gothic Mannerism in the search for naturalism and the rendering of human feelings. The face, the shoulders and the bust are still idealized, while the hands and the fold of cloth over the legs are more realistic. Between 1415 and 1426, Donatello created five statues for the campanile of Santa Maria del Fiore in Florence, also known as the Duomo. These works are the Beardless Prophet; Bearded Prophet (both from 1415); the Sacrifice of Isaac (1421); Habbakuk (1423–1425); and Jeremiah (1423–1426); which follow the classical models for orators and are characterized by strong portrait details. Between 1425–1427, Donatello collaborated with Michelozzo on the funerary monument of the Antipope John XXIII for the Battistero in Florence. In the same period, he executed the relief of the Feast of Herod and the statues of Faith and Hope for the Baptstery of San Giovanni in Siena. The relief is mostly in stiacciato, while the foreground figures are done in bas-relief. Around 1430, Cosimo de' Medici, the foremost art patron of his era, commissioned the bronze David for the court of his Palazzo Medici. This is now Donatello's most famous work. According to some historians, Donatello made no secret of his homosexuality and his behaviour was tolerated by his friends, certainly Cosimo is known to have played a part in patching up at least one lover's quarrel between Donatello and one of his young assistants. Frequently his violent outbursts would result from passionate entanglements. When one of his assistants ran away, Donatello is said to have chased him as far as Ferrara with the intention of killing him. Donatello's David that he produced for Cosimo was one of the most overtly homosexual works of its era, its sensuous nudity emphasised by the young David's calf-length ornamented leather boots and curly tresses. Donatello died in Florence in 1466 and was buried in the Basilica of San Lorenzo, next to Cosimo de' Medici the Elder.

Louis-Michel-Clément Faille *(1881, Nurlu – 1938, Nurlu) was a French architect from Picardie. He was responsible for much reconstruction in the eastern Somme département of northern France after the end of World War I. Very early in his career, he was interested in the local architectural tradition and had grasped the basic principles of layout and construction.*

By 1916, the Somme, his native département, was already devastated by the battles of World War I. During the conflict, he applied his architectural thoughts to the reconstruction of these devastated areas, hoping that one day they would come to fruition. In 1917, he took part in a competition launched by S.A.D.G. (Société des architectes diplomes par le gouvernement) for the establishment of typical models of homes and farms for the devastated region. His idea of a large Picardy farm at the heart of a commune showed his understanding of the local building tradition. In the days following the end of the war, in accord with the territorial divisions alloted for reconstruction, he was assigned to the cantons of Roisel and Combles, where he designed and built many new schools, churches and town-halls.

Giovanni Duprè (1 March 1817 - Florence, 10 January 1882) was an Italian sculptor, of distant French stock long settled in Tuscany, who developed a reputation second only to his contemporary Lorenzo Bartolini. He began in his father's carving workshop and that of Paolo Sani, where he was occupied with producing fakes of Renaissance sculptures. In an open contest run by the Accademia di Belle Arti, he won first prize with A Judgment of Paris and made his reputation with the life-size figure of the dead Abel, which was purchased for Grand Duchess Maria Nikolaievna, Duchess of Leuchtenberg and was replicated in bronze, c. 1839. The raw naturalism of the figure, greeted with shock at the time, presaged the beginning of the end of Neoclassicism in Italian sculpture and gained Duprè the encouragement of Lorenzo Bartolini. He followed this with a more classical Cain, and followed with figures of Giotto and Saint Antonino of Florence for façade niches on the Uffizi. On a trip to Naples he passed through Rome and saw Antonio Canova's funeral monument to Pope Pius VI, which influenced his style in a classical direction. A period of ill-health was followed by renewed vigour, which resulted in the brooding and melancholy Sappho of 1857-61, with its Michelangelesque flavour contemporary critics acclaimed it as his best work to date. In 1851 he was called upon to provide the model for the bronze base for the grand table inlaid in pietra dura with Apollo and the Muses, executed by the Grand Ducal Opificio delle pietre dure; Duprè's figures of the Seasons with putti was cast in bronze by Clemente Papi. In 1863 Duprè created his finest work, the Pietà (1860-65), for the family tomb of the marchese Bichi-Ruspoli in the cemetery of the Misericordia, Siena. This group was awarded the Grande medaille d'honneur at the International Exhibition in Paris. His last work, the St. Francis inside the Cathedral of S. Rufino in Assisi, was finished by his eldest daughter and pupil, Amalia.

Jean-Honoré Fragonard (5 April 1732 - 22 August 1806) was a French painter and printmaker whose late Rococo manner was distinguished by remarkable facility, exuberance and hedonism. One of the most prolific artists active in the last decades of the Ancien Régime, Fragonard produced more than 550 paintings (not counting drawings and etchings), of which only five are dated. Among his most popular works are genre paintings conveying an atmosphere of intimacy and veiled eroticism. He was born at Grasse, Alpes-Maritimes, the son of François Fragonard, a glover. He was articled to a Paris notary when his father's circumstances became strained, but showed such talent and inclination for art that at the age of eighteen he was taken to François

Self-portrait

Boucher, who, though recognizing the youth's rare gifts , was disinclined to waste his time with someone so inexperienced. Instead, he sent Fragonard to Chardin's atelier (workshop). Fragonard studied for six months under the great luminist, then returned more fully equipped to Boucher, whose style he soon acquired so completely that the master entrusted him with the execution of replicas of his paintings. Though not yet a pupil of the Academy, Fragonard gained the Prix de Rome in 1752 with a painting of "Jeroboam Sacrificing to the Golden Calf", but before proceeding to Rome he continued to study for three years under Charles-André van Loo. In the year preceding his departure he painted the "Christ washing the Feet of the Apostles". On 17 September 1756, he took up his place at the French Academy in Rome, then presided over by Charles-Joseph Natoire. Here, Fragonard became friends with a fellow painter, Hubert Robert. In 1760, they toured Italy together, executing numerous sketches of local scenery. It was in these romantic gardens, with their fountains, grottos, temples and terraces, that Fragonard conceived the dreams which he was subsequently to render in his art. He also learned to admire the masters of the Dutch and Flemish schools (Rubens, Hals, Rembrandt, Ruisdael), imitating their loose and vigorous brushstrokes. Added to this influence was the deep impression made by the florid sumptuousness of Giovanni Battista Tiepolo, whose works he had an opportunity to study in Venice before he returned to Paris in 1761. Back in Paris, Marguerite Gérard, his wife's 14-year-old sister, became his pupil and assistant in 1778. In 1780, he had a son, Alexandre-Évariste Fragonard (1780-1850), who eventually became a talented painter and sculptor. The French Revolution deprived Fragonard of his private patrons - they were either guillotined or exiled, but he found shelter in the house of his friend Maubert at Grasse, which he decorated with the series of decorative panels known as the Les progrès de l'amour dans le cœur d'une jeune fille. He returned to Paris early in thenineteenth century, where he died in 1806, almost completely forgotten.

Francesco Saverio Geminiani (5 December 1687 – 17 September 1762) was an Italian violinist, composer and music theorist. Born in Lucca, he received music lessons from Alessandro Scarlatti studied the violin under Carlo Ambrogio Lonati in Milan and later under Arcangelo Corelli. From 1711, he led the opera orchestra in Naples, as Leader of the Opera Orchestra and concertmaster, which gave him many opportunities to collaborate with Alessandro Scarlatti. In 1714, he arrived in London, where he was taken under the special protection of William Capel, the 3rd Earl of Essex, who remained a patron. In 1715 he played his violin concerti with Handel at the keyboard, for the court of George I. Geminiani made a living by teaching and writing music and tried to keep pace with his passion for collecting by dealing in art, not always successfully. Many of his students went on to have successful careers such as Charles Avison, Matthew Dubourg, Michael Christian Festing, Bernhard Joachim Hagen and Cecilia Young. After visiting Paris and residing there for some time, he returned to England in 1755. In 1761, on one of his stays in Dublin, a servant robbed him of a musical manuscript on which he had spent a great deal of time and labour. His distress is said to have hastened his death.

Théodore Géricault (26 September 1791 – 26 January 1824) was a profoundly influential French artist, painter and lithographer, known for *The Raft of the Medusa* and other paintings. Although he died young, he became one of the pioneers of the Romantic movement. Born in France, Géricault was educated in the tradition of English sporting art by Carle Vernet and classical figure composition by Pierre-Narcisse Guérin, a rigorous classicist who disapproved of his student's impulsive temperament, but recognized his talent. Géricault soon left the classroom, choosing to study at the Louvre instead, where he copied from paintings by Rubens, Titian, Velázquez and Rembrandt for about six years, from 1810 to 1815. There he found a vitality which he preferred to the prevailing school of Neoclassicism.

His first major work, The Charging Chasseur, exhibited at the Paris Salon of 1812, revealed the influence of the style of Rubens and an interest in the depiction of contemporary subject matter. This youthful success, ambitious and monumental, was followed by a change in direction and for the next several years Géricault produced a series of small studies of horses and cavalrymen. A trip to Florence and Rome (1816–17), prompted in part by the desire to flee from a romantic entanglement with his aunt, ignited a fascination with Michelangelo, while Rome itself inspired the preparation of a monumental canvas, the 'Race of the Barberi Horses', a work of epic composition and abstracted theme. Géricault never completed the painting and returned to France, after which he continually returned to the military themes of his early paintings and the series of lithographs he undertook on military subjects after his return from Italy. Géricault's last efforts were directed toward preliminary studies for several epic compositions, including the Opening of the Doors of the Spanish Inquisition and the African Slave Trade. The preparatory drawings suggest works of great ambition, but Géricault's waning health intervened. Weakened by riding accidents and chronic tubercular infection, he died in Paris in 1824 . His bronze figure reclines, brush in hand, on his tomb at Père Lachaise Cemetery in Paris, above a low-relief panel of The Raft of the Medusa.

Domenico Ghirlandaio (1449—11 January 1494) was an Italian Renaissance painter from Florence. Among his many apprentices was Michelangelo. Domenico, the eldest of eight children, was at first apprenticed to a jeweller or a goldsmith, most likely his own father. The nickname "Il Ghirlandaio" (garland-maker) came to Domenico from his father, a goldsmith who was famed for creating the metallic garland-like necklaces worn by Florentine women. In his father's

Self-portrait

shop, Domenico is said to have made portraits of the passers-by and he was eventually apprenticed to Alessio Baldovinetti to study painting and mosaics. In 1480, Ghirlandaio painted the 'Saint Jerome in His Study' and other frescoes in the Church of Ognissanti, Florence and a life-sized 'Last Supper' in its refectory. From 1481 to 1485, he was employed on frescoes in the Sala dell'Orologio of the Palazzo Vecchio. He also painted the Apotheosis of St. Zenobius, an over-life-sized work with an elaborate architectural framework, figures of Roman heroes and other secular details, striking in its perspective and structural/compositional skill. In 1483, Ghirlandaio was summoned to Rome by Pope Sixtus IV to paint a wall fresco in the Sistine Chapel, 'Christ calling Peter and Andrew to their Apostleship'. On returning to Florence in 1485, Ghirlandaio painted fresco cycles in the Sassetti

Sassetti. One of the great legacies of Ghirlandaio is that he is commonly credited with having given some early art education to Michelangelo, who cannot, however, have remained with him long. Francesco Granacci is another among his best-known pupils. Ghirlandaio died of a fever and was buried in Santa Maria Novella. He had been twice married and left six children. One of his three sons, Ridolfo Ghirlandaio, also became a noted painter.

Benozzo Gozzoli *(c. 1421 – 1497), an early Italian Renaissance painter, was the son of the tailor Lese di Sandro, his original name Benozzo di Lese di Sandro. His father was from a citified branch of a family of farmers. Gozzoli's formative collaborations included those with Lorenzo and Vittorio Ghiberti on the third bronze door of the Baptistery, Florence (1444), with Fra Angelico on the pictorial decoration of the Dominican convent of San Marco in Florence (1444-45), with Fra Angelico on some frescoes in the chapel of Pope Nicholas V in the Vatican (1447) and again with Fra Angelico on the ceiling of the Chapel of San*

Self-portrait

Brizio in the cathedral at Orvieto (1448). In 1450 he was in Montefalco in Umbria where his first independent works were executed. He left frescoes in the churches of S. Fortunato and produced a panel painting of the Madonna della Cintola for the high altar. For the church of S. Francesco, the Franciscans commissioned from him the fresco cycle with Scenes from the Life of St Francis (1450-52). At Viterbo he painted nine frescoes of scenes from St Rose's life (after 1453), which were lost during the course of extension work in the church in 1632. Between 1456 and 1459 Benozzo put in an irregular appearance in various places in Central Italy. He painted an altarpiece at Perugia for Collegio Gerolominiano (1456); at Sermoneta he painted a Madonna in Glory for the cathedral (1458). He was in Rome in 1458, working on the displays (flags and standards) for the coronation ceremony of Pius II. In Rome he also frescoed the Albertoni chapel in Santa Maria d'Aracoeli of which a St Anthony of Padua survives. In 1459 Benozzo was summoned to Florence by the city's most illustrious patrons, the Medici, to carry out the prestigious commission - the most important of his career - of decorating the walls of the chapel in their palace. The subject chosen was the Journey of the Magi which he used to portray various members of the Medici family, with its young princes handsomely, even flamboyantly dressed and all set against a wonderful landscape, creating a fairy tale of the Renaissance (1459-60). In 1461 he produced the altar painting of a Sacra Conversazione for the Compagnia delle Purificazione in Florence. The painting has since been taken apart and is kept in various museums. By 1463 he was working in San Gimignano on a cycle of 17 scenes from the life of St Augustine in the choir of Sant'Agostino (last scene signed and dated 1465) and on a fresco of St Sebastian (1464). In 1467 he painted the Tabernacle of the Executed and the Shrine of the Visitation, the detached frescoes are now on display in the Palazzo Pretorio, Certaldo and in the Biblioteca Comunale, Castelfiorentino, respectively. In 1471 he executed a panel painting of the Triumph of St Thomas Aquinas (now in the Louvre, Paris), in 1484 the Shrine of the Madonna delle Tosse, the detached frescoes of which can be seen also in Castelfiorentino. Between 1469 and 1485 he painted his most extensive commission, a series of 25 frescoes of Old Testament scenes for the Campo Santo (cemetery), Pisa. In 1944 a bombing raid, followed by a fire, destroyed or damaged the greater part of the frescoes. Forced to leave Pisa, along with other Florentine residents of the city, following the invasion by

Charles VIII and the expulsion of the Medici, Benozzo returned to Florence. In 1497 he moved to Pistoia where his sons were already working. Benozzo died in Pistoia on October 4, 1497, probably of plague and was buried in the cloister of the convent of San Domenico.

Francisco José de Goya y Lucientes (30 March 1746 – 16 April 1828) was born in 1746 in a small town near Zaragoza. When he was 14 he began a 4 year apprenticeship to a local master, José Luzan. Goya then left for Madrid with the intention of winning a prize at the Academy of San Fernando. Although he didn't win, he met the court artist Francisco Bayeu who was to prove influential in forming Goya's early style. Bayeu was heavily influenced by the German painter Anton Taphael Mengs and passed elements of this style on to Goya. Bayeu was also instrumental in Goya's first involvement in a commission. This was the fresco decoration of the Church of the Virgin in El Pilar in Zaragoza. From 1773, after spending a year in Italy, Goya worked on a number of other fresco projects, including one for the Charterhouse of Aula Dei, near Zaragoza. However, it was in 1798 that he worked on his greatest fresco project for the Church of San Antonio de la Florida, Madrid. Goya had now begun working on prints based on paintings by one of his two greatest sources of inspiration, Velázquez. Goya began working on official portraits commissioned by King Charles III around 1786. He also worked on several tapestry cartoons depicting Spanish life and these revolutionized the Spanish tapestry industry. However, in the winter of 1792, Goya's life took a dramatic turn when he became totally deaf after a serious illness. This led to much of his subsequent work having a pessimistic air to it. He drew and etched the first in a series of prints, the satirical Los Caprichos (The Caprices). Others followed, including the Desastres de la Guerra (Disasters of War) and Disparates (Absurdities). Goya had witnessed the horrors of war, at first hand, during the French occupation of Spain and he drew on this for two of the paintings that he completed in 1814. The Second of May, 1808 and Third of May, 1808 both depict brutal massacres of his countrymen by the French. The thick, bold strokes of dark colour that he used were typical of many of his later paintings. Another characteristic of Goya's paintings towards the end of his life was that they had an openness and honesty, especially his portraits. His portrait, Family of Charles IV, portrays the Royals in a realistic manner and not idealized as many other artists did. Towards the end of his life, Goya painted a series of fresco scenes on the walls of his country house. These were the Black Paintings and he used mainly blacks, browns and greys to depict scenes of witchcraft. Goya was evidently becoming depressed by the political situation in Spain and these paintings reflected his mood. He was forced to leave Spain in 1824, because of the oppression in his native land and moved to France. Goya began to pursue the then new art of lithography and he produced a series of bullfight scenes that are among the best lithographs ever made. He died, in France, in 1828.

Self-portrait

Jean Auguste Dominique Ingres (1780 - 1867) son of a sculptor and landscape artist, he showed precocious talent and studied first in Toulouse, then with Vien, Vigan and Briard in Paris before entering David's workshop in 1797. Ingres won the Prix de Rome in 1801, but could not go to Italy until 1806. During the interim period he supported himself by painting portraits in a style that was

Self-portrait

147

already rhythmic in line and indicative of great powers of character observation. While in Italy, Ingres spent four years in Florence studying Italian primitives, Greek vase paintings and Flaxman's illustrations for Homer. He then spent fourteen years in Rome, where he came more and more under the influence of Raphael. Ingres was named director of the Beaux-Arts in 1829. He was very popular as a teacher and became the principal advocate of David's Neoclassical school, upholding line and drawing, sculpturesque form and balanced composition against the expressive movement and the emotionalism of the Romantic school. In 1834, he returned to Italy where he served as director of the French Academy in Rome until his final return to Paris in 1841. He was triumphantly received in Paris and enjoyed both homage and honor until his death in 1856. A highly complex and very talented artist, Ingres was more severe in his theories of art than in his own production - his subjects are exotic even romantic, both in concept and in the handling of tone and texture. His many odalisques, the female nudes, are executed with great delicacy and are placed in exotic, foreign surroundings and his "troubadour" paintings present equally romantic moments in the history of French kings. His drawings, often carefully corrected, are the most purely classical of his works. As a portraitist, Ingres was a superb master of physical exactness and of psychological understanding. His influence affected such diverse artists as Renoir, Degas, Modigliani, Seurat and Picasso, in their use of form and line. His classical drawing influenced nineteen-century sculpture. His basic belief in "art for art's sake," his rich colour and his brilliant drawing make Ingres a truly universal artist.

Jacob Jordaens (1593 - 18 October 1678) a Flemish artist, was born in 1593 into the family of an Antwerp linen merchant. He was the pupil of Adam van Noort under whom Rubens had studied briefly. Later Jordaens married van Noort's daughter, Catharina. In 1615, he joined the St. Lukas Guild and, in 1621, became its deacon. Jordaens painted religious, mythological, historical subjects, portraits and genre scenes and big monumental decorations. In his early period, marked by the influence of Caravaggio, the night scenes with candle and moon light prevail. The young master's individuality was revealed on big-scaled compositions, where several full-length figures fill all the surface of the picture, which lack depth. This method did not change during his working life. Maybe it was the result of his work on wall-hangings, which he designed and painted on linen and which his father sold. Jordaens did not visit Italy and never tried to imitate the Italian style but remained stylistically close to Rubens, in whose workshop he was employed several times. Jordaen's talent revealed itself in genre painting. He took subjects from folklore, fables and proverbs. After Rubens' death, Jordaens became the leader of the Antwerp school, carrying out innumerable commissions for Church and Court between 1640 and 1650, including 22 pictures for the salon on Queen Henrietta Maria at Greenwich, work for the Scandinavia and French courts. In 1650, he adopted Calvinism, but continued to receive commissions from the Catholic Church. Jordaen died in 1678 in Antwerp.

Baldassarre Lanci *(1510-1571) A military engineer from Urbino, Lanci was in the service of*

the Republic of Lucca between 1547 and 1557. In this period, he also worked for the French who were occupying Montalcino on behalf of the Republic of Siena (1549) and for Marcantonio Colonna in Paliano and Nettuno. He made surveys of the walls of Rome and the fortresses of Ancona, Ostia and
View of
Firenze
Civitavecchia for Pius IV (1499-1565, Pope from 1559). In 1557, he entered the service of Cosimo I de' Medici (1519-1574), who commissioned him to fortify just-conquered Siena and other Tuscan towns. The surveying instruments made for the Grand Duke's collection date from this period. He worked in the Maremma region as a hydraulic engineer, supervising the construction of the Sovana aqueduct and other infrastructure. Lanci took part in the improvement of Leghorn harbor (1566-1567), where he tested a dredger of his invention. He also distinguished himself as a civil architect. He seems to have designed the church of Santa Maria della Rosa in Chianciano and he is mentioned as a perspectivist in Egnazio Danti's (1536-1586) commentary on Le due regole della prospettiva (The two rules of perspective).

Ambrogio Lorenzetti *(or Ambruogio Laurati; c. 1290 – June 9, 1348) was an Italian painter*

of the Sienese school. He was active between approximately 1317 to 1348. His elder brother was the painter Pietro Lorenzetti. The earliest dated work of the Sienese painter is a Madonna and Child. His presence was documented in Florence up until 1321. He would return there after spending a number of years in Siena. The frescoes on the walls of the Room of the Nine (Sala dei Nove) or Room of Peace (Sala della Pace) in the Palazzo Pubblico of Siena are one of the masterworks of early renaissance secular painting. The "nine" was theoligarchal assembly of guild and monetary interests that governed the republic. Three walls are painted with frescoes consisting of a large assembly of allegorical figures of virtues in the Allegory of Good Government. In the other two facing panels, Ambrogio weaves panoramic visions of Effects of Good Government on Town and Country, and Allegory of Bad Government and its Effects on Town and Country. The better preserved "well-governed town and country" is an unrivaled pictorial encyclopedia of incidents in a peaceful medieval "borgo" and countryside. Like his brother, he is believed to have died of bubonic plague 1348.

Filippino *(c. 1457 - April 18, 1504) was an early Renaissance painter of the Florentine school*

whose works influenced the Tuscan Mannerists of the 16th century. The son of Fra Filippo Lippi and his wife, Lucrezia Buti, he was a follower of his father and of Botticelli. After Fra Filippo Lippi's death, Filippino entered Botticelli's workshop. The style of Filippino's earliest works stems from that of Botticelli, though Filippino's use of line is less sensitive and subtle. In a group of paintings executed about 1480–85 he developed a harder and more individual style. Among
Self-portrait
the most notable works of this period is the "Journey of Tobias" in the Galleria Sabauda, Turin, Italy. He was employed, along with Botticelli, Perugino and Ghirlandaio, on the frescoed decoration of Lorenzo de' Medici's villa at Spedaletto and at the end of 1482 was commissioned to complete work left unfinished by Perugino in the Palazzo della Signoria

in Florence. No trace of either work survives. Soon after (probably 1483–84) he was entrusted with the completion of the frescoes in the Brancacci Chapel in the Carmine, which had been left unfinished on Masaccio's death in 1428. His most popular picture, the beautiful altarpiece of "The Vision of St. Bernard" (Badia, Florence), has been variously assigned to the years 1480 and 1486. In Rome Filippino decorated the Carafa Chapel in Sta. Maria sopra Minerva. Nothing in Filippino's earlier works prepares for the vein of inspiration that he struck in the Carafa Chapel, which became one of his most influential works. After his return from Rome, Filippino executed a fresco of the "Death of Laocoön" for the villa of Lorenzo de' Medici at Poggio a Caiano, in which some of the decorative devices used in the Carafa Chapel are again employed and resumed work in the Strozzi Chapel (completed 1502), the frescoes of which anticipate Tuscan Mannerism of the 16th century. Lippi's last work is the Deposition for the Santissima Annunziata church in Florence, which at his death in April 1504 was unfinished. He was so renowned that all the workshops of the city closed on the day of his burial.

Simone Martini (c. 1284 – 1344) was an Italian painter born in Siena. He was a major figure in the development of early Italian painting and greatly influenced the development of the International Gothic style. It is thought that Martini was a pupil of Duccio di Buoninsegna, the leading Sienese painter of his time. His brother-in-law was the artist Lippo Memmi. Very little documentation survives regarding Simone's life, but he was doubtlessly apprenticed from an early age, as would have been the normal practice. Among his first documented works is the

Virgil

Maestà of 1315 in the Palazzo Pubblico in Siena. A copy of the work, executed shortly thereafter by Lippo Memmi in San Gimignano, testifies to the enduring influence Simone's prototypes would have on other artists throughout the fourteenth century. Perpetuating the Sienese tradition, Simone's style contrasted with the sobriety and monumentality of Florentine art and is noted for its soft, stylized, decorative features, sinuosity of line and unsurpassed courtly elegance. Simone's art owes much to French manuscript illumination and ivory carving: examples of such art were brought to Siena in the fourteenth century by means of the Via Francigena.

Henri Matisse (31 December 1869 – 3 November 1954) Matisse was born in Le Cateau-Cambrésis in northern France on December 31, 1869. The son of a middle-class family, he studied and began to practice law. In 1890, however, while recovering slowly from an attack of appendicitis, he became intrigued by the process of painting. In 1892, having given up his law career, he went to Paris to study art formally. He joined Gustave Moreau's studio at the Ecole des Beaux-Arts where he met Camoin, Manguin, Marquet and Jean Puy. His first teachers were academically trained and relatively conservative; Matisse's own early style was a conventional form of naturalism and he made many copies after the old masters. He also studied more contemporary art, especially that of the impressionists and he began to experiment, earning a reputation as a rebellious member of his studio classes. Matisse's true artistic liberation, in terms of the use of colour to render forms and organize spatial planes, came about first through the influence of the French painters Paul Gauguin and Paul Cézanne and the Dutch artist Vincent van Gogh, whose work he studied closely beginning about 1899. Then, in 1903 and 1904, Matisse encountered the pointillist painting of Henri Edmond Cross and Paul Signac. Cross and Signac were experimenting with juxtaposing small strokes (often dots or "points") of pure pigment to create the strongest visual vibration of intense colour. Matisse adopted their technique and modified it repeatedly, using broader strokes. By 1905 he had produced some of the boldest colour images ever created, including a striking picture of his wife, Green Stripe (Madame Matisse). The title refers to a broad stroke of brilliant green that defines Madame Matisse's brow and nose. In the same year Matisse exhibited this and similar paintings along with works by his artist companions, including André Derain and Maurice de Vlaminck. Together, the group was dubbed "les fauves" (literally, "the wild beasts") because of the extremes of emotionalism in which they seemed to have indulged, their use of vivid colours and their distortion of shapes. While he was regarded as a leader of radicalism in the arts, Matisse was beginning to gain the approval of a number of influential critics and collectors, including the American expatriate writer Gertrude Stein and her family. Among the many important commissions he received was that of a Russian collector who requested mural panels illustrating dance and music. Such broadly conceived themes ideally suited Matisse; they allowed him freedom of invention and play of form and expression. His images of dancers and of human figures in general, convey expressive form first and the particular details of anatomy only secondarily. Matisse extended this principle into other fields; his bronze sculptures, like his drawings and works in several graphic media, reveal the same expressive contours seen in his paintings. Although intellectually sophisticated, Matisse always emphasized the importance of instinct and intuition in the production of a work of art. He argued that an artist did not have complete control over colour and form; instead, colours, shapes and lines would come to dictate to the sensitive artist how they might be employed in relation to one another. He often emphasized his joy in abandoning himself to the play of the forces of colour and design and he explained the rhythmic, but distorted, forms of many of his figures in terms of the working out of a total pictorial harmony. From the 1920s until his death, Matisse spent much time in the south of France, particularly Nice, painting local scenes with a thin, fluid application of bright colour. In his old age, he was commissioned to design the decoration of the small Chapel of Saint-Marie du Rosaire at Vence (near Cannes), which he completed between 1947 and 1951. Often bedridden during his last years, he occupied himself with decoupage, creating works of brilliantly coloured paper cutouts arranged casually, but with an unfailing eye for design, on a canvas surface. Matisse died in Nice on November 3, 1954. Unlike many artists, he was internationally popular during his lifetime, enjoying the favor of collectors, art critics and the younger generation of artists.

Ludovico Mazzanti (5 Dec 1686 - 29 Aug 1775) an Italian painter who served his apprenticeship under Giovanni Battista Gaulli from 1700 onwards and was influenced by the classicism of Maratti as well as by the Baroque tendencies of Lanfranco in the refined form found in the work of Giovanni Battista Beinaschi (1638-88). His painting was

Suicide of Cleopatra

produced in the cultural climate of the Society of Arcadia and the Accademia di S Luca, which included Odazzi and other Roman decorative artists. He took part in the Concorsi Clementini in 1703-5 and 1708, becoming a member of the Accademia di S Luca in 1744 and of the Accademia Clementina in 1748.

Lippo Memmi *(c. 1291 – 1356) was an Italian painter from Siena. He was the foremost*

follower of Simone Martini, who was his brother-in-law. Together with Martini, in 1333 he painted one of the masterworks of the International Gothic, the Annunciation for the Sienese church of Sant'Ansano (now in the Uffizi). He was one of the artists who worked at the Orvieto Cathedral, for which he finished the Madonna dei Raccomandati. Later he followed Martini at the Papal court in Avignon, where he worked until the mid-14th century. After his return to Siena Memmi executed several works until his death in 1356.

Madonna

Michelangelo *di Lodovico Buonarroti Simoni (6 March 1475 – 18 February 1564) was one of*

the greatest sculptors of the Italian Renaissance and one of its greatest painters and architects. He was born in Caprese, a village where his father, Lodovico Buonarroti, was briefly serving as a Florentine government agent. The family moved back to Florence before Michelangelo was one month old. Michelangelo's mother died when he was six. From early childhood Michelangelo was drawn to the arts, but his father considered this pursuit below the family's social status and tried to discourage him. However, Michelangelo prevailed and was apprenticed at the age of thirteen to Domenico Ghirlandaio (1449-1494), the most fashionable painter in Florence at the time. After a year Michelangelo's apprenticeship was broken off and he gained access to the collection of ancient Roman sculpture of the ruler of Florence, Lorenzo de' Medici (1449–1492). He dined with the family and was looked after by the retired sculptor who was in charge of the collection. This arrangement was quite unusual at the time. Michelangelo's earliest sculpture, the Battle of the Centaurs, a stone work created when he was about seventeen, is regarded as remarkable for the simple, solid forms and squarish proportions of the figures, which add intensity to their violent interaction. Soon after Lorenzo died in 1492, the Medici family fell from power and Michelangelo fled to Bologna. In 1494 he carved three saints for the church of San Domenico. They show dense forms, in contrast to the linear forms which were then dominant in sculpture. After returning to Florence briefly, Michelangelo moved to Rome. There he carved a Bacchus for a banker's garden of ancient sculpture. This is Michelangelo's earliest surviving large-scale work and his only sculpture meant to be viewed from all sides. In 1498 the same banker commissioned Michelangelo to carve the Pietà (refers to a type of image in which Mary supports the dead Christ across her knees) now in St. Peter's. On Michelangelo's return to Florence in 1501 he was recognized as the most talented sculptor of central Italy and was commissioned to carve the David for the Florence Cathedral. From this time on, Michelangelo's work consisted mainly of very large projects and many he did not finish because he felt unable to turn down the vast commissions of his important clients. In 1508 Pope Julius II commissioned Michelangelo to decorate the ceiling of the chief Vatican chapel, the Sistine. The traditional format of ceiling painting contained only single figures. Michelangelo introduced dramatic scenes and an original framing system, which was his earliest architectural design. The chief elements are twelve male and female prophets (the latter known as sibyls) and nine stories from Genesis. Michelangelo stopped for some months halfway along. When he returned, his style underwent a shift toward a more forceful grandeur and a richer emotional tension than in any previous work. The images of the Separation of Light and Darkness and Ezekiel illustrate this greater freedom and mobility. Michelangelo devoted himself almost entirely to architecture and poetry after 1545, including rebuilding of the Capitol area, the Piazza del Campidoglio, for Pope Paul III. The pope also appointed him to direct the work at St. Peter's in 1546. Michelangelo's sculpture after 1545 was limited to two Pietàs that he executed for himself. The first one, begun in 1550 and left unfinished, was meant for his own tomb. He began the Rondanini Pietà in Milan in 1555 and was working on it in February 1564 when he became ill. He died six days later in Rome and was buried in Florence.

Igor Mitoraj (born 1944) is a Polish artist born in Oederan, Germany. Mitoraj's sculptural style is rooted in the classical tradition with its focus on the well modelled torso. However, Mitoraj introduces a post-modern twist with ostentatiously truncated limbs, emphasising the damage sustained by most genuine classical sculptures. He studied painting at the Kraków School of Art and at the Kraków Academy of Art under Tadeusz Kantor. After graduating, he had several joint exhibitions, and held is first solo exhibition in 1967 at the Krzysztofory Gallery in Poland. In 1968, he moved to Paris to continue his studies at the National School of Art. Shortly afterwards, hebecame fascinated by Latin American art and culture, spending a year painting and travelling around Mexico. The experience led him to take up sculpture. He returned to Paris in 1974 and two years later he held another major solo exhibition at the Gallery La Hune, including some sculptural work. The success of the show persuaded him that he was first and foremost a sculptor. Having previously worked with terracotta and bronze, a trip to Carrara, Italy, in 1979 turned him to using marble as his primary medium and in 1983 he set up a studio in Pietrasanta. In 2006, he created the new bronze doors and a statue of John the Baptist for the basilica of Santa Maria degli Angeli in Rome. However report hot controversy as a result of installation (April 5 2008) of his work in Piazza Trento in Tivoli, opposite the church of St. Maria Maggiore and the Villa d'Este. The location of the fact has put at risk the celebration of the rite dell'Inchinata. The work was moved on August 11, in this way was made possible the sacred ceremony. The statue was then called in situ on August 20, 2008. The citizens of Tivoli, which already signed a petition People (4800 signatures, the source Il Messaggero) against the installation of sculpture, even aesthetically and historically totally alien to the site, hope that in future the removal can be definitive.

Bernardino di Betto, called **Pintoricchio or Pinturicchio** (1454 – 1513) was an Italian painter of the Renaissance, born in Perugia. He may have trained under lesser known Perugian painters such as Bonfigli and Fiorenzo di Lorenzo. After assisting Perugino in his frescoes in the Sistine Chapel, Pinturicchio was employed by various members of the Della Rovere family and others to decorate a series of chapels in the church of Santa Maria del Popolo in Rome, where he appears to have worked from 1484 to 1492. The earliest of these is an altarpiece of the Adoration of the Shepherds, in the first chapel (from the west) on the south, built by Cardinal Domenico della Rovere; a

Madonna Adoring
the Child

portrait of the cardinal is introduced as the foremost of the kneeling shepherds. In 1492 Pinturicchio was summoned to Orvieto, where he painted two Prophets and two of the Doctors in the Cathedral. He then returned to Rome and was employed by Pope Alexander VI (Borgia) to decorate a recently completed suite of six rooms, the Appartamenti Borgia in the Vatican. These rooms now form part of the Vatican library and five still retain a series of Pinturicchio frescoes. Pinturicchio worked in these rooms till 1498, assisted by his pupils. His other chief frescoes in Rome, still existing in a very genuine state, are those in the Cappella Bufalini at the south-west of Santa Maria in Ara Coeli, probably executed from 1497 to 1500.

Pablo Diego Picasso *(25 October 1881- 8 April 1973) Pablo Picasso was born in Málaga in*
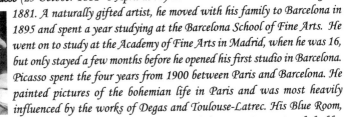
1881. A naturally gifted artist, he moved with his family to Barcelona in 1895 and spent a year studying at the Barcelona School of Fine Arts. He went on to study at the Academy of Fine Arts in Madrid, when he was 16, but only stayed a few months before he opened his first studio in Barcelona. Picasso spent the four years from 1900 between Paris and Barcelona. He painted pictures of the bohemian life in Paris and was most heavily influenced by the works of Degas and Toulouse-Latrec. His Blue Room, painted in 1901, is the best example of this. He finally settled in Paris in 1904 and the blue was replaced by pink. This Rose Period lasted for the next year or so and a common theme of the paintings that he produced during this time was the circus. In 1906, Picasso produced pieces that were heavily influenced by Greek, Iberian and African art and entered his Cubism period. Later, his cubism took on another dimension when he began working on collages with paper and cloth. Picasso also revolutionized sculpture by creating pieces from everyday materials. One example, Guitar, is made of cardboard, paper and string and is on display in the Musée Picasso in Paris. As this technique was taken up by other sculptors of the time, it became known as Constructivism. Picasso's love life also had an influence on his work. He painted realistic portraits of his first wife and son, in the early years from 1917. However, as the marriage disintegrated he moved into darker, more surrealistic images during the mid-1920s. He fell in love again, in the early 1930s and his paintings took on another lighter mood. However, his most important work, Guernica, was a far darker picture. It was influenced by events during the Spanish Civil War. It now hangs in the Reina Sofia Art Centre in Madrid. Picasso died in 1973.

Nicola Pisano *(c. 1220/1225 - c. 1284) was an Italian sculptor whose work is noted for its*

classical Roman sculptural style. Pisano is sometimes considered to be the founder of modern sculpture. His birth date or origins are uncertain. He was born in Apulia and probably trained in the local workshops of the emperor Frederick II. Around 1245 he moved to Tuscany to work in the Prato Castle. In September 1265 he began work on a marble pulpit for the Siena Cathedral. Nicola Pisano pushed 13th century Tuscan sculpture in the direction of a Gothic art that already integrated the noble features of Roman art, while simultaneously staying attached to the Gothic art from Northern Europe.

Nicola Pisano, statue

Portrait of a Girl

The *Florentine brothers Antonio and Piero del Pollaiuolo were born some 10 years apart and started on different paths. Piero trained as a painter, perhaps with Andrea dal Castagno. Antonio is usually considered the greater artist. He developed design skills which were the basis of the painting and sculpture for which he is famous. Antonio had his own workshop by 1459 and styled himself painter and sculptor. He was and remains, famous for his work in other media such as designs for embroidery, engraving and enamel-work. His engraving of the 'Battle of the Ten Nudes' was the largest and most influential print of the 15th century, providing models of the male body in action.*

Self-portrait

Pietro Perugino *(1446–1524) was the leading painter of the Umbrian school. According to Vasari, he was apprenticed iunder Andrea del Verrocchio alongside Leonardo da Vinci. In 1472 he enrolled as a painter in the confraternity of St Luke. Perugino was one of the earliest Italian practitioners of oil painting. Some of his early works were extensive frescoes for the convent of the Ingesati fathers, destroyed during the siege of Florence. Perugino, aged forty, left Rome after completion of the Sistine Chapel work in 1486 and by autumn he was in Florence. In July 1487 he and another Perugian painter named Aulista di Angelo were convicted, on their own confession, of having attacked someone in the streets near Pietro Maggiore. Perugino was fined ten gold florins and Aulista di Angelo was exiled for life. Between 1486 and 1499 Perugino worked chiefly in Florence, making one journey to Rome and several to Perugia, where he may have maintained a second studio. He had an established studio in Florence and received a great number of commissions. Perugino's last frescoes were painted for the church of the Madonna delle Lacrime in Trevi (1521, signed and dated), the monastery of Sant'Agnese in Perugia and in 1522 for the church of Castello di Fortignano. He died in 1524 of the plague and like other plague victims, was hastily buried in an unconsecrated field, the precise spot now unknown.*

Giacomo Puccini *(22 December 1858 - 29 November 1924) an Italian composer, born into a family of organists and choirmasters, he was inspired to write operas after hearing Giuseppe Verdi's Aïda in 1876. At the Milan Conservatory he studied with Amilcare Ponchielli (1834 -86). Puccini entered his first opera, Le villi (1883), in a competition. Though it lost, a group of his friends subsidized its production and its premiere took place with immense success. His second, Edgar (1889), was a failure, but Manon Lescaut (1893) brought him international recognition. His mature operas included La Bohème (1896), Tosca (1900), Madam Butterfly (1904) and The Girl of the Golden West (1910). All four are tragic love stories; his use of the orchestra was refined and he established a dramatic structure that balanced action and conflict with moments of repose, contemplation and lyricism. They remained exceedingly popular into the 21st century. He was the most popular opera composer in the world at the time of his death; his unfinished Turandot was completed by Franco Alfano (1875 – 1954).*

Jacopo della Quercia *(c. 1374 - October 20, 1438) anItalian sculptor in Siena, he was the son of a goldsmith and wood carver. His earliest major work is the tomb of Ilaria del Carretto in Lucca Cathedral (c.1406 - 08). His most important commission for Siena was the fountain known as Fonte Gaia (1408 - 19) in the Piazza del Campo. He worked with Donatello and Lorenzo Ghiberti on reliefs for the baptismal font in the Baptistery in Siena (1417 – 30). His last and greatest work was the sculptural reliefs around the portal of San Petronio in Bologna (1425 - 30). In 1435 he was appointed supervising architect of Siena Cathedral. and elevated Sienese sculpture to a place of prominence and influenced subsequent Sienese painters. The greatest non-Florentine sculptor of the 15th century, he was a major influence on the young Michelangelo.*

Madonna of Humility

Luca Della Robbia *(1400-1482) Luca Della Robbia is ranked alongside Donatello and Lorenzo Ghiberti; the architect Filippo Brunelleschi and the painter Masaccio. Born in 1400 in Florence, Robbia's father is recorded as Simone di Marco Della Robbia, a Florentine citizen and member of the Wool Makers Guild. Facts about Robbia's early life or training in the art of sculpture are scarce. It has been suggested that he may have trained as a goldsmith and it is possible that he worked with masters such as Niccolò di Piero Lamberti and Nanni di Banco (with whom he may have worked in 1420 on the decoration of the Porta della Mandorla in Florence Cathedral). Robbia's first documented commission is the Singing Gallery (Cantoria) for Florence Cathedral in 1431. Although Robbia must have been a relatively unknown artist at this time, the prestigious commission demonstrates that he must have demonstrated his skill prior to this, enough to impress his patrons at least. No doubt the fact that more established sculptors like Donatello and Michelozzo were otherwise occupied on works in Rome helped his case. The Singing Gallery consists of 10 marble panels of sculptural reliefs, showing singing infants, teenagers and angels praising the Lord in the words of Psalm 150. Where Donatello's carved figures are vigorous and dramatic, Robbia's figures are serene and graceful. The relief was originally placed above the North Sacristy door in the Cathedral, but was dismantled in 1688. It was eventually painstakingly reassembled and is now housed in the Museo dell'Opera del Duomo, Florence. In 1432, Robbia joined the Sculptors Guild and continued to work for the next ten years in marble and bronze. In 1437 he began a series of marble reliefs for the bell tower of Florence. Around this time, he also started experimenting with marble and enamelled terracotta. According to the Renaissance author Giorgio Vasari, in his historical review of the history of sculpture during the Renaissance, Luca experimented with a glaze consisting of a mixture of tin oxide, litharge antimony and other minerals. This glaze made his sculptures more durable and would go on to keep his family in work for generations. His earliest documented work using this technique are two lunettes, the Resurrection (1445) and the Ascension (1446) over the Sacristy doors of Florence Cathedral (1442–45). By covering the baked clay model in a hard glaze, his figures*

Panel of the Cantoria.

looked like they were bathed in light, the polished surface reflecting light and colour. The Cathedral Vestry Board were so pleased with his lunettes, they offered him several more commissions. His last major work in was an altarpiece in the Palazzo Vescovile at Pescia (1472).

August Rodin (12 November 1840 – 17 November 1917) is considered to be one of the greatest and most prolific sculptors of the 19th and 20th centuries. His artworks were so innovative  and non-conventional that Parisian art critics initially denounced them. Despite these rejections, Rodin's works were well received outside of France and eventually won the recognition of his countrymen. Born in Paris on November 12, 1840, Rodin expressed an interests in art at an early age. When he was 14, he attended "la Petite Ecole", a school for drawing and mathematics. However, devastated by the death of his sister, Rodin turned towards religion and joined the Order of the Holy Sacrament in 1862. It was during this time that Rodin sculpted the bust of Father Piere-Julien Eynard. Realizing that religion was not his calling, he returned to Paris in 1963. After a brief employment as a corporal in the French National Guard, Rodin traveled to Belgium and Italy, where he studied Michelangelo's works. Rodin was greatly impressed and influenced by the Italian sculptor's portrayal of muscles and human body. Contrary to artistic tradition of his time, Rodin believed that sculptures should reflect the subjects as they truly are and not as the ideal that they should be. In 1877, Rodin exhibited his nude masterpiece L'Age d'Airin (The Age of Bronze) in Brussels and Paris. Unfortunately, this realistic work of art was not well received. Critics accused Rodin of casting the statue directly from living models, instead of sculpting it. In time, Rodin's true genius was recognized and the French government purchased The Age of Bronze as the first of many state acquisitions of his artworks. The French government commissioned Rodin in 1880 to sculpt the entrance of the planned Museum of Decorative Arts. This project, called La Porte de l'Enfer (The Gates of Hell), was inspired by The Inferno, the first chapter of Dante's Divine Comedy. The museum site was later moved from the bank of Seine to Louvre and Rodin's commission was then canceled. Despite the setback, Rodin continued to work on this project and created one hundred and eighty-six figures. These statues represented mainly scenes and characters from the famous poem. Some of them, such as The Thinker (a portrayal of Dante himself), Adam and Eve, are among Rodin's most famous artworks. The Kiss was originally part of The Gates of Hell until Rodin realized that the sculpture's joyful nature conflicted with the theme of The Gates of Hell. Unfortunately, Rodin never finished the project and the statues were cast in bronze only after his death. Rodin's most controversial artwork, The Nude Balzac, was created under commission in 1891. This sculpture of the famous French writer drew criticisms from French papers for the next 10 years. Eventually, the commission was given to another sculptor and the resulting statue was installed at the Avenue Friedland in 1902. Rodin refused to sell his Nude Balzac despite numerous offers. It was not until years after his death that the sculpture was placed at the intersection of Boulevards Raspail and Montparnasse and viewed as the masterpiece that it truly is. In 1908 Rodin moved his studio to the ground floor of the Biron Hotel, which was established as the official Rodin Museum

Florence Cathedral (1442–45, now in the Museo in 1919. He died in the Hotel on November 17, 1917 at the age of 77.

Raphael - Raffaello Sanzio da Urbino (April 6 or March 28, 1483 – April 6, 1520). As a

member of Perugino's workshop, he established his mastery by 17 and began receiving important commissions. In 1504 he moved to Florence, where he executed many of his famous Madonnas; his unity of composition and suppression of inessentials is evident in The Madonna of the Goldfinch (c. 1506). Though influenced by Leonardo da Vinci's chiaroscuro and sfumato, his figure types were his own creation, with round, gentle faces that reveal human sentiments raised to a sublime serenity. In 1508 he was summoned to Rome to decorate a suite of papal chambers in the Vatican. The frescoes in the Stanza della Segnatura are probably his greatest work; the most famous, The School of Athens (1510 – 11), is a complex and magnificently ordered allegory of secular knowledge showing Greek philosophers in an architectural setting. The Madonnas he painted in Rome show him turning away from his earlier work's serenity to emphasize movement and grandeur, partly under Michelangelo's High Renaissance influence. The Sistine Madonna (1513) shows the richness of colour and new boldness of compositional invention typical of his Roman period. He became the most important portraitist in Rome, designed 10 large tapestries to hang in the Sistine Chapel, designed a church and a chapel, assumed the direction of work on St. Peter's Basilica at the death of Donato Bramante and took charge of virtually all the papacy's projects in architecture, painting and the preservation of antiquities. When he died on his 37th birthday, his last masterpiece, the Transfiguration altarpiece, was placed at the head of his bier.

Cosimo Rosselli (1439 - after 1506) a Florentine painter, a pupil of Cosimo Rosselli, whose

Christian name he adopted as a patronym. There are no signed, documented, or dated works by him and reconstruction of his oeuvre depends on the account given in Vasari's Lives. It is one of Vasari's most entertaining biographies, for he portrays Piero as a highly eccentric character who lived on hard-boiled eggs, "which he cooked while he was boiling his glue, to save the firing". The paintings for which he is best known are appropriately idiosyncratic - fanciful mythological inventions, inhabited by fauns, centaurs and primitive men. There

Madonna and Child with Angels

is sometimes a spirit of low comedy about these delightful works, but in the so-called Death of Procris he created a poignant scene of the utmost pathos and tenderness. He was a marvellous painter of animals and the dog in this picture, depicted with a mournful dignity, is one of his most memorable creations. Piero also painted portraits, the finest of which is that of Simonetta Vespucci, in which she is depicted as Cleopatra with the asp around her neck. His religious works are somewhat more conventional, although still distinctive. One of his outstanding religious works is the Immaculate Conception, which seems to have been the compositional model for the Madonna of the Harpies by his pupil Andrea del Sarto.

Self-portrait

Andrea del Sarto *(1486 – 1531) an Italian painter active in Florence. After an apprenticeship with Piero di Cosimo, he became established as one of the outstanding painters of Florence, most notably as a fresco decorator and painter of altarpieces in the style of the High Renaissance. His feeling for colour and atmosphere was unrivaled among Florentine painters. One of his most striking achievements was the series of grisaille frescoes on the life of St. John the Baptist (1511 – 26) in the Chiostro dello Scalzo. His work is noted particularly for its exquisite composition and craftsmanship. It was instrumental in the development of Florentine Mannerism.*

Deeds of the Antichrist

Luca Signorelli *(c. 1445 – October 16, 1523) trained under Piero della Francesca and his earliest work reflects his debt to Piero, especially in the use of broad planes to model forms. But Signorelli rejected Piero's static figures and was most concerned with depicting the human body in action, an interest he may have acquired from the Florentine painter and sculptor Antonio Pollaiuolo. Among Signorelli's most important early works are the frescoes (late 1470s) in the Sacristy of the Basilica of the Holy House, Loreto; the Flagellation (1480-1481) in the Brera, Milan; the Testament and Death of Moses (ca. 1482) in the Sistine Chapel in the Vatican, Rome; the S. Onofrio altarpiece (1484) in the Cathedral Museum, Perugia; and the frescoes (mid-1490s) in the cloister of the Abbey of Monte Oliveto Maggiore near Siena. Called to Orvieto in 1499 to complete the vault decorations begun by Fra Angelico and Benozzo Gozzoli, Signorelli worked until 1504 painting the walls with a vivid narrative, including the Preaching of the Antichrist, the End of the World, the Resurrection of the Dead and the della Damned and the Elect. He suppressed details of environment to concentrate attention on the numerous nude figures that dominate the compositions. Signorelli never equaled the expressive power of these works in the paintings of his last 20 years. His late works were mainly formal altarpieces in which the hands of assistants may be seen.*

Jacob's Dream

Vincenzo Tamagni *(1492 - c. 1516) was a pupil of Sodoma, whom he assisted on the frescoes in the monastery of Monte Oliveto Maggiore, near Siena. In 1510-12 he executed frescoes of the Virgin and Child with Saints and Others in the ex-pharmacy of the Ospedale di S Maria Croce at Montalcino (Siena) and these show clearly the influence of Sodoma. He then moved to Rome, where he entered the shop of Raphael and probably worked on the decoration of the Loggetta of Cardinal Bernardo Bibbiena in the Vatican; his frescoes of 1516 in the apse of S Maria at Arrone (Terni) reflect contemporary Roman ideas, in particular from Raphael's Vatican Stanze and from Baldassare Peruzzi. He then assisted in the decoration of the Vatican Logge, where several scenes can be attributed to him. On his return to San Gimignano in 1522, Tamagni executed a Virgin and Child Enthroned for S Gerolamo and in 1523 the Birth of the Virgin for S Agostino. Also from this period is the Assumption of the Virgin in the Badia at Isola (Siena) and the Virgin and Child with Saints in the parish church of Pomarance, signed and dated 1525. About this date* he returned to Rome, where he completed three ceiling frescoes at Villa Lante, of illustrious men and women surrounded by grotesque decoration. After the Sack of Rome in 1527, he returned to San Gimignano, where he executed works including the Mystic Marriage of St Catherine and the Meeting of Joachim and Anne (S Salvatore, Istia d'Ombrore, Grosseto), signed and dated 1528.

Jacopo Robusti Tintoretto (1518-1594) one of the foremost Mannerist artists of the later 16th

Self-portrait

century. His work inspired the development of baroque art. Tintoretto, originally named Jacopo Robusti, was called Il Tintoretto ("the little dyer") in allusion to his father's profession. As a young man he studied briefly with Titian, who soon discharged him from his studio. The animosity between these two great painters lasted throughout their careers. Unlike Titian, Tintoretto lived and worked exclusively in Venice. His immense output was produced entirely for the churches, confraternities and rulers of Venice and for the Venetian state. In the first decade of his career (circa 1538-48), Tintoretto searched for a style, turning to diverse sources for inspiration. Important among these were Florentine Mannerist paintings, the work of Michelangelo and the relief sculpture of Jacopo Sansovino; from them Tintoretto learned modes of figure drawing and composition. From the Dalmatian painter Andrea Schiavone he learned an extraordinarily broad, free, sketchy way of applying paint. These elements were combined in varying ways to striking effect in Tintoretto's paintings of the 1540s. His artistic coming of age is marked by the large St. Mark (1548, Accademia, Venice), painted for the Scuola di San Marco, in which Tintoretto's daring foreshortenings, spatial illusions and high-keyed lighting mesh triumphantly to create an overwhelming impression of spontaneous action. In the decades that followed, Tintoretto's style intensified without essentially changing and the huge number of commissions he received attests to its enthusiastic reception. Even his staggering facility as a designer and executant could not cope with the work load and he was increasingly aided by a large corps of assistants, notable among them being his daughter, Marietta and his son, Domenico, whose contributions are often difficult to distinguish from Tontoretto's own. As a mature artist, Tintoretto tended progressively to rely on contrasts of brilliant light and cavernous dark on eccentric viewpoints and extreme foreshortening and on flamboyantly choreographic groupings to heighten the drama of the events portrayed. After his death on May 31, 1594, in Venice, Venetian painting precipitously declined.

Titian (c. 1473/1490[1] - 27 August 1576) is generally regarded as the leading painter of the

Self-portrait

Venetian school. Born in a small village in the Dolomite range of the Alps near Belluno, Titian removed to Venice where he worked first with the mosaicist Sebastiano Zuccato, then in the studio of Gentile and Giovanni Bellini. Titian was significantly influenced by Giorgione, whom he assisted in executing the external fresco decoration of the Fondaco dei Tedeschi on the Grand Canal in Venice. Upon Giorgione's death, 1510, Titian completed several of Giorgione's works-in-progress. Titian's career escalated rapidly after he received a commission, 1511, to execute three frescoes for the Scuola del Santo in Padua. By 1513 he had begun painting a Battle for the Chamber of the Grand Council in the Doge's Palace in Venice. Upon the death of Giovanni Bellini, 1516, Titian became official painter to the Republic. Some of Titian's most acclaimed works of the ensuing ten years were the Assumption for the Church of S. Maria Gloriosa dei Frari (1518) (in which the soaring movement of the Virgin is said to anticipate the later Baroque period), three paintings for Alfonso d'Este in Ferrara (the Worship of Venus, the Bacchanal and Bacchus and Ariadne) (1518-23), an altarpiece in Ancona (1520), a polyptych in Brescia centred on a Resurrection of Christ (1520-2) and the altarpiece for the Pesaro family side altar in the Church of S. Maria Gloriosa dei Frari (1519-26). Later Titian's work became more heavily weighted toward portraiture. Young Giorgio Cornaro (H-4) was one of his subjects in a 1538 painting. Among other prominent subjects were Pope Paul III (1546) and Charles V (1548), Emperor of the Holy Roman Empire. The Emperor appointed Titian court painter and gave him the rank of Count Palatine and Knight of the Golden Spur. In the 1540s Titian's work became more heavily influenced by the Mannerism of central and north Italy. He travelled to Rome in 1545-6 for his only visit there. In 1550 he was in Augsburg to paint portraits of Emperor Charles V's son, who was to become Phillip II of Spain and an important later patron of Titian. A detail from his 1567-8 self-portrait, now at the Prado, Madrid, is shown above. Titian remained active until his death in Venice at about age 91. His last work was a Pieta' (now in the Accademia Museum in Venice) created for his own tomb and completed after his death by Palma il Giovane.

Luigi Vanvitelli (May 12, 1700, Naples - March 1, 1773, Caserta) was an Italian engineer and architect. The most prominent eighteenth-century architect of Italy, he practiced a sober classicizing academic Late Baroque style that made an easy transition to Neoclassicism. Vanvitelli was born in Naples, the son of a Dutch painter, Caspar van Wittel, who also used by the name Vanvitelli. He was trained in Rome by Nicola Salvi, with whom he worked on the construction of the Trevi Fountain. Following his notable successes in the competitions for the facade of the Basilica di San Giovanni in Laterano (1732) and the facade of Palazzo Poli behind the Trevi Fountain, Pope Clement XII sent him to the Marche to ork on a number of papal projects. At Ancona, in 1732, he devised the vast Lazzaretto, a pentagonal building covering more than 20,000 square meters, built to protect the military defensive authorities from the risk of contagious diseases potentially reaching the town with the ships. Later it was used also as a military hospital or as barracks. In Rome, Vanvitelli stabilized the dome of St. Peter's Basilica when it developed cracks and found time to paint frescos in a chapel at Sant Cecilia in Trastevere. He also built a bridge over the Calore Irpino in Benevento. In the beginning of 1742 Vanvitelli designed (along with Nicola Salvi) the Chapel of St. John the Baptist for King John V of Portugal. It was built in Rome, disassembed in 1747, and shipped to Lisbon where it was reassembled in the Church of St. Roch (Igreja de São Roque). It was completed in 1750, although the mosaics in it were not finished until 1752. Built of many precious marbles and other costly stones, as well as gilt bronze, it was the most expensive chapel in Europe at the time. Vanvitelli's technical and engineering capabilities, together with his sense of scenographic drama led Charles VII of Naples to commission the great Palace of Caserta, intended as a fresh start for administering the ungovernable Kingdom of Naples. Vanvitelli worked on the project for the rest of his life, for Charles and for his successor Ferdinand IV. In Naples he designed the city's Palazzo Reale (1753) and some aristocratic palaces and churches. His engineering talents were also evident in his design for Caserta, the great aqueduct system that brought water to run the cascades and fountains. Luigi Vanvitelli died at Caserta in 1773.

Francesco Villamena (1564 - 7 July 1624) an Italian engraver. According to tradition, he was

a pupil of Cornelis Cort, whose engravings he copied and was associated in his youth with Agostino Carracci. He made few original engravings but reproduced designs of artists including Raphael, Paolo Veronese, Federico Barocci, Girolamo Muziano and Giulio Romano. His output also included frontispieces and book illustrations. Closely related to such northern late adherents of Mannerism as Hendrick Goltzius and Jacques Bellange, he employed an elegant and

Street Fight

expressive calligraphic style with perfect control of the burin. In addition to religious and

Francisco de Zurbarán (November 7, 1598 - August 27, 1664) was a Spanish painter apprenticed to a painter in Sevilla (Seville), where he lived until 1658. He had a few royal

commissions, but remained throughout his life a provincial painter of religious pictures. He had numerous commissions from monasteries and churches throughout southern Spain. Zurbarán's piety was influenced by Spanish Quietism, a religious movement that taught inner withdrawal, the discovery of God in humbly submissive silence and the use of penitential exercises to subdue the senses and calm the intellect. Although this influence had a profound effect upon his art, it in no way limited his artistic activities. The contracts for this period are so numerous that he would have been obliged to

Self-portrait

assign many of them to assistants. In addition, he was commuting to Seville (a 2-day trip) to execute works for the Dominican, Trinitarian, Mercedarian and Franciscan monasteries arrived with his wife, children and eight servants. The following year the painters' Guild of St. Luke ordered him to submit to an examination; he refused and the town council supported him. In April 1634 the painter Diego Velázquez, who was in charge of the decorations for the new Royal Palace in Madrid, commissioned Zurbarán to execute for the Hall of Realms two battle scenes, which were to belong to a series that included Velázquez's Surrender of Breda and ten Labors of Hercules. Zurbarán returned to Seville in November with the honorary title of Painter to the King and the happy memory that Philip IV had called him the king of painters. Zurbarán was at a peak of creativity and felicity in 1639, when his wife died. His art production declined markedly and his style became more grave. He married for the third time, in 1644, but his artistic star was descending as the popularity of the young Bartolomé Esteban Murillo rose. Lacking sufficient commissions at home, Zurbarán was obliged to produce the majority of his works for South America, particularly Lima and Buenos Aires. With four more children born of his new marriage, he even sold Flemish landscapes and paints and brushes to the South American market. He continued to produce mostly for South America until 1658, when he decided to try to change his luck in Madrid. His art, however, was little appreciated there and he died destitute on Aug. 27, 1664.

exercises to subdue the senses and calm the intellect. Although this influence had a profound effect upon his art, it in no way limited his artistic activities. The contracts for this period are so numerous that he would have been obliged to assign many of them to assistants. In addition, he was commuting to Seville (a 2-day trip) to execute works for the Dominican, Trinitarian, Mercedarian and Franciscan monasteries arrived with his wife, children and eight servants. The following year the painters' Guild of St. Luke ordered him to submit to an examination; he refused and the town council supported him. His patrons continued to be mostly monasteries: the Capuchins, Carthusians and Jeronymites were added to the list. In April 1634 the painter Diego Velázquez, who was in charge of the decorations for the new Royal Palace in Madrid, commissioned Zurbarán to execute for the Hall of Realms two battle scenes, which were to belong to a series that included Velázquez's Surrender of Breda and ten Labors of Hercules. Zurbarán returned to Seville in November with the honorary title of Painter to the King and the happy memory that Philip IV had called him the king of painters. Zurbarán was at a peak of creativity and felicity in 1639, when his wife died. His art production declined markedly and his style became more grave. He married for the third time, in 1644, but his artistic star was descending as the popularity of the young Bartolomé Esteban Murillo rose. Lacking sufficient commissions at home, Zurbarán was obliged to produce the majority of his works for South America, particularly Lima and Buenos Aires. With four more children born of his new marriage, he even sold Flemish landscapes and paints and brushes to the South American market. He continued to produce mostly for South America until 1658, when he decided to try to change his luck in Madrid. His art, however, was little appreciated there and he died destitute on Aug. 27, 1664.

LaVergne, TN USA
10 November 2010
204307LV00001B